CUBA

Also by JAIME SUCHLICKI

Mexico: From Montezuma to the Fall of the PRI
University Students and Revolution in Cuba
Historical Dictionary of Cuba

CUBA
FIFTH EDITION

from

COLUMBUS TO CASTRO AND BEYOND

JAIME SUCHLICKI

BRASSEY'S, INC.
Washington, D.C.

Library of Congress Cataloging-in-Publication Data

Suchlicki, Jaime.
 Cuba : from Columbus to Castro and beyond / James Suchlicki.—5th ed.
  p. cm.
 Includes bibliographical references and index.
 ISBN 1-57488-436-0 (alk. paper)
  1. Cuba—History. I. Title.
 F1776 .S93 2002
 972.91—dc21   2002003953

Printed in the United States of America on acid-free paper that meets the American National Standards Institute Z39-48 Standard.

Brassey's, Inc.
22841 Quicksilver Drive
Dulles, Virginia 20166

FIFTH EDITION

10 9 8 7 6 5 4 3 2

CONTENTS

PREFACE TO THE
FIFTH EDITION

SINCE the publication of the fourth edition of *Cuba: From Columbus to Castro* several important events are having an impact on Cuba and the Castro regime. The rise to power of Hugo Chavez in Venezuela, the willingness of the Chinese to expand trade and investments in Cuba, the growth of the island as a major tourist attraction, and the increasing remittances of dollars by Cuban-Americans all are helping the Cuban leadership muddle through the difficult period following the collapse of the Soviet Union.

While not likely to improve substantially or solve Cuba's continuing economic difficulties, the Chavez presidency is proving highly significant for Castro. Chavez signed agreements to provide Cuba with Venezuelan petroleum at subsidized prices that Castro can repay with services to Venezuela. This allows Cuba to divert some of the sugar it's trading for Russia's petroleum to be sold for hard currency in the world market. In addition, Castro can resell some of the Venezuelan petroleum for hard currency. Both of these maneuvers could provide the Cuban economy with a timely infusion of dollars. Chavez's support for Cuba's political positions and his criticism of U.S. policies toward Cuba are welcomed by the Cuban leadership. For years prior to his electoral victory in Venezuela, Chavez lived in Cuba and received Castro's support and counsel. In August 2001, Castro spent several days in Venezuela visiting his successful protégé and heir apparent to the leadership of Castroism in Latin America.

Perhaps the most astonishing development in the past few years is the growth of Chinese investments and involvement with the Castro regime. The Chinese have built a variety of factories on the island and have invested in Cuba's biotechnology industry. But more important is the close military relationship that has developed between China's People's Liberation Army (PLA) and Castro's Fuerzas Armadas Revolucionarias (FAR). The PLA is providing Cuba with military spare parts, munitions, and technology. Raúl Castro and Defense Minister Chi Haotian have exchanged visits, and a variety of Cuban military officers have spent time observing the Chinese economic and political experiment.

Of significant concern to the United States is China's establishment of an eavesdropping station in Cuba and its provision of equipment to interfere with Radio Martí and monitor U.S. military and commercial transmissions. After the release of the congressional Cox Report detailing Chinese espionage at a U.S. nuclear laboratory, it is hardly a secret that the Chinese are operating an extensive spy network in the Western Hemisphere. So it should be no further surprise that the Chinese might want an electronic espionage base close to American shores. China is not in the same league as the Soviets were in the 1960s or 1970s, but the People's Liberation Army hardly regards itself as a friend of the West. If it were, it would not have engaged in such potentially destabilizing practices as shipping advanced weapons to the Syrians and the Iranians. Indeed, Chinese foreign policy is patient and farsighted. In Cuba, the Chinese seem to be taking a calculated gamble: that the United States' complex relations with and economic interest in China will prevent the United States from raising a big fuss over China's activities in Cuba.

Internally there have been several ominous developments in Cuba. Castro continues to cling to an outmoded economic model. The economic reforms of the mid-1990s, which indicated a mild opening toward the market, have been stopped and in several cases even reversed. Politically Castro continues to oppose even the most minimal opening. The visit of Pope John Paul II in 1998 encouraged those who expected greater religious and political freedom. Neither has developed. As a matter of fact, at the beginning of the new century, the regime is increasing the persecution of dissidents and human rights activists. Cuba is undergoing a Chinese-type cultural revolution, albeit slower and less dramatic than in China, in which an aging leader insists on purifying and rejuvenating "his" exhausted revolution before departing from this world.

The Castro government has shown very few signs of making meaningful or durable concessions in the political and human rights arenas recently or in the past four decades. There has been no indication that Castro intends to truly open up the island's political or economic system or promote a peaceful solution to Cuba's deepening crisis. History reveals various instances in which strong and even autocratic political leaders have mellowed with age and softened their positions, but there is scant evidence that this is the case with Castro. On the contrary, as the Cuban leader has aged he has become more intransigent and difficult. At the Fifth Party Congress in 1997, he reaffirmed his staunch opposition to the United States and his unwillingness to relinquish personal power even after more than thirty-nine years at the helm of this troubled island.

The Clinton Administration, for the most part, seemed willing to depart from the policies of previous, Republican administrations toward Cuba in two areas. The administration was willing to relax restrictions on travel to Cuba for Cuban-Americans and Americans and was ready to increase telecommunications and other media contacts with the island. Former secretary of state Warren Christopher issued statements regarding "U.S. calibrated responses" to Castro's actions, an indication of U.S. willingness to consider moving in a direction of gradually normalizing relations with Cuba. There was the hope among U.S. policy makers that this policy of engagement would lead to economic changes on the island, the building of a civil society, and finally the undermining of Castro's personal power. The speed of the U.S. response would be conditioned by internal changes in Cuba, the actions of the U.S. Congress, pressures from the Cuban-American community, and specific policy priorities of the executive branch of the American government.

Castro encouraged this U.S. policy of engagement. He mobilized significant resources to force the United States to lift the embargo and the travel ban. He invited U.S. religious, political, business, and academic leaders to the island. He reached out to moderate Cuban-Americans to begin a dialogue and to weaken Cuban-American opposition to a Cuban-U.S. rapprochement. He portrayed Cubans' suffering as a result of the U.S. embargo while covering the reality that it is the result of a failed economic system.

Castro's calculated moves were designed to gain time and to force the United States into unilateral concessions regarding the embargo and the travel ban. He hoped that U.S. and world opinion would force the Clinton Administration to soften its policies and that U.S. attempts at subverting his revolution could be handled by Cuba's efficient security apparatus. His short-term tactically motivated actions did not envision the dismantling of communism in Cuba or the weakening of his personal power over the Cuban people.

In early 1996, Cuban-U.S. relations took a turn for the worse. The slowing of the pace of reforms in Cuba was an indication of Castro's unwillingness to move Cuba toward a market-oriented economy. The government's repression unleashed against Concilio Cubano, an umbrella organization of dissident groups in the island, and the arrest of more than one hundred of its members in February also emphasized Castro's opposition to a political opening. Then, on February 24, two small, unarmed civilian aircraft flown by a Cuban-American humanitarian group based in Miami, Brothers to the Rescue, were destroyed by Cuban MIG aircraft over international waters, killing the four occupants of the planes. Although Brothers to the Rescue had dropped anti-Castro leaflets in Havana, its mission was to spot Cuban rafters fleeing the island and advise the U.S. Coast Guard so they could be rescued.

The United States reacted swiftly. The Clinton Administration supported the passage of the Helms-Burton Act. This act punished foreign companies and nationals that invested in properties confiscated by the Castro government, prohibiting the principals in those companies from traveling to the United Sates and allowing American citizens to sue foreign companies in U.S. courts to obtain compensation. The law aimed to discourage foreign investment in Cuba and to set a standard of morality and fairness regarding properties illegally confiscated by the Castro government. Although the law generated significant criticism, particularly in Canada, Europe, and Latin America, the Clinton Administration and Congress refused to budge, claiming it was important to punish the Castro government for its actions. Subsequently, provisions allowing for legal action against foreign companies were suspended. By the end of the Clinton Administration, the United States and its allies had achieved an understanding whereby the Europeans would limit their investments in Cuba and continue to pressure the Castro regime to provide political and economic concessions in return for the United States' not implementing the most onerous of the Helms-Burton provisions.

The Bush Administration seems willing to continue these policies while tightening the prohibition of Americans traveling as tourists to Cuba. The president has made strong statements critical of

Castro's abuses of human rights and emphasized his unwillingness to change U.S. policy until the Castro regime provides meaningful concessions in the political and economic arenas. The appointment of several Cuban-Americans to key foreign-policy positions also indicates the new administration's willingness to maintain a hard line against the Cuban regime. Statements regarding changes at Radio Martí and the possibility of improving TV Martí, so it can be seen in Cuba, augur a continued period of tense U.S.-Cuban relations.

By its actions, the Castro government served notice that even limited economic liberalization would not be implemented. Castro risked upsetting the mild thaw in U.S.-Cuban relations, trade deals with the European Union, and condemnation by the world community in order to maintain internal control and external security. Fearful that a broader economic opening would lead to a political opening, he rejected both.

At the Fifth Party Congress in 1997 and later, Castro showed that in Cuba politics dictates economic decisions. Despite mounting economic problems, Castro has not introduced any major reforms that would propel Cuba into the market. "We will do what is necessary without renouncing our principles," Castro said. "We don't like capitalism, and we will not abandon our Socialist system."

Castro also reiterated his long-standing anti-American position, accusing the United Sates of waging economic war against his government and calling for "military preparedness against imperialist hostility."

The final party document and Castro's long speech to the Congress showed a determination to stay the course. Aware of his advancing age, Castro tried to ensure that his revolutionary legacy of anti-Americanism and Marxism-Leninism would endure beyond his life. He showed determination and confidence that despite the collapse of communism in Eastern Europe and Cuba's current difficulties, his hard line would be vindicated. Immediately following the Party Congress, Castro held a meeting of communist leaders from foreign countries to reassert the supremacy of Communist ideology and to plan for a "comeback" when capitalism fails. "Neo-liberalism and globalization create consumer societies like the U.S. throughout the world," he emphasized, "and this is not a model for anyone."

The Party Congress was also significant in other ways. It reasserted Raúl Castro's position as the undisputed heir to Fidel Castro's dynasty. Both in the party's private meetings and in public, Fidel praised his brother and summoned the faithful to support him so as to ensure the continuity of the revolution. Raúl's position as vice president, head of the military, and second secretary of the party makes him the obvious replacement for Fidel. Clearly, the older brother wanted the party cadres and the population at large to understand that the younger brother, as his anointed heir, should be supported and obeyed and that his leadership would be best for the future of Cuba.

For the past four years a process to ensure succession from Fidel to Raúl and continuity of the revolution has been taking place. The military has assumed greater and wider control of the economy. Close military allies of Raúl's have been promoted to key military and civilian positions. Raúl has increased his role in the daily management of state affairs, and Fidel has continued to emphasize that his brother is the "best suited" to carry on with the revolution. This has been accompanied by massive anti-American rallies, public demonstrations, and television programs whereby the leadership is attempting to infuse with new fervor the anti-U.S. rhetoric and to imbue the masses with a new sense of purpose and mission, by all accounts not very successfully.

Castro's brief public fainting spell in August 2001 accentuated the fragility of the 75-year-old leader and the proximity of a succession. Seeing their leader collapse on TV for the first time, the Cubans wondered about a future without Fidel. American policy makers scrambled to decipher the complex issues created by a succession. Cuban-Americans rejoiced at the spectacle of a feeble enemy nearing the end of his life and hoped for a real transition rather than succession on the island.

Faced with the approaching end of his life and his fear that once he is gone "his" revolution will change course and Cuba will end up another friendly Caribbean island close to the United States, Castro is not likely to open up either the economy or the political system. Concessions and constructive engagement did not work for the Europeans and Canadians and has not worked for the United States. They are not likely to shake Castro's belief in a communist, anti-American future for Cuba. Commitment to anti-Americanism, personal rule, and violent internationalism remain the cornerstones of Castro's policies. It may well be the case that better relations with the United States will be seen and feared by the Cuban leadership and will lead to further tightening of political control. On the basis of stated beliefs and recent actions, Cuba under Castro, and probably under his brother, will remain for the immediate future a communist project undertaken in stark isolation and opposition to the course of history in the Americas and the rest of the contemporary world.

JAIME SUCHLICKI
Coral Gables, Florida
September 2001

I

THE COLONIAL YEARS

1

THE LAND AND
THE PEOPLE

Upon landing in Cuba in 1492, Columbus marveled at the physical beauty he found, "the most beautiful land that human eyes have ever seen." And indeed it was an impressive sight. Essentially a palm-studded grassland, Cuba also boasted approximately five thousand different species of flowers, plants, and trees—among them yucca, tobacco, pineapple, and sweet potatoes, all native to the island. A rich variety of small tropical birds and animals further enlivened the scenery.

The largest and most westerly of the Caribbean islands, Cuba has an estimated area of 42,827 square miles and extends approximately 745 miles from east to west. Less than 90 miles from the Florida Keys, it commands the entrance to the Gulf of Mexico and the Panama Canal. The island's strategic location as well as its size made it a valuable possession for Spain as well as a desirable prize for other European powers seeking supremacy in the Caribbean during the seventeenth and eighteenth centuries.

The Cuban coastline, including the larger keys, is about 2,500 miles in length and is indented by hundreds of bays and inlets. The harbors of Havana, Guantánamo, Nipe, Cienfuegos, and Bahía Honda rank among the best in the world. The northern coast is mostly steep and rocky and along the southern coast are long stretches of lowlands and swamps, including the great Zapata swamp (*Ciénaga de Zapata*). Slightly more than half the island consists of flat or rolling terrain with many fertile valleys such as the Yumurí in Matanzas. The remainder is hilly or mountainous. In general, Oriente Province is dominated by the Sierra Maestra, culminating in Pico Turquino (6,389 feet); Camagüey has rolling plains and low mountains; Las Villas contains the Escambray mountains; Matanzas and Havana are flat or rolling; and Pinar del Río is dominated by the Sierra de los Organos. Rivers are generally short, narrow, and shallow and are navigable only for short distances. The largest river, the Cauto, flows westward for two hundred miles north of the Sierra Maestra but is used little for navigation.

Although situated within the Tropic Zone, Cuba is in the tradewind belt and thus its climate is semitropical. The surrounding seas give the island a moderate and stable climate and temperatures vary throughout the year by only 10°. The average minimum temperature is 70° F; the average maximum, 81° F with July and August the hottest months of the year. The tropical hurricanes that afflict the island usually from August to October are perhaps the most striking as well as dangerous aspect of the climate.

Knowledge about the early inhabitants of Cuba is generally sketchy. The Indians that inhabited the island at the time of Columbus's landing, estimated at about 60,000*, possessed no written language and most of them, although peaceful, were annihilated, absorbed, or died out as a result of the shock of conquest. Whatever information is available comes primarily from the writings of early explorers and from later archeological discoveries and studies of village sites, burial places, and middens. These sources indicate that at least three cultures, the Guanahatabeyes, the Ciboneyes, and the Taínos swept through the island before the arrival of the Spaniards.

The first of these cultures, the Guanahatabey, was the oldest in the island and has been described as a shell culture, characterized by its use of shell gouge and spoon as its principal artifacts. The Guanahatabeyes might have come from the south of the United States, for their artifacts display certain similarities with those of some early inhabitants of Florida. Yet some archeologists and anthropologists

---

*Estimates range from a low of 16,000 to a high of 600,000. See the *Handbook of the South American Indians* (Washington: United States Government Printing Office, 1941), IV, p. 542.

are more inclined to accept the theory that they migrated from South America through the chain of islands in the West Indies until finally settling in Cuba. By the time of the Spanish arrival, they had retreated to the most western part of Cuba, primarily the Peninsula de Guanahacabibes.

The Guanahatabeyes built no houses and lived mostly in caves. They were fruit pickers and food gatherers and did little fishing or hunting. They seemed to have relied on molluscs as their principal foodstuff. Cuba's first governor, Diego Velázquez, was shocked by the way the Guanahatabeyes lived: "like savages, without houses or towns and eating only the meat they are able to find in the forests as well as turtles and fish."* They avoided contact with the Spaniards and their civilization seemed to have been declining by the time the Europeans arrived.

The second culture, the Ciboney, was part of the larger South American Arawak group. They inhabited western Cuba and the southwestern peninsula of Hispaniola. It is generally agreed that the Ciboneyes, as well as the more advanced Taínos, the other Arawak group found in Cuba, originated in South America and had island-hopped along the West Indies. The Ciboneyes were a Stone Age culture and were more advanced than the Guanahatabeyes. It is believed that they migrated to Cuba already carrying with them a stone culture. They were highly skilled collectors, hunters, and fishermen, and inhabited towns particularly near rivers or the sea. Some lived in caves while others had begun to inhabit primitive dwellings called *bajareques* or *barbacoas*. The Ciboneyes practiced some form of elementary agriculture and their diet, more varied than that of the Guanahatabeyes, included turtles, fish, birds, and molluscs. Two of the more typical artifacts they developed included a stone digger (*gladiolito*) and a ball (*esferolito*), both symbols of authority or high social status also considered as magical objects. The Ciboneyes fell prey to the more advanced Taínos and became their servants or *nabories*. Father Bartolomé de las Casas, an early chronicler, described the Ciboneyes as "a most simple and gentle kind of people who were held like savages."

The second and more advanced Arawak group to enter the island, about two hundred years before the conquest, were the Taínos. They

---

*José Alvarez Conde, *Revisión Indoarqueológica de la Provincia de las Villas.* (La Habana: Publicaciones de la Junta Nacional de Arqueología y Etnología, 1961), p. 52.

occupied the central and eastern parts of Cuba, as well as most of Hispaniola, Jamaica, and Puerto Rico. The Taínos made extensive use of pottery and stone artifacts, which are reminiscent of Old World neolithic artifacts. The short, olive-skinned people subjected their children to artificial cranium changes by binding the frontal or occipital regions of their heads during early childhood; hence, their faces and particularly foreheads were unusually wide. They preferred high and fertile terrain close to sources of fresh water and lived in small villages in round houses with conical roofs made up of bamboo and thatched palm called *caneyes* or rectangular ones called *bohios*. An eyewitness described them as "meek, humble, obedient, and very hospitable, little given to sexual pleasures or other exerting physical activities."

Sexually promiscuous or not, the Taíno men went about naked. Girls at puberty wore a small cloth and married women wore a longer skirt. One of their favorite activities was bathing. The Spaniards seemed to have been annoyed at the frequency and time spent by the Taínos in the rivers, for a royal decree was issued recommending that they limit their number of baths. The Taínos also enjoyed a sort of soccer game called *juego de batos* played between two teams in an open court or *batey*. The *batey* also served as the meeting place for the *areitos,* a most important fiesta in which the Taínos sang and danced for several hours and recited their past to the young.

Compared with the Ciboneyes, the Taínos developed a rather advanced economic system based on agriculture with commonly cultivated fields. The cultivation and preparation of *yuca* (manioc), a sturdy tuber, played a significant role. By means of a *coa* or stick they opened a hole in the ground dropping the slip of the *yuca*. They also developed the more modern technique of cultivation in beds. They piled the soil around the *yuca* into mounds or *montones,* thus concentrating the nourishing power of the soil around the slip and preventing soil erosion. After the *yuca,* which had a period of growth over a year, had been harvested, it was grated, drained of its poisonous juice, and baked into unleavened bread called *cassava,* which the Spaniards labeled "bread of the earth." This bread was both nutritious and tasty and kept for several months, even in humid weather.

Tobacco, cotton, corn, and white and sweet potato were also an important part of the Taíno economy. Tobacco was used for smoking as well as for religious ceremonies and for curing the ill. After the Spanish occupation it became an important item for export. Cotton was mostly used for hammocks, bags, and fishing nets. Textiles together with pottery making represented the incipient Taíno industrial development. Both the manufacture of textile and of pottery items were tasks performed by women, while men engaged in hunting, fishing, or agriculture. The Taíno also developed a number of wooden artifacts, such as powerful canoes, which gave them great mobility by water.

Society was organized along distinct class lines. At the top was the chief or *cacique,* who managed all the affairs of the community and ruled over a specific territory. The line of inheritance to become a *cacique* was not direct; the eldest son of the *cacique*'s eldest sister became chief when the former *cacique* died. If the *cacique* did not have any sisters, then his eldest son would inherit the post. The *caciques* were aided by the *nitaínos,* a group of advisors who supervised communal work and seemed to have been in charge of various sectors of the population. Aware of the *nitaínos'* importance in controlling the labor supply, the Spaniards used them later on as overseers in their plantations. Next to the *nitaínos* was the medicine man or *behique.* Through dreams and fasting the *behique* determined the will of the gods or *cemis* and conversed with the dead ancestors. This was done at a special ceremony in which snuff was inhaled. Naturally the *behique* also healed the sick or wounded. The lower class were the *nabories* who did most of the work of the village. At the time of the Spanish conquest the Ciboneyes had been incorporated into this group and seemed to have accepted their lot with little resistance.

The Taínos believed in a supreme invisible being and their religion was dominated by a series of gods represented by idols. Ancestor-worshiping was common and they carved special idols resembling their ancestors. The souls of the dead were thought to reside in a nearby island and to return at night to hunt the living. Taíno burials were elaborate and often accompanied by numerous offerings. The dead were buried in a bent position, usually in caves or in open camp sites.

By 1492 the Taínos were being challenged by the Caribs, a warlike group moving north from South America. The Caribs (the word means "cannibal") had made a number of incursions into Cuba and terrorized its population with their practice of eating, either for ritual purposes or merely for food, the male warriors they captured. Little is known of their early culture, even less than about the Arawaks. The Caribs never settled permanently in Cuba, making only periodic raids on the terrorized Taínos and Ciboneyes.

The arrival of the Spaniards in the Caribbean prevented the further expansion of the Caribs. A contest soon erupted between the two for control of the land and the native population. The Spaniards proved superior and the Caribs retreated to the Lesser Antilles. A sort of stalemate developed, with Spain occupying the larger islands and the Caribs the smaller ones. As time went by and European contenders such as the Dutch, English, and French appeared on the scene, Spain's failure to occupy the small islands proved a costly mistake. These European nations divided the smaller islands among themselves, challenging Spain's predominant position in the Caribbean.

In terms of economic development, social organization, technological advances, and art, the Indians of Cuba were far inferior to the more advanced Indians of the mainland, such as the Maya and Aztec of Mexico or the Inca of Peru. The Ciboneyes and Taínos left only a mild imprint on Cuba's later culture; the Guanahatabeyes left almost none. There was little mingling of races between Spaniards and Indians. A new society first of Spaniards and then of Spaniards and blacks supplanted the Indian society. New institutions, new values, and a new culture replaced the old ones. Some Indian words, foods, and habits, as well as agricultural techniques were retained by later generations, as was the *bohio,* the typical and picturesque dwelling of many Cuban farmers, which still can be seen today and remains perhaps the most visible legacy of the Indian society.

For the most part, however, the Cuban Indians' contribution to the development of a Cuban nationality must be considered minor. For generations after the conquest, Indian warriors such as Hatuey, who fought the Spanish conquest in eastern Cuba, were glorified in the pages of Cuban history books and raised to the status of folk heroes. They represented for Cuban children a symbol of the native resistance against the oppressive Spanish *conquistador.* The Indian's innocence and kindness was contrasted with the cruelty of the Spanish invader. But for those in search of the roots of a uniquely Cuban national identity, this was not enough of a foundation. In their search for a nationalistic identity, Mexicans could look back to their Indian past, and revolutionary regimes in this century found in *indianismo* a rallying point. The Cubans could not. The glory of the Aztec past was just not there for the Cubans to turn to. Instead, Cuban writers in search of the roots of Cuban nationality would later look to African or Spanish contributions and try to find in them the missing link with the past—but with little luck. The Spanish heritage was dismissed as part of the rejection of colonialism and the former were never totally recognized, particularly by white Cuban society. This search for a nationalistic or distinctly Cuban identity is still an unresolved and highly critical problem of present-day Cuba.

2

ENTER THE SPANIARDS

THAT it was the Spaniards who arrived in the New World in 1492 was no accident. By then navigational instruments and ships capable of a transatlantic voyage had been developed. Clergymen, scientists, and monarchs had accepted the belief in the earth's sphericity and laymen's curiosity had been aroused by Marco Polo's voyages to the Far East and the tales of exotic, faraway lands. Meanwhile, the marriage of Isabel of Castile and Ferdinand of Aragon had consolidated the Spanish monarchy and Spain was emerging as a proud, aggressive nation after several hundred years of bitter but successful fighting against the Moorish invader.

With the Moors expelled from most of the Iberian Peninsula and the unity of Spain achieved, the Catholic monarchs now looked to new horizons to expand their faith as well as their commercial interests. War gave way to exploration and conquering souls became as important as conquering lands. Competition also played a key role in Spain's new outward look. A strong maritime nation, Portugal was exploring the western coast of Africa as far south as the Cape of Good Hope. The Spanish monarchs looked with envious eyes at the exploits of Henry the Navigator, and longed for an opportunity to challenge Portugal's growing supremacy.

Christopher Columbus provided that opportunity. Although others had visited the New World before him, it was his determination as well as the propitious conditions that existed in Spain and in

Europe that made possible now a permanent contact between the two worlds. Tall, blue-eyed, this proud and stubborn Genoese seaman first visited Portugal, proposing his scheme for a westerly voyage in search of the Indies. The Portuguese, however, were bent on reaching the Far East by rounding the southern tip of Africa and rejected his ideas. Discouraged, Columbus left for Spain. There he convinced the Spanish monarchs to finance his venture and with ninety men and three ships, the *Niña,* the *Pinta,* and the *Santa María,* he sailed westerly in 1492 on a voyage that changed the fate of the world.

The first voyage was indeed an epic of courage and determination. The unknown sea, a rugged climate, and a mutinous crew were all subdued by Columbus's faith that beyond the horizon lay the Indies. Finally, on October 12, 1492, land was discovered, the small island of San Salvador (Watlings Island) in the Bahamas. From there Columbus touched on Santa María de la Concepción, later renamed Rum Cay, and on October 27 he sighted Cuba. For several weeks he explored the northeast coast of Cuba. He communicated with the natives who received the Spaniards with hospitality and obedience, perhaps fearing them as being of divine origin. Turning east, Columbus explored the north coast of Hispaniola—modern day Haiti—and with timber from the wrecked *Santa María* he established a little settlement, La Navidad, not far from Cap Haitien. There he left a few of his men and set course back for Europe with several Indians and some gold to show the Spanish monarchs.

While exciting, the material results of this first voyage were disappointing. The venture proved costly. Columbus lost one of his ships and had to leave behind almost half his men. The little wealth and the few Indians he brought back did not seem to compensate for the crown's investment. Yet new islands had been discovered and new wealth would soon begin to flow into Spain's depleted treasury. Although Columbus claimed he had reached the Far East, Spain soon began negotiations with the papacy and Portugal to secure a monopoly of navigation and settlement over the new lands.

This proved an easy task. Pope Alexander VI, himself a Spaniard who was seeking Ferdinand's support for the establishment of a principality in Italy for his son, issued a series of bulls which established the Line of Demarcation from north to south a hundred leagues west of the Azores and Cape Verde islands and provided that the sea and land west of the line should belong to Spain. In the 1494

Treaty of Tordesillas between Spain and Portugal, the papal bulls were confirmed but the line was pushed westward. By doing so, Spain unwittingly relinquished to Portugal a significant part of the yet to be explored South American continent, that which later became Brazil.

By the time of the signing of the Treaty of Tordesillas, Columbus had initiated his second voyage. This one aimed at establishing a permanent, self-sufficient settlement in Hispaniola, one that would produce gold to be sent back to Spain while at the same time serve as a base for further exploration and colonization. Columbus left Spain in September 1493, touched on several islands in the Lesser Antilles, and landed finally in Hispaniola only to find the colony destroyed by an Arawak rebellion. A second settlement, Isabela, was soon founded on a poor site on the north coast. Traveling west in search of the empire of the Great Khan, Columbus spent several months exploring the southern coast of Cuba and made a short landing in Jamaica. Then he sailed almost to the western tip of Cuba but thinking it a peninsula of the mainland he turned around, having failed to prove that Cuba was an island. Columbus returned to Isabela where he found the settlers weakened by sickness and at odds among themselves and with the Indians. After restoring order by harshly punishing the much abused Taínos, he left his brother Bartolomé in charge with plans to move the settlement south to what later became Santo Domingo and then sailed back to Spain.

Two other voyages followed. Although the Spanish monarchs were somewhat disappointed with the profits of exploration, suspicious about Columbus's loyalty, and unhappy over the many complaints against him from fellow colonizers, they still permitted the admiral to organize new expeditions. In 1498 Columbus sailed following a more southerly course, landing first in Trinidad and then sighting the mouth of the Orinoco River on the north coast of South America. Sailing north to Santo Domingo, he found the colony torn by internal dissension and Indian warfare. Columbus's efforts to harmonize the various factions proved futile. One group complained to the Spanish monarchs, who sent Francisco de Bobadilla as chief justice and royal commissioner. Bobadilla listened to violent complaints against Columbus's rule and without taking time to determine the accuracy of the charges, he ordered that Columbus be returned to Spain in chains.

In Spain Columbus managed to exonerate himself of all charges and to organize a fourth and final voyage. Yet he was never again allowed to make use of his titles of admiral and viceroy or to become involved in the government of Hispaniola. In this voyage (1502–1504) Columbus explored the coast of Central America and spent a year marooned in Jamaica. Disillusioned and physically exhausted, Columbus finally returned to Spain where he died in 1506.

By the time of Columbus's death other explorers had made their way into the Caribbean. Alonso de Ojeda touched on the northern coast of South America and gave Venezuela its name. He was accompanied by Amerigo Vespucci, whose letters portraying the new world received widespread attention in Europe and led to the adoption of the name "America" for the newly discovered lands. Rodrigo de Bastidas explored in Central America while others traveled to the northeast coast of South America.

Exploration soon gave way to conquest and colonization. Hispaniola, first settled by Columbus, continued to grow, but it was hindered primarily by the lack of a steady labor supply. As the Indian population died out as a result of the conquest, diseases, and overwork, this became a critical problem. The little mineral wealth that was found in Hispaniola and the precarious pastoral existence of its settlers discouraged further colonization of new lands. Also, the various Indian raids conducted by the Spaniards on adjacent islands and especially the fact that several ships were wrecked on the swampy southern coast of Cuba convinced the Spaniards that the new lands to the west offered little different from Hispaniola.

As time went by, however, the Spanish crown became increasingly intrigued over the possibility of finding gold in Cuba. Spanish officials, desirous of increasing their labor supply as well as exploring possible new sources of wealth, also began to look toward Cuba. Christopher Columbus's son, Diego, who had been appointed governor of the Indies and resided in Hispaniola, was particularly interested in extending the territory under his control. As a preliminary step to colonization, Hispaniola's governor, Nicolás de Ovando, sent an expedition headed by Sebastián de Ocampo that circumnavigated Cuba in 1508 bringing back tales of wealth and a more detailed picture of the island's fine terrain and harbors.

Finding a *conquistador* who combined military skill, administrative talent, and loyalty to the crown as well as to Diego Columbus himself, was no easy task. The choice finally fell on Diego Velázquez, Ovando's lieutenant and one of the wealthiest Spaniards in Hispaniola. Although not as heroic or daring as later *conquistadores* such as Francisco Pizarro, conqueror of Peru, or as cunning as Hernán Cortés, conqueror of Mexico, Velázquez had achieved a reputation for courage and sagacity because of his role in subduing Indian *caciques* in Hispaniola. An able administrator, he was nevertheless extremely jealous of his authority and enjoyed the great pomp and ceremony attached to an important position in the Spanish bureaucracy.

After obtaining an agreement or *asiento* from Columbus and permission from the crown for the venture, Velázquez recruited over a hundred men and prepared for the conquest. In early 1511 he landed near Baracoa on the eastern tip of Cuba where he established the first permanent settlement and prepared for the colonization of the rest of the island.

From the start, Velázquez faced an outraged and hostile Indian population. Led by Hatuey, a fugitive Indian chieftain from Hispaniola, the natives of eastern Cuba resolved to resist the Spanish onslaught. It was a futile gesture, for the peaceful Taínos lacked the military skills and weapons to face the better armed and trained Spaniards. Spanish horses and hounds—both unknown in Cuba—played a decisive role in terrorizing the Indians, who soon surrendered or fled into the mountains to escape the wrath of the *conquistadores*. Hatuey himself was captured, tried as a heretic and a rebel, and burnt at the stake.

Indian hostility diminished considerably after Hatuey's death, but it did not end. Other *caciques* continued to harass and ambush the Spaniards as they moved into the interior of the island. Some of Velázquez's lieutenants, in particular Pánfilo de Narváez and Francisco de Morales, dealt harshly with Indian resistance and permitted the soldiers to plunder Indian villages and abuse Indian women. Both the crown and Velázquez attempted to end these abuses; Morales was relieved of his task and sent back to Hispaniola. The crown insisted, partly for religious and humanitarian reasons, partly for economic reasons, that abuses against the natives should stop and that the Indians should be Christianized and made a productive part of society. The rapid dwindling of Indian labor that had occurred in Hispaniola had to be avoided at all costs in Cuba, and Velázquez knew that if he failed in this respect, the conquest of Cuba could also be a failure.

Velázquez set out to pacify the country and end the abuses against the Indians. He induced groups of them to depose their weapons and work near the several new towns he established throughout the island.*

In this task he was decisively aided by the work of Fray Bartolomé de las Casas, the famous "Protector" of the Indians. The Dominican friar preceded the Spaniards into Indian villages on many occasions and succeeded in convincing the natives to cooperate with the *conquistadores.* Las Casas, however, was horrified by the massacres of the natives, particularly the one at Caonao, and he became an outspoken critic of the conquest of Cuba. He wrote extensively condemning the Spaniards' cruelty and claiming that the Indians were rational and free and therefore entitled to retain the lands. He clashed with those who defended the doctrine of just conquest which advanced the idea that the Spaniards were naturally superior and had divine authorization to use force to convert the natives to Christianity. The writings of las Casas, particularly his *History of the Indies,* received widespread attention throughout Europe. They influenced Spanish Indian policy in the New World and gave rise to the Black Legend about exaggerated Spanish cruelty.

To strengthen his own power and gain supporters both in Cuba and in Spain, Velázquez began to issue *encomiendas,* a practice already in existence in Hispaniola which entailed assigning Indian families or other inhabitants of a town to the Spaniard who would extract labor and tribute from them while providing for their Christianization. The granting of an *encomienda* did not carry with it title to the land on which the Indians lived and labored nor ownership of the Indians. The crown took the position that the natives were "free" subjects, although they could be compelled to pay tribute and to work like other such subjects. Many *encomenderos,* however, interested only in exploiting the resources of the island, disregarded their moral, religious, and legal obligations to the Indians, as did others elsewhere in the New World. Acting as absentee owners, in many instances they delegated actual control of their *encomiendas* to overseers who overlooked the provisions about Christianization, abused the Indians, and extracted from them an unreasonable amount of labor.

A conflict soon developed between the crown and the Spanish settlers over the control and utilization of the labor and also between

---

*Among these were Baracoa, Bayamo, Trinidad, Sancti-Spiritus, La Habana, Puerto Principe, and Santiago de Cuba.

the crown's stated objective to Christianize the natives and its own economic motivations. Not that Christianizing and extracting labor were incompatible, but in the reality of the New World the sixteenth-century Christian ideal of converting souls was many times sacrificed for a profit. Christianization was reduced to mass baptism; and despite the crown's insistence that Indians were not slaves, many were bought and sold as chattels. The Spanish monarchy itself profited from the *encomienda* system, using Indians as miners and taxing the *encomenderos* for the number of Indians they received. Despite attempts to regulate the functioning of the *encomienda* and prevent further abuses, the crown lacked a means of enforcement. Such legislation as the Law of Burgos (1512–1513) or, later, the New Laws (1542) which sought to end the *encomienda,* were more intended as statements of purpose rather than as practical legislation that could be implemented in the New World wilderness.

In Cuba, the *encomienda* was used by the crown as a political instrument to consolidate its control over the Indian population. No doubt, Ferdinand of Aragon and later Spanish rulers were in great part motivated by the religious characteristic of the sixteenth century, but they also may have recalled the profitable financial and political results brought about in Spain by the conversion of the Moors and the Jews and in so doing hoped perhaps that the conversion of the Indians would lead to similar political control and financial gain.

3

THE EMERGING COLONY

As soon as the conquest was completed and the Indians subjugated, the crown began introducing into the island the institutional apparatus necessary to govern the colony. The governor, highest representative of the crown in the island, ruled Cuba with almost complete authority over administrative, political, and judicial affairs. The governor was technically subject to the *audiencia* in Santo Domingo and viceroy in New Spain. In practice, however, he exercised much autonomy, particularly after the wealth of Mexico was discovered, diverting the crown's interests away from Cuba and its lack of resources. Diego Velázquez acted as the first governor from the time of his landing until his death in 1524.

In the late sixteenth century the governor also received the title of captain-general. This added military powers to the extensive civil authority he already exercised and made him of similar rank to the commanders of the fleets that called at the port of Havana.

Nominally responsible for the collection and expenditures of revenues and all financial affairs, the governor delegated these functions to several *oficiales reales* appointed directly by the crown. The latter worked very closely, discussing ways to increase royal revenue with both the governor and the *Casa de Contratación* (House of Trade) located in Seville, an institution devoted to finance, taxation, and maritime operations between Spain and America. The *oficiales* consisted of a treasurer, an accountant, and sometimes a factor who was appointed to administer the king's property. They also joined the governor as judges in cases involving contraband. In the early eighteenth century Cuba's growing population and increasing wealth, as well as the crown's mounting demands for more revenue to support its growing involvement in European affairs, forced the *oficiales* to appoint deputies to represent them in cities throughout the island. When in 1765 the intendancy was established, the whole organization was revamped to fit the more rational and efficient Bourbon monarchical system.

At first the seat of government remained in Baracoa, the first village founded by Velázquez. But later it was transferred to Santiago and finally in 1538 to Havana because of its geographic location and excellent port. In 1607 Cuba was divided into two provinces with their capitals at Santiago and Havana. The governor-captain general at Havana ruled in military matters over the entire island, but the governor at Santiago was able to exercise considerable political independence.

Although the governor-captain general was nominally subject to the viceroy of New Spain, highest royal official in the New World, the viceroy exerted little control over the affairs of the island. Of more direct influence, and a powerful check on the governor, was the *audiencia* of Santo Domingo. This tribunal heard criminal and civil cases appealed over the decisions of the governor. But it soon became more than, as in Spain, a court of law; it was also an advisory council to the governor and always exercised its right to supervise and investigate his administration. This was done sometimes by a royal order to conduct a *residencia* or formal hearing held at the end of the governor's term in office. At such time, witnesses testified before a specially appointed judge concerning the performance of the official. If found guilty of any misbehavior while in office, he was required to make restitution to those whom he had mistreated; in some instances harsher punishments were administered. A second and important check on the power of the governor was the inspection or *visita,* performed by a special crown-appointed official who reported back to the monarch on the operation of the colony and the performance of its officials.

At the local level the most important institution was the *cabildo.* Presided over by the governor or his lieutenant, and composed of *alcaldes* (judges), *regidores* (councilmen), and other minor officials, the *cabildo* was the political, judicial, and administrative unit of each new settlement. It imposed local taxes, provided for local police, and maintained public buildings, jails, and roads. The *alcaldes* acted as judges of first instance and in the absence of the governor or his lieutenant they presided at meetings of the *cabildo*. They also visited the territories under their jurisdiction and dispensed justice in the rural areas.

In the early days the *cabildo* emerged as a fairly representative institution of local government. Although the governor appointed its president, the *teniente de guerra,* members were either elected by the settlers or appointed by the *conquistadores*. Away from the direct control of the governor and following the Spanish tradition of independence, these Spaniards exercised a significant amount of autonomy.

The *cabildos* selected a *procurador* (solicitor) who represented the interests and desires of the community and served as liaison between the settlers and the Spanish crown. *Procuradores* from various towns met annually at Santiago to discuss the island's needs and to choose a general *procurador* to carry their grievances and requests to the king. Yet this budding development of representative government was soon crushed by various governors' attempts to centralize the government, and in 1532 the last meeting of *procuradores* was held in Santiago amidst bitter quarrels and opposition from the governor.

By mid-century, representative and autonomous government gave way to centralization and political interference from Spain. The crown began appointing *regidores* for life and initiated the practice of selling offices. *Regidores* in turn appointed the *alcaldes*. These changes were accompanied by frequent quarrels between the *cabildo* members and the *teniente de guerra* over the distribution of power. Differences occurred also between the *cabildo* and the governors. The latter were not all too happy to allow local government to be carried out independently of their control. They also complained that councilmen, under the protection of their office, were speculating, organizing monopolies of necessary commodities, and hording groups of Indians for their personal benefit. In an attempt to reassert their authority, some governors appointed deputies, *tenientes de gobernadores,* with extensive powers to represent them in far-away towns. The *cabildos* in turn were unwilling to see their powers curtailed by the governors and in 1583 appealed to the *audiencia* of Santo Domingo. Although the *audiencia* decided in their favor and ordered the *tenientes* removed, the practice continued to the detriment of municipal government.

As royal government became better organized and more entrenched in Cuba the powers and prerogatives of the *cabildo* were progressively curtailed. By the end of the colonial period few responsible citizens wanted to become involved in local government. Those who did were more interested in their personal well-being than in the affairs of the colony. Peninsular Spaniards who bought their offices sought rewards for their investments and enriched themselves at the expense of public funds. Creoles, Spaniards born in the New World, also joined the Spanish bureaucracy. Unable to find wealth and other opportunities controlled by peninsular Spaniards, they looked to local government as one of the few potential areas of employment in which they could succeed. Very few Creoles ever attained a position of importance in the political hierarchy of the island. As the bureaucracy grew in the colonial period, a latent hostility developed between peninsular Spaniards and Creoles—a hostility that erupted into hatred and violence during the wars for independence in the nineteenth century.

In the early years *cabildo* members were content to eke out an existence until such time as new opportunities might arise for them to migrate to better lands or until mineral wealth might be discovered in Cuba that would bring them instant wealth. Those who expected to enrich themselves from Cuba's mineral resources were greatly disappointed. The island did not enjoy the large deposits of gold and other minerals that were later found in Mexico and in South America. Gold found in the river banks did not represent any great wealth, although it did require a large labor supply as well as costly equipment to wash the gold near the rivers. A handful of Spanish entrepreneurs controlled the business and used Indians for a labor supply. The crown was also involved from the earliest times in controlling what looked like a possibly lucrative business. The Spanish monarchs took one-fifth of all production as a tax for the right of mining and especially when this mining was done by Indians in *encomienda*.

Despite the problem of finding a suitable labor supply, washing gold was the basis of Cuba's economy in the earlier years. It increased and focused Spain's attention on the island and led to much speculation about the possible wealth to be found. It was also the source of widespread unhappiness among the much abused Indians and led to numerous uprisings, particularly toward the end of Velásquez's administration.

Foodstuffs also were an important part of the economy. The Indian agricultural practices were taken over by the Spaniards who continued to grow some of the native foodstuffs, particularly yucca. New crops and new grains from the Old World were also brought to the island. Sugar, which had been grown by the Spaniards in the Canary Islands, was also a part of the island's economy. As early as 1523 the crown instructed the *Casa de Contratación* to lend money to settlers in Cuba to help finance the construction of a sugar mill. Other similar loans were made in later years but it was not until the eighteenth century and particularly the nineteenth century that sugar assumed any importance. Without large amounts of capital, an adequate labor supply, and official encouragement, sugar remained overshadowed in importance by the more lucrative and important business connected with the cattle industry and its derivative products.

Cattle raising became one of the most prosperous businesses, especially in the seventeenth century. Although the activity called for daring horsemanship, it required no sustained effort, for Cuba's abundant pasture lands facilitated breeding. (As early as 1514 Velázquez informed the crown that there were over thirty thousand hogs and an unspecified number of horses in the island.) The cattle were let loose on Cuba's savannahs, where they multiplied rapidly. They were used as a means of transportation as well as for feeding purposes. Salted meat became an important item sold to the Spanish ships that touched on Cuba's ports. Perhaps the chief value of cattle lay in the hides. In the seventeenth and eighteenth centuries, as demand for leather grew in Europe, cattle hides became Cuba's chief export, yielding considerable profit.

Spaniards preferred such pastoral pursuits as cattle raising to farming. Tilling the soil required manual labor and had been the work primarily of the Moors in Spain. Now this was to be left to the Indians or the blacks in the New World. Besides, as a result of the Reconquest, the Spanish struggle that culminated in the expulsion of the Moorish domination from Spain in the late fifteenth century, Spaniards had become used to cattle, which could be transported to the new lands as these were captured from the Moors. Enterprising Spaniards brought cattle to Cuba and received large grants of land from the crown, which was interested in encouraging the settlement of vast unpopulated areas.

Tobacco also made some modest gains, particularly in the seventeenth century. Since it was not too bulky and commanded high prices in Europe, it was a favorite item for smuggling. By the eighteenth century it became an important export item to the French. Throughout this period the tobacco business remained in private hands. But under the administration of Charles III (1759–1788) it was converted into a government monopoly. The crown advanced money to the growers who would sell their crops to the government at a fixed price. In the early nineteenth century the value of tobacco as an export began to decline. By then the price of land had increased tremendously, partly as a result of the growth of sugar estates. Tobacco growers found themselves either squeezed out of their lands or selling them to the sugar capitalists. The crown's emphasis on coffee and sugar growing was also detrimental to the tobacco industry. In desperate need of capital, the Spanish monarchs encouraged the more lucrative sugar business as a source of revenue.

The economy was oriented toward importing the bare necessities, with little or no provision for domestic manufacturing. Such essential items as tools, paper, and even foodstuffs were brought in from the outside. Spain followed a thoroughly mercantilistic economic policy, encouraging Cuba's dependence on outside sources of supply for its needs and looking at the island as a producer of raw materials to satisfy the needs of the mother country.

Commercial relations developed first with Hispaniola. Much of the gold found in Cuba was shipped there and then on to Spain. But Hispaniola could not satisfy the needs of her neighbor and soon commerce developed directly with Spain. In addition, it was cheaper for the inhabitants of Cuba to buy directly than to go through Hispaniola. Cubans were thus allowed to trade with the Spanish port of Seville, where the *Casa de Contratación* stored all goods imported from and exported for the New World, and supervised the trade between Seville and the colonies. It was mainly gold that was exported in the early years, but later on some *cassava,* some native plants, and hides were sent to Spain.

Cuba became the source of support for the conquest of nearby lands. It was from the island that Hernán Cortés's expedition sailed in 1519 to conquer the Aztec Empire. The conquest of Mexico meant temporary prosperity and great euphoria, but it also meant the decline of Cuba's importance. The days of boom soon gave way to years of bust. Farmers and adventurers all left the island in search of El Dorado in Mexico, or joined the ill-fated expeditions of Pánfilo de

Narváez in 1527 and Hernando de Soto in 1539 to conquer Florida. Exodus of population, decline of food production, and economic misery afflicted the island. Estates were abandoned by their owners and bought cheaply by less adventurous Peninsular Spaniards, humble folks willing to produce for the passing ships and live a modest existence.

For the next two centuries Spain focused most of its attention on the continental colonies from where it obtained much needed mineral wealth. A complex and at times cumbersome political and defense system developed to ensure the uninterrupted flow of this wealth. Cuba was relegated to a mere stopping point for passing ships. It remained valuable only because of its strategic location as the gateway to the New World, not because of the products it produced.

Cuba's population diminished continuously throughout this period. The Indians continued to die out and there was little new influx of Spanish immigrants. An economy of scarcity and a hot, sickness-ridden tropical climate offered little incentive for new immigration. In other parts of the continent abundant land, mineral wealth, and labor supply attracted those Spanish settlers willing to leave their homeland and cross the Atlantic in search for a different and perhaps better world. Those who did come to Cuba were mostly Spanish officials, soldiers, and members of the clergy; there was also a good number of transient migrants on their way to Mexico or South America. By 1544 Cuba had a population of less than 7,000, composed of 660 Spaniards, some 5,000 Indians, and 800 black slaves.

This early society was characterized by little social mobility as well as lack of interest in the arts or in education. Creoles were less educated and seemed less interested in a formal education than their ancestors. Living in small towns, surrounded by an unknown and at times hostile environment, fearful of Indian or later of black rebellion, or of foreign attacks, most had little time for cultural activities and were mainly concerned with the daily problems of existence. Brutality, opportunism, corruption, and smuggling characterized this society. Violence and lack of observance of the law flourished as the struggle for survival became harsher. Whatever education existed was offered within the Catholic Church. In the cathedral of Santiago de Cuba, for example, a chair of grammar was established in the 1530s, and elementary and religious education was provided for Spanish as well as for selected Indian children.

In this society the Church played an important role. As in the rest of Latin America, it was under the direct control of the crown, except for doctrinal affairs. The *patronato real,* a body of rights and privileges granted by the pope, permitted the Spanish monarch to nominate all higher Church dignitaries coming to the New World as well as to control the administration of ecclesiastical taxation. In practice, the king and his officials in the New World became the secular heads of the Church. The Church became a political arm of the state and was to dominate Indians and blacks, as well as colonists.

In the meantime, protected by the power of the state, the Church grew in numbers and influence. By mid-seventeenth century there were about two hundred friars and priests and about one hundred nuns in the island. Churches were built in every new city and Church wealth increased through the continuous acquisition of lands donated to the Church and through the collection of rents, as well as of a special tax called *diezmo.* With wealth came not only prestige and influence, but also the loss of the Church's early missionary zeal. The priesthood began identifying with the wealthier classes to the neglect of Indians and blacks and became a conservative institution interested in preserving the *status quo.*

The uninterrupted arrival of blacks throughout the colonial period decisively influenced this developing society. African slavery existed in Spain and the first slaves had come to Cuba with the early *conquistadores.* Later they were brought in greater numbers to work in the washing of gold. Stronger, better suited for hard labor, they replaced the weaker indigenous groups. The importation of black slaves was costly, however; as gold reserves became exhausted, there was little need for a large and expensive labor supply, and so their importation slowed down. Not until the full-scale development of the sugar industry was there again a significant need for manpower. The growth of the sugar industry, especially in the late eighteenth and nineteenth centuries, caused a major revolution in the island with the small plantation giving way to the large sugar estate and the small entrepreneurs being replaced by the large capitalist. But it was in the racial composition of the island that the far-reaching impact of this sugar revolution was most strongly felt. Thousands of black slaves entered Cuba in the nineteenth century, and by 1825 the black population had surpassed the white one.

Conditions of the slaves, while not unbearable, were not good. Blacks were much more valuable and seemed to have received better treatment than did the Indians earlier. Yet Spanish officials complained to the crown that the blacks were given little food or clothing and that they were subjected to abusive corporal punishment forcing many to escape into Cuba's mountains. These runaway slaves or *cimarrones,* as they were called, were a constant concern to the Spaniards, since by their example they encouraged other slaves to escape captivity and to rebel. As early as 1538 black slaves rioted and looted Havana while French privateers were attacking the city from the sea.

While most blacks worked in rural areas, some performed a variety of jobs in the cities. A considerable number labored in artisan industries, in construction, in the wharves, and in domestic service. Some were able to obtain their own earnings and thus liberate themselves or pay the price of their manumission. Others were freed after they had performed services their master was willing to reward. The number of slaves decreased continuously until reaching the low figure of 38,879 out of a total population of 171,620 in 1774.

These opportunities to become free contributed to the development of a uniquely Cuban society. Spanish law, the Catholic religion, the economic condition of the island, and the Spanish attitude toward the blacks all contributed to aid the blacks' integration into Cuban society. While the black population in the English sugar-producing colonies in the Caribbean lived under the tight political control of a small, exploiting minority of overseers and government officials, blacks in Cuba coexisted with the rest of the population and lived mainly by farming and grazing. Prior to the eighteenth century, the island avoided the plantation system with its concomitant large-scale capital investment, *latifundios* (large estates), and disciplined black slave labor force. Instead, society developed slowly with little outside interference. Cuba thus began to find its own identity in a society that combined within a Spanish framework, racial balance, small-scale agriculture, and folk-Catholicism. As Professor Sydney W. Mintz has pointed out, "Cuba as a Spanish colony had more nationhood than the colonies of other European powers in the Antilles might have had as sovereign states."*

---

*See Professor Mintz's Foreword to Ramiro Guerra y Sánchez, *Sugar and Society in the Caribbean* (New Haven: Yale University Press, 1964), p. xxiv.

4

THE FOREIGN
CHALLENGE

DURING the first decades of the sixteenth century Spanish settlements in Cuba and throughout the Caribbean were little challenged
by European powers. The remoteness and apparent poverty of the
newly discovered lands discouraged European nations from coloniz-
ing ventures. Furthermore, the spread of the Reformation and religious problems in Europe consumed the attention and finances of
possible challengers to Spain. The Spanish monarchy itself was powerful enough to claim supremacy over the seas and to expel intruders
from the Caribbean.

Yet from mid-century on foreign interlopers visited what Spain
considered its exclusive waters. These came primarily in two groups:
the pirates who owed allegiance to no country and were mostly
interested in plundering Spanish shipping and new settlements, and
the privateers who sailed under the flag of a particular European
nation and were concerned with trading with the colonists or
attacking Spanish colonies and ships at times of war in Europe.

While the colonists distinguished between the two groups, the
Spanish crown did not. For Spain both were unwelcome. The colonists, on the other hand, feared the pirates but welcomed the smugglers who brought cheaper goods than the Seville monopolists. They
also deplored Spanish naval policy which proved ineffective against

pirates but was curtailing smuggling. A conflict of interest soon developed between Spain and the settlers that was to persist throughout the colonial period. The former was mostly interested in seeing gold, silver, and other New World products arrive safely in Spain, while the latter were primarily interested in defending their exposed harbors and obtaining European goods at the cheapest possible price.

Until 1580, when the Spanish and Portuguese crowns were united, the principal smugglers were Portuguese and the most important contraband trade was in African slaves. It was the French privateers, however, who became particularly active in the Caribbean and threatened Spanish commerce. The outbreak of hostilities between Spain and France and the Treaty of Lyon between France and Portugal, which prohibited France from attacking Portuguese shipping, focused French attention on Cuba and other Spanish possessions in the Caribbean and led to numerous forays on towns and harbors. The most notorious of these was the attack by Jacques de Sores, who captured Havana and burnt a significant part of the city in 1555. Fortunately for Spain, these attacks coincided with rising religious strife in France. The French soon agreed to peace with Spain, thus halting, at least temporarily, French incursions into the Caribbean.

The increasing volume of trade and of silver coming from the New World whetted the appetite of yet another European power: Protestant England. Under Elizabeth, Anglo-Spanish relations deteriorated and the English showed a growing interest in trade with the Spanish Caribbean. In the 1560s John Hawkins made four trading trips to the area and, although not financially rewarding, these alerted the Spaniards to English intentions.

Spain reacted swiftly. It entrusted one of its most able strategists, Pedro Menéndez de Avilés, the task of coordinating sea and land defenses and unifying command in the Caribbean. A tough disciplinarian and a fine administrator, Menéndez was fiercely loyal to Spain and to Philip II who supported him throughout his career. Philip appointed him *adelantado* (royal deputy entrusted to found a colony) of Florida and later governor of Cuba. Since most shipping was by then done through the convoy system, Menéndez took steps to secure the safe passage of the fleets and to fortify key Spanish ports in the Caribbean. He oversaw construction at Havana harbor, where a fine dockyard was built, and made the city an almost impregnable fortress. He also fortified the cities of Cartagena, Santo

Domingo, Santiago de Cuba, and San Juan. Venting his wrath against the Protestant intruder, he destroyed a French Huguenot settlement in Florida and built a Spanish fort in its place. After his death in 1574, his successors continued his work, and for the next half-century Spanish fleets were able to return to Spain without much interference. Not until 1628 when the Dutch pirate Piet Heyn captured a Spanish fleet off the northern coast of Cuba did Spain lose a whole shipment of gold and silver to a foreign power.

If Menéndez was brilliant as a strategist, he was less successful in winning the support of the settlers in Cuba. They complained that as governor Menéndez had delegated most of his functions to subordinates while he worried about Florida and Spanish shipping and that he was unduly concerned with Havana to the detriment of Santiago, the most important settlement in the island at the time. Undoubtedly, from Spain's point of view Menéndez was successful. Yet his policies emphasized Spain's declining interest in the island settlements in relation to the wealthier and better populated mainland colonies and the relegation of Havana to a mere stopping point for the fleets.

Also despite Menéndez's successes, Havana, Santiago, and other Spanish cities in the Caribbean could never feel completely safe from foreign attacks. The English in particular looked with envious eyes at the growing wealth coming from the New World and hammered away at the possessions and shipping of its Catholic rival. In the 1570s and 1580s England unleashed Francis Drake, one of its most brilliant corsairs. An impoverished gentleman-landholder turned seaman, Drake attempted unsuccessfully to wrest the whole Caribbean away from Spain. In 1585 he captured and plundered Santo Domingo and Cartagena and almost captured the Spanish fleet off Panama. He sailed past Havana harbor where over 1,000 Spaniards, some brought especially from Mexico, waited unnecessarily to engage him. Instead of landing in Cuba he went on to St. Augustine in Florida, destroyed the Spanish fortifications being built there, and finally returned home. In 1595 Drake together with Hawkins again attacked the Caribbean. This time, however, the Spaniards were ready and inflicted heavy losses on the English. Drake and Hawkins themselves died and their decimated fleet barely made it back to Europe.

Spain's problems were further complicated by the revolt of its colonies in the Netherlands. The rebellion added a powerful anti-

Spanish naval power to the Caribbean and, although the Dutch were primarily interested in Brazil and Venezuela's salt deposits, their corsairs plundered the islands while their businessmen kept contraband with the Spanish settlers at a brisk pace.

The Dutch and the English worked together and by the beginning of the seventeenth century were ready to establish permanent settlements in the Caribbean. In the Treaty of London (1604) which ended Anglo-Spanish hostilities and in the Truce of Antwerp (1609) which ended the Netherlands' war with Spain, they both put forth the principle that they would not recognize Spanish rights in unoccupied parts of America and that they would respect Spanish claims only in effectively occupied territories. The Dutch and the English thus served notice on the Spaniards that the contest now was not only for plunder and trade but also for colonies.

Conditions were aggravated by Oliver Cromwell's accession to power in England. Like Drake in the sixteenth century, Cromwell in the seventeenth century fancied the idea of capturing the whole Caribbean and placing it under the English flag. His "Western Design" included capturing first Santo Domingo and then Cuba. An expedition launched in 1654, however, failed to capture Santo Domingo and the defensive measures taken in Cuba discouraged the English from attacking the island. The expedition instead turned south and took Jamaica in 1655.

The capture of Jamaica increased Cuba's vulnerabilities to English smugglers and pirates. In October 1662 the English launched an invasion from Jamaica which succeeded in capturing Santiago. They sacked the town and set it afire, taking with them slaves, church bells, and whatever artillery was available. Fearful that reinforcements might arrive, they returned safely to Jamaica, leaving the settlers and the Spanish government deeply distressed over the possible repetition of such attacks.

The rush for colonies and the English, French, and Dutch settlements in the Caribbean created a new challenge for Spain. These contenders now had local bases from where attacks on Spain's possessions could be launched. Jamaica provided for the English an ideal location from which goods could be smuggled to the welcoming Spaniards. Contraband increased as did the price of slaves, for now there was greater demand due to the growing sugar industry.

A new and different type of pirate emerged, too. The buccaneers, as they were called, were mercenaries with no political allegiance.

They served European nations in times of war and plundered for themselves in times of peace. Their source of hatred and interest was Catholic Spain. The buccaneers made the Caribbean their home and the islands of Tortuga and Jamaica their headquarters. Even the Isle of Pines off the southern coast of Cuba became a refuge for them.

The best known of these was Henry Morgan who terrorized Spanish settlers with his daring exploits. A cut-throat mercenary, he sacked northern South America, Porto Bello, and Camagüey and Oriente provinces in eastern Cuba, butchering or torturing to death those Spaniards who were not fortunate enough to escape his wrath. Until the end of the seventeenth century the inhabitants of the island lived under the fear of attack of these buccaneers, "the debased and brutalized successors of the Protestant corsairs of the sixteenth century."*

Buccaneering was not limited to England and France. After emerging out of the period of Spanish captivity in 1630, the Portuguese also became active in the area. Spain itself armed ships to raid the colonies of its enemies. Supported by business groups and the governor of Cuba, Spanish buccaneers attacked Port Royal in Jamaica and Saint Domingue, the French settlement on the western side of Hispaniola, and ventured as far north as Charleston. Many of these buccaneers left the Spanish service to engage in private looting.

As time went by and Jamaica and other English and French colonies became more productive, the two powers began to have second thoughts about buccaneering and raids on Spain. Now that the Spanish were willing to unleash their own buccaneers, the cost in lives and ruined property was growing and neither England nor France were willing to pay the price of this continuous warfare. Influential sugar planters pressured their governments to end hostilities with Spain and instead begin an era of economic competition. England itself realized that by continuing a policy of hostility toward Spain it was reducing its opportunities to supply Spanish colonies with many needed English products. England came to accept the idea that it would be best to trade peacefully with an increasingly weak Spain than to continue to harass Spain's distant empire.

The ambitions of Louis XIV, especially as were seen in his attacks

---

*J. H. Parry and P. M. Sherlock, *A Short History of the West Indies* (New York: St. Martin's Press, 1966), p. 87.

against the Spanish Netherlands, increased Spanish and English apprehensions. Holland, in particular, feared that if he succeeded in adding the Spanish Netherlands to France, his next move would be an effort to annex the Dutch provinces. The Dutch and the English soon put aside their mutual antagonisms and joined with Sweden in 1668 to form the Triple Alliance against France. Although the Alliance forced Louis to sign the Treaty of Aix-la-Chapelle (1668) and to renounce his claims to the Spanish Netherlands, he was bent on revenge against the Dutch. Soon he was successful in detaching England and Sweden from the Alliance, and Charles II of England even signed a short-lived secret treaty whereby he agreed, in return for financial assistance, to aid Louis in a war against the Dutch. It is no wonder then that England and Spain were most interested in maintaining harmonious relations at such critical times. In the Treaty of Madrid (1670), Spain acknowledged English possessions in the Caribbean and promised to end buccaneer raids. Over two decades later, in the Peace of Ryswyck (1697) which ended nine years of fighting between France and the League of Augsburg (Spain, Holland, Savoy, Austria, and England), formed to curb Louis's expansionist designs, war-weary France was forced to surrender all the European territory it had taken during the war, except Strasbourg; to acknowledge William III of Orange as king of England; to grant a favorable commercial treaty to the Dutch; and to promise to end buccaneer raids in the Caribbean, in return for permanent control of Saint Domingue.

The Treaty of Ryswyck marked the decline of the buccaneering era. England and France curtailed the activities of the buccaneers and in the Treaty of Utrecht (1713), which ended the War of the Spanish Succession, England obtained from Spain an *asiento* to bring African slaves to the Spanish colonies. The newly organized London's South Sea Company was also permitted to bring one ship full of English goods to be sold to the Spanish possessions. Soon English ships flooded Caribbean markets. Smuggling grew as did the unhappiness of the Spanish crown which saw a reduction in revenues collected from the islands. The economy of Cuba, on the other hand, received a shot in the arm from the availability of a relatively cheap labor force as well as supplies to support the slaves. Unfortunately for Cuba, this situation lasted only for a few years until the new outbreak of hostilities between England and Spain. The War of Jenkin's Ear (1740) was used by the latter to clamp down on smuggling and to attempt to eradicate the fastidious English merchants from the Caribbean.

By the eighteenth century the character of the struggle in the Caribbean changed. Instead of the undisciplined, disorganized buccaneers and privateers of the seventeenth century, disciplined and organized navies would confront each other. The Caribbean became the arena where European rivalries would be aired. As time went by and the economic and strategic value of colonies increased, European powers went to war to defend their possessions and to cripple the commercial capabilities of its enemies. Wars no longer started because of incidents in Europe and moved to the Caribbean; instead, as evidenced by the War of Jenkin's Ear and even the Seven Years' War (1756–1763), they started in the New World and then moved to Europe. While dynastic ties and succession, the search for a balance of power in Europe, and monarchical ambitions were in many instances behind these wars, commercial rivalries and control of Caribbean lands came to play a growing part in European conflicts.

Also, Spain was no longer the object of English and French attacks. Instead the two great powers now faced each other. In frank decadence, impoverished and weakened after years of conflict, and governed by inept and vacillating monarchs, Spain retreated to the position of a second-rate power, usually supporting France's policies and being drawn into wars not of her own making.

Caribbean islands increasingly became mere pawns in the chessboard of international politics. Captured in times of war by rival powers, they were usually later returned at the peace table or changed hands permanently in return for lands in Europe or for some trade concession. For most islands and especially for Cuba, war dislocated trade, increased taxation, and produced human suffering.

5

THE RISE OF
KING SUGAR

OF all the wars that ravaged the Caribbean, one in particular, the Seven Years' War (1756–1763), had a profound effect on Cuba. At first only France and England were at war; soon Spain came in on the French side. Motivated by dynastic connections with France, by grievances against England and its colonies in the New World, especially in Central America, and by an awareness that if France lost the war England would be supreme in the Caribbean, Spain cast its lot with the French. Spain's entrance into the war proved disastrous, since she lacked the naval power to confront the English or to prevent them from capturing its possessions. In August 1762 the English destroyed a large Spanish naval force and captured Manila and Havana, only to trade the latter back to Spain for Florida at the Treaty of Paris in 1763.

Before the late eighteenth century, Cuba had lived an uneventful and meager existence, threatened only by pirate attacks and minor internal disturbances. Yet, lying on the path of the fleets, Havana had become a thriving commercial and naval center and had grown faster than the other cities of the island. The passing Spanish fleets encouraged the development of a variety of businesses related to tourism. Cattle and pig raising also developed, as well as the growing of fruits and vegetables to be sold to the fleets.

Cattle attained a privileged position. During the seventeenth and part of the eighteenth centuries, most of the island was covered by large cattle ranches. Although these had first been obtained through individual grants, they were later transformed into collective properties or *haciendas comuneras* through property transfers and sales or inheritances. Each *comunero* received, instead of a piece of land as in the early days, a share or *peso de posesión* of the appraised value of the farm, and branded his own livestock within the collective farm. As time went by, these practices limited somewhat the growth of large cattle estates and encouraged, instead, small-scale land ownership.

Another factor preventing large-scale landholdings or latifundism was the growth of the tobacco industry, especially in the seventeenth and early eighteenth centuries. Aided by an increasing demand in Europe, and Cuba's ideal soil, tobacco farms or *vegas* sprung up all around Havana and Pinar del Río. The small labor force and amount of capital required for cultivating tobacco helped *vegas* to spread, in spite of government monopolies and restrictions. Grown principally on small independent farms by immigrants from the Canary Islands, tobacco soon rivaled the privileged position of cattle and was one of the factors contributing to the subdivision of the cattle estates.

As the demand for tobacco grew in Europe, Spain tightened its control over the industry in Cuba. In an attempt to increase revenues, a government monopoly was set up by which the crown purchased Cuban tobacco at a cheap price and then sold it in Europe at considerable profit. All tobacco production was placed under a government monopoly early in 1717, and a general purchasing agency was set up in Havana with offices in several other important cities.

Tobacco growers complained about these oppressive economic policies, but to no avail. Unhappiness with Spain's mercantilistic policies took several forms. Smuggling, which had existed almost since the establishment of the colony, now increased substantially. Resistance and opposition grew to the point of armed rebellion. A series of unsuccessful tobacco growers' revolts against Spanish mercantilism, and particularly the tobacco monopoly, occurred in the 1720s, but Spain continued its policies. It was not until a bloody, but successful revolt in 1812, at the time of growing Spanish liberalism, that Spain ended the monopoly.

The tobacco planters were not the only ones hurt by Spanish policies. The establishment of the Royal Company of Commerce in 1740 placed all the island's commerce in the hands of a few businessmen from Cadiz and Havana, with the backing of the crown. Cuban producers were now forced to sell their sugar, tobacco, and hides to the company at low prices. Cost of imports also increased as the company sought to realize a handsome profit from their privileged position as chief exporter and importer. During the two decades of its existence, the company proved a very successful venture for its Spanish stockholders, but Cuba's commercial development was hampered and production lagged. Small planters and producers, as well as the population in general, suffered from these practices.

Cattle and tobacco, together with the sugar industry, which now began to make inroads into the economy, helped to shape Cuba's developing society into distinctive classes. At the top was a small group of owners who ran the large cattle, tobacco, and sugar industries, and who, together with the city merchants and lawyers, decisively influenced the politics of the island. In close contact with Spanish authorities both in the island and in Spain, they used their influence to further their economic interests. At first city merchants and rural planters worked together, but during the nineteenth century a conflict developed between the two groups, with the planters requesting freer trade, and the merchants clinging to a protectionist and monopolistic policy.

Next came the small landholder, principally the individual tobacco grower who struggled to eke out a living and shared his meager existence with a variety of sharecroppers and leaseholders. A group of overseers, bookkeepers, and plantation employees formed a class apart entrusted to take care of the properties of the often absentee bosses. In the cities, their counterparts included skilled tradesmen, carpenters, and other artisans. Further down came a large body of landless peasants, the rural proletariat, who worked for wages and had little hope of obtaining any land. Their numbers grew as the sugar industry developed in the nineteenth and twentieth centuries. In the cities a similar group, the poor white, worked for wages or commuted to plantations for seasonal employment. During the sugar harvest, these lived side by side with a good number of free blacks and mulattoes, and intermingled freely with them. At the very bottom of the scale were the black slaves, who worked primarily in the sugar estates. With little hope of mobility, many just resigned themselves to their unhappy fate. Some, however, escaped the plantations and joined, particularly in the nineteenth century, secret organizations which promised an end to their condition of servitude. In the late nineteenth century, when they realized that liberation would come only by breaking Cuba's ties with Spain, many joined the wars for independence (1868–1898).

The growth of the sugar industry imbalanced this social scheme. By the first quarter of the nineteenth century the number of people on the island increased significantly, and there were now considerably more blacks than whites.* Up to this time, sugar had grown slowly, primarily because of lack of markets and the difficulties and cost of bringing in slaves and equipment. Spain itself was unable to absorb Cuba's sugar production, and the Laws of the Indies prevented Cuba from trading with other nations, thus curtailing the dynamic growth of the industry.

Several factors converged in the late eighteenth century to bring Cuba out of its isolation and to give the sugar industry the boost it needed. The relaxation of Spanish trade restrictions; the emergence, with the establishment of the United States in 1776, of an important and close market for Cuban products; and the devastation of Haiti's sugar and coffee estates following the rebellion of the slaves in the 1790s, all had an impact on bringing the island into the mainstream of world affairs. But it was the English capture and occupation of Havana that really shocked the Cuban society out of its lethargic sleep.

During the brief eleven months of English occupation, the oppressive Spanish trade restrictions were lifted, and Havana was thrown open to trade with England and particularly with the North American colonies. Over seven hundred merchant ships visited the port during those months, more than the number that had visited Havana in the preceding decade. English capital, as well as large numbers of low-priced slaves, entered the island, boosting sugar production. For the most part, England maintained Spanish administrative institutions, although an attempt was made to purify the judicial system by ending some of the existing privileges and streamlining judicial practices.

The impact of the occupation was long range. It made the Cubans aware of the benefits of trading with the English and particularly with a close and growing market like the United States. The large

---

*By 1791 there were already 138,700 blacks and 133,500 whites. In 1872, out of a population of 700,000, there were 286,942 slaves and 106,949 freed blacks.

quantities of English goods that entered the island gave the Cubans a taste for those products and increased their demands for freer trade. Similarly, the occupation focused the attention of North American entrepreneurs on Cuba's economic potential as an area for investment, a source of raw materials, and a market for English and North American products. Finally, Spain was forced to reexamine its policies toward Cuba. The island was no more the stopping point of the fleets, but a bone of contention among European powers, one important enough to have merited English effort at conquest. Spain had to look at her Caribbean possession and try to satisfy, or at least placate, the demands and aspirations of her tropical subjects.

The English occupation had given the island the initial economic boost it needed. When the slave uprisings and the destruction of properties occurred in Haiti, Cuba was ready to become the sugar bowl of the Caribbean, and she soon replaced Haiti as the supplier of European sugar. Cuban planters pleaded with the Spanish crown for the easing of trade relations and for the free importation of slaves. In particular, Francisco de Arango y Parreño, one of the island's most prominent Creole planters who was in Madrid at the time of the Haitian rebellion, fully realized the opportunities that the development afforded Cuba, and he carried his group's message to the monarchs in Spain. Through his influential pleadings he obtained the elimination of many trade barriers and permission for the free and unlimited importation of slaves beginning in 1791.

In the years that followed, the sugar industry grew substantially. Annual production rose from 14,000 tons in 1790 to over 34,000 tons in 1805, and the number of sugar mills grew to 478, more than twice as many as had existed prior to the English capture of Havana. Sugar also benefited from the close commercial relations that developed between Cuba and the United States. The wars of the French Revolution isolated Spain from her colonies thus helping the growth of trade between Cuba and the United States. By the turn of the century, Cuba enjoyed substantial trade with the United States and when Cuban ports were thrown open to free trade with all nations in 1818, commercial relations between the two grew even closer.

Throughout the nineteenth century sugar as well as coffee became increasingly important in the Cuban economy. Large cattle estates were subdivided and sold to enterprising Spaniards for sugar or coffee cultivation. Aware of the profit possibilities, the Spanish crown encouraged and aided the subdivisions of land. Prior to this time, much suitable land was often part of large estates whose owners could neither divide nor sell the land since it had been granted to them for use, not ownership. Alejandro Ramírez, distinguished economist and Cuba's finance intendant from 1816 until 1821, studied the situation and obtained the crown's approval in 1819 to consider landowners all those who could prove they had been on the land for the past forty years. This facilitated the breakdown of large estates, contributed to the growth of the sugar industry, and benefited a new class of proprietors who could either sell their land at a profit, become sugar producers themselves, or lease their land to other less fortunate and smaller planters who did not receive title to a piece of real estate. In 1827 there were in Cuba, 1,000 sugar mills, 2,067 coffee estates, and 5,534 tobacco farms. By 1860 it is estimated that there were about 2,000 sugar mills, perhaps the greatest number in Cuban history. A prosperous and large class of rural proprietors who based their prosperity on the cultivation of sugar and tobacco had emerged.

Despite its rapid growth, the development of the sugar industry was not without serious problems and setbacks. Overproduction, fluctuations in price, competition from the English islands in the Caribbean, and the appearance of a dreaded competition, beet sugar, in the second decade of the century, depressed the sugar market and slowed down Cuba's sugar boom. These problems were further complicated by the English-imposed legal suppression of the slave trade in 1821 which deprived the island of a continuous source of labor and by the lack of an appropriate network of internal transportation which could facilitate the moving of the sugar to the mills and the ports of embarkation.

In the 1840s, however, two events renewed the acceleration of the sugar industry. Coffee, which had come to occupy an important position in the island's economy, was seriously affected by a fall in prices which almost ruined coffee planters. Capital and labor fled from coffee into sugar and much land was shifted toward the growing of cane. The second event was the introduction of the railroad. Cane could now be brought from remote areas to the mills and then to the ports for shipment. Bitter rivalries developed among mill owners for control of individual cane growers and nearby lands. As railroads came into wider use and demand for sugar grew, mill owners purchased idle land as well as that of small producers. What started out as a not too large business grew into a powerful capitalistic enterprise based on large landholding, slave labor, and mass production.

The wars for independence in the last three decades of the century slowed down this trend somewhat. The conditions that prevailed on the island during those bloody years of war were not conducive to new investments. Capital retracted and production fell. The war, together with the still limited resources of the sugar mill owners, only awaited a new infusion of capital. This occurred after the island became independent in 1902. Protected by a policy which favored foreign investment, American capital invaded the sugar industry, accelerating the concentration of land as well as cementing Cuba's dependence on one export crop.

In the early decades of the nineteenth century, most Cubans seemed content with their status. The new aristocracy of wealth that had developed around the sugar industry enjoyed its recently acquired wealth and feared that a repetition in Cuba of the continental wars would upset the social order upon which its prosperity depended. These "aristocrats" were willing to tolerate a limited number of political and economic reforms, so long as the *status quo* was not endangered: to them that *status quo* meant the presence of a foreign power to protect their position against the possibility of a black rebellion similar to the one in Haiti. By the 1840s there was real concern about preserving Cuba's colonial status. Still fearful of a slave rebellion, or even an actual end to slavery forced upon a weak Spain by England, they looked toward the United States for a possible permanent relationship. Painfully aware of the problems in the English Caribbean since the abolition of slavery and its impact on sugar production, the property owners saw in the United States, particularly in the southern states, a slave-owning society similar to Cuba's own plantation economy. A series of slave revolts in Cuba in the early 1840s increased apprehension and the desire for a permanent relationship with the United States.

Since the administration of Thomas Jefferson, the United States had shown an interest in Cuba and looked sympathetically at the possibility of annexing the island. At a time when the new nation was expanding westerly, some U.S. leaders saw Cuba as a valuable acquisition and feared that England might wish to acquire the island. In 1825 Henry Clay reaffirmed U.S. concern, explaining that his country "could not see with indifference" Cuba's passing into the hands of another European power.

United States interest in Cuba and in its strategic location grew, particularly after the war with Mexico and the acquisition of California. In the 1840s and 1850s, Presidents James K. Polk, Franklin Pierce, and James Buchanan attempted unsuccessfully to buy Cuba from Spain. In 1854 three United States ministers to Europe signed a secret report, later known as the "Ostend Manifesto" which called for the U.S. purchase of Cuba or, if this failed, the forceful wresting of the island from Spain.

The Ostend Manifesto was the high watermark of U.S. interest to acquire Cuba peacefully in the 1850s. Other efforts, however, proved bolder. During the administrations of Presidents Zachary Taylor (1849–1850) and Millard Fillmore (1850–1853), pro-slavery elements were discouraged by lack of official support and some turned to filibustering expeditions hoping that this might lead to the overthrow of Spanish power in the island. The principal filibusterer was Narciso López, a Venezuelan-born Spanish general who lived in Cuba and became involved in a conspiracy to annex Cuba to the United States.

Exiled to the United States, López resumed his conspiratorial activities and organized an expedition with the support of southern leaders. In 1850 he sailed from New Orleans with a force of over six hundred men, mostly American veterans of the Mexican War, and landed in Cárdenas, Matanzas province. The expeditionaries overwhelmed the small Spanish force and captured the town. But finding little support from the population and faced with Spanish reinforcements, López retreated and escaped to the United States. The untiring and daring Venezuelan sailed again in 1851 with over four hundred men, mostly Southerners, some Hungarians and Germans, and a few Cubans. He planned to join with conspirators in the island, but these rebelled prematurely and were rapidly annihilated. López landed in Pinar del Río in a desolate area far from the uprisings. He found little support and was soon defeated and captured by the Spanish army. When he was publicly garroted in Havana on September 1, 1851, he insisted: "My death will not change the destiny of Cuba."

Historians still disagree about López's real objectives. Some point out that he wanted the island's independence; others insist that he desired Cuba's annexation to the United States. Perhaps he wanted a free Cuba, but one where slavery could be preserved. Whatever his motivations, López's actions helped arouse anti-Spanish sentiment in the island and paved the way for later uprisings.

López's failure and the United States Civil War ended, at least temporarily, the clamor for annexation. The abolition of slavery in the United States deprived Cuban slaveholders of the reason for wanting to tie themselves permanently to their northern neighbor. Abraham Lincoln's coming to power also had a significant effect on the Cuban policy of the United States, for Lincoln and his advisers were willing, as long as Spain remained unaggressive, to allow Cuba to stay under Spanish control. The expansionist attempts of the 1840s and 1850s thus gave way to the less aggressive era of the 1860s. The proponents of the acquisition of Cuba were not defeated, however, only silenced. What their brethren were unable to achieve in mid-century, the expansionists of the 1890s accomplished at the turn of the century when the United States occupied Cuba during the Spanish-American War and later exerted considerable political and economic influence over the affairs of the island.

Cuba's destiny seemed inexorably tied to sugar and to the United States. Sugar was king and sugar dictated the political and economic direction of the island. As the nineteenth century progressed, latifundism supplanted small landholding, black slaves drove away white workers, and the United States began to cast its shadow over the future development of Cuba.

II

TOWARD INDEPENDENCE

6

THE GOLDEN CENTURY

By the beginning of the nineteenth century, Cuba was experiencing an economic prosperity that was closely tied to the development of the sugar industry. The progressive changes known as the Bourbon Reforms, initiated throughout Latin America by Charles III (1759–1788), quickened economic and political activities and started a complete transformation of Cuban society. Population increased, agricultural production and profits expanded, and contacts with various Spanish ports as well as with the rest of Europe became closer, leading to the introduction of new ideas into the colony. The old order began to decay. To the forefront of Cuban society came a new and active class of Creole *hacendados* and entrepreneurs who based their prosperity on sugar, coffee, land speculation, and the slave trade.

It was only natural that members of this group made their point of view felt concerning economic and social matters. As the century progressed and their power increased they began questioning Spanish mercantilistic policies. In the press, in treatises, and through their visits to Spain they advocated freer trade for Cuba, cheap and unlimited importation of slaves, and reduced tariff for products imported into the island. Their primary focus concerned their immediate economic interests. Yet, at a time when Europe was undergoing profound intellectual changes resulting partly from the Enlightenment, their questioning of Spain's economic policies naturally led to the growth of a more critical attitude on the part of many Creole writers and intellectuals on the island. The desire for economic reforms was later translated into a desire for political and even social change. Intellectual activity flourished so intensely during the century that the period has come to be known as Cuba's Golden Century.

Two individuals in particular were instrumental in shaping the intellectual climate of the island, Captain-General Don Luis de las Casas and Bishop Díaz de Espada. A truly enlightened ruler in both cultural and economic matters, las Casas was sent to Cuba as captain-general in 1790. After he acquired a sugar mill, his own interests became tied to those of the Creole planting class, in particular to the Creole planter and economist Arango y Parreño. The two men joined in founding in 1792 the Sociedad Económica de Amigos del País (the Economic Society), a center of learning and discussion; the Junta de Fomento, an agricultural and development board; and the *Papel Periódico,* Cuba's first newspaper.

The Sociedad Económica became the headquarters of a tightly organized and influential group of Creoles from Havana. In their meetings they discussed science and arts, culture and education, and commerce and industry. But their consuming interest was agriculture, especially sugar. They were instrumental in obtaining from Spain permission for the free and unlimited importation of slaves. When war broke out between Spain and France in 1793, they prevailed on las Casas to open Cuba's ports to neutral and allied nations; the resulting purchase of Cuban sugar by the United States and England resulted in growing prosperity. The Sociedad also became the most influential advocate for significant changes in the landholding structure of the island. By 1815 the group had succeeded in convincing the Spanish government to permit the outright ownership of land previously held in usufruct, to sell crown lands, and to devote hardwood forests to agricultural production thus paving the way for the rapid expansion of the sugar industry.

The influence of the members of the Sociedad rested not in their numbers, which reached about two hundred, but on their economic power. The corruption and inefficiency of the Spanish bureaucracy in the island weakened royal control and made Spanish officials easy tools of the Creole planters. Particularly on the issue of slavery, Creoles, Peninsulars, and slave traders or *negreros* developed an uneasy alliance to preserve the institution and Spanish officials were therefore powerless to implement legislation on behalf of the slaves. In desperate need of capital for its depleted treasury, war-exhausted Spain also bowed to the demands of the Cuban planters to sell crown lands for sugar growing.

The members of the Sociedad found an important ally in Bishop Espada. Sent to Havana in 1802, he became a director of the Sociedad and the mentor of numerous reforms and educational institutions. He sponsored a crusade for smallpox vaccination and the building of a new cemetery and opened his own library to students and friends. It was he more than anyone else who, although belatedly, brought the ideas of the Enlightenment to Cuba, thus paving the way for the period of intellectual ferment that spanned the nineteenth century.

Espada encountered two centers of higher learning in Havana, the Real y Pontificia Universidad de San Gerónimo, established in 1728, and the Real Colegio Seminario de San Carlos, founded in 1773. Of the two, the seminary had perhaps the strongest impact on intellectual developments during the nineteenth century. Out of its classrooms came such influential Creoles, some later prominent members of the Sociedad Económica, as José Agustín Caballero, Arango y Parreño, José de la Luz y Caballero, Félix Varela, and José Antonio Saco. Founded after the expulsion of the Jesuits, the seminary trained those entering the priesthood as well as those pursuing lay professions. Espada liberalized available readings and under his guidance the traditional scholastic methods were abandoned.

Scholasticism, which consisted of theological and philosophical thought based on Aristotelian logic and church dogma, had permeated education in Cuba as well as throughout Latin America. Students were subjected to memorization and recitation of the Latin materials read by the professor. Through the workings of Espada and some of his disciples, most notably Father Félix Varela, much of this was changed. Varela began to teach modern philosophy at the seminary, and established the explicative method of teaching in the vernacular. Aided by the bishop, who provided him with the necessary equipment and protection, Varela also offered the first physics classes. Of all of Espada's protégés, he in particular exerted a strong influence among the youth of the island, especially toward the latter half of the century when he became an ardent exponent of Cuban independence.

Espada enthusiastically convinced Varela to lecture on constitutional law at San Carlos, an experience that prepared him for his later participation in the Spanish Cortes. A staunch defender of the liberal Spanish constitution of 1812, Varela fostered among his students a growing sympathy for liberal ideas and a dislike for the absolutism of Ferdinand VII. Unlike las Casas, Varela claimed that the abolition of slavery was necessary for the future well-being of Cuba. A Creole intellectual liberal, he differed from the Creole planters in Cuba who still advocated the retention of slavery. Varela's position, which he maintained before the Spanish Cortes, left a profound impact upon his students and Cuban society.

After the failure of liberalism in Spain, and the restoration of Ferdinand VII's authoritarian rule with the aid of the Holy Alliance and the invading French armies in 1823, Varela left for the United States, where he began to call for the complete separation of Cuba from Spain. It was mostly through his newspaper, *El Habanero,* published in New York and smuggled secretly into Cuba, that Varela expounded the need for Cuba's independence. His appeal became so widespread that the worried Spanish authorities even sent an assassin to the United States in an unsuccessful attempt to kill him. Fearful that his writings might incite his youthful followers to a premature and futile revolt, and aware that the Cuban planters would not yet join an independent movement, Varela ceased publishing his newspaper in 1826 and refrained from further political involvement.

Varela's significance goes well beyond the teachings and reforms he introduced at San Carlos with the aid of Bishop Espada. His importance resides in the fact that he was representative of a growing number of Creole intellectuals who were becoming increasingly disillusioned with the possibility of reform within the Spanish empire. These Creoles formed a cosmopolitan, articulate, and well-educated elite. Contrary to the rural *hacienda* elite of Mexico and other parts of Latin America, which looked inward and was mostly concerned with the maintenance of its self-sufficient landed estates, Cuba's Creole elite was urban and more oriented toward the outside world. The nature of the sugar industry forced it to wrestle with a budding capitalistic enterprise and with the problems of labor, technology, transportation, marketing, and finances. Cuba became very much part of the world scene with an economy tied to and dependent on the international commercial centers of the world, a feature that survived its colonial period.

Naturally, many of the attitudes and actions of the group that came to dominate the Cuban economy and politics in the nineteenth century were influenced by these ties with the international community and particularly with Spain's inability to satisfy the island's economic needs. It finally became clear that Spanish policy had little to offer in exchange for increased taxation, ineffective administration, and virtual exclusion of Creoles from responsible positions in government—the Cubans turned away from any hopes of reform and toward independence.

Varela, a constitutional reformer and an early admirer of Spanish liberalism, by the 1820s had accepted the idea that the only road open to the Cubans was complete separation from Spain. He and other Creole intellectuals, particularly José Antonio Saco, sociologist, journalist, and author of the multivolume *Historia de la Esclavitud* (1879), and José de la Luz y Caballero, came to expound a vague and romantic form of nationalism.

But it was perhaps in the poetry of the time that Cuba's emerging soul found its best expression. Some poets like Fornaris and El Cucalambé eulogized the Indian past and used Indian themes to attack oppression and to foster a love for the island's traditions. As the century progressed, the bellicosity of Cuban poetry increased, especially from the 1830s until the wars for independence in the 1860s. A number of poets, such as José María Heredia and Juan Clemente Zenea, were exiled while others like Hernández Echerri were executed for their anti-Spanish activities. Miguel Teurbe Tolón in his famous poem "Mi proposito" attacked Spanish despotism and called upon Cubans to sacrifice for their country. It was through the verse and prose of these men that a national consciousness and a separate identity began to be fostered in a society previously oriented toward self-enrichment and permeated by political cynicism.

The desire for separation from Spain had focused, particularly in the first half of the century, on annexation to the United States. Fearful that England might force Spain to abolish slavery in the island or that a Haitian-type rebellion might occur and seeing numerous commercial and security advantages in a close relation with the North, some Cubans looked toward the slave society of the United States in hopes of establishing a lasting relationship. Composed mainly of Creole planters and slaveowners, and some writers and intellectuals, the annexationists realized the dangers involved in a struggle to annex Cuba to the United States. Threatened with losing Cuba, Spain might liberate the slaves and use them against the white planters, or the blacks themselves might see the struggle as an opportunity for liberation. The end result of the annexationists' attempts could thus be the opposite of their main objective: the maintenance of the slave system. Yet, the example of Jamaica where a slave uprising had been crushed in the 1830s and the awareness of their own power encouraged the annexationists. They seriously questioned the future of Cuba under Spain and characterized the Cuban as "a slave, politically, morally, and physically." Annexation, they emphasized, would ensure "Cuba's peace and future success; her wealth would increase; liberty would be given to individual action, and the system of hateful and harmful restrictions which paralyzed commerce and agriculture would be destroyed."

Several events in mid-century weakened the annexationist movement. For one thing, the fears of the Cuban planters were somewhat appeased when Spain stiffened its resistance to English pressure to end the slave trade and emancipate the slaves. The lack of official United States encouragement, particularly in the 1850s, and the violent expansion of the United States into Texas, northern Mexico, and California, somewhat discouraged annexationist effort. The development of an incipient nationalism, particularly among Creole elements within the island, also weakened the feeling for annexation among the already small minority who advocated it; indeed, the great majority of the Cubans certainly did not sponsor annexation. Finally the United States Civil War dealt a death blow to those who still hoped for a close relation with a similar slave society.

Partly representative of this stage of the movement was the distinguished Creole writer José Antonio Saco. An early advocate of annexation, Saco had come to realize by mid-century that it was not the way to attain the political liberty denied to Cuba. He admired the neighbor to the north, but felt that the United States would not fight to incorporate Cuba and without its aid any rebellion in the island would prove disastrous for the white population. He saw numerous advantages in annexation to the United States but he feared the powerful influence that the Anglo-Saxon population and ideas would have on the Cubans. Inevitably, because of its growing population and emerging expansionism, the United States would impose its will and culture on the island. The Cubans would then be converted into an oppressed minority within their own country. Saco warned that Cuba would not only be annexed but absorbed, thus preventing the development of a Cuban nationality.

With the annexation movement faltering and the possibility of independence still remote, some Cubans again turned to attempts at reform within the Spanish empire. Reformism, which had existed in Cuba since the beginning of the nineteenth century, took new impetus in mid-century partly due to the failure of a number of conspiracies aimed at expelling Spanish power and to black uprisings against slavery in the island. Also, Spain seemed at the time to be following a more conciliatory policy toward Cuba. Under the administration of Captain-Generals Francisco Serrano (1859–1862) and Domingo Dulce (1862–1865), Spain initiated a period of tolerance perhaps in an attempt to arrest independent tendencies. Cubans were permitted to publish a newspaper outlining the reforms they desired in the colonial regime. Serrano even prepared a law project which would restore Cuban participation in the Spanish Cortes.

The reformers sought to obtain from Spain numerous political and economic concessions. They called for more equitable taxation and freer trade as well as political representation at the Spanish Cortes. Contrary to some of their predecessors who had advocated not only the continuation of slavery but the expansion of the slave trade, these reformers advocated the ending of the slave trade and even the gradual abolition of slavery.

Several factors—among them the pressure of reformers, British insistence on abolition, and the example of the Civil War in the United States—gravitated in favor of abolition. A number of large estate owners had come to realize the economic disadvantages of slavery at a time of increased mechanization. Also, in the late 1840s and 1850s a number of Chinese laborers and Indians from the Yucatán had arrived in Cuba to work in the sugar fields and in railroad construction, providing a cheap, although still small, labor supply whose maintenance was less problematic than that of the slave population. A significant number of white workers, many with skills needed to operate the new machinery, also joined the labor force in the mills. Finally, those seeking the overthrow of Spanish power in Cuba looked at the black population as a strong and necessary ally in any attempt to liberate Cuba. Yet, despite these strong forces at work, emancipation came about slowly. In 1865 the slave trade was partially curtailed, but it was not until 1886, long after the end of the Ten Years' War, Cuba's first major attempt at independence, that slavery was completely abolished.*

---

*On November 5, 1879 the Spanish government issued a law abolishing slavery in Cuba. It established an eight-year state of tutelage (*patronato*) for all liberated slaves. Patterned somewhat on the earlier apprenticeship system introduced by England for its Caribbean possessions, the *patronato* guaranteed the continued labor

In 1865 the reform movement was strong enough to organize the Partido Reformista, the first such political party to exist in the island. The party was not a cohesive political organization. Some of its members had been previously involved with the annexation movement and a few still flirted with the idea. Others wanted some form of political autonomy for Cuba within the Spanish empire. Still others called for the island's representation at the Cortes. A few felt that *reformismo* could be a step that would eventually lead to complete independence. In general the party advocated equal rights for Cubans and Peninsulars, limitation on the powers of the captain-general, and greater political freedom in the island. It also supported freer trade and gradual abolition of slavery, and called for an increase of white immigrants into Cuba. The newspaper *El Siglo,* published in Havana since 1862, was purchased a year later by the Reformists and placed under the editorship of the able Francisco Frías, count of Pozos Dulces, a renowned statesman and economist.

The activities of the Reformists soon met with strong opposition from a group of Peninsulars who formed the Partido Incondicional Español (the Unconditional Spanish party). Trying to prevent any economic or political change, especially if it affected their interests, the Peninsulars used their newspaper, the *Diario de la Marina,* to attack the reformers. They cautioned that any concessions from Spain could only strengthen the Creoles, weakening continuous Spanish control over Cuba.

The work of the reformers and their clash with the Peninsulars had an impact on Spain. Following the successful movement for independence in Santo Domingo against Spanish rule in 1865, and at a time when Spain was experiencing renewed economic and political difficulties, the Spanish monarchy felt it would be best to moderate its policy toward Cuba. It therefore called for the election of a reform

---

of the blacks for their masters. Masters were required to furnish their wards with proper food and clothing, and to furnish them monthly wages. It proved more profitable, however, for the masters to free the blacks and hire them as laborers, thereby avoiding the necessity of maintaining them during slack seasons. With sugar developing as a modern, mechanized industry, without a continuous supply of new slaves, and with the availability of an alternate labor supply composed of poor whites and Asians, black slavery became increasingly uneconomical. The abolitionists themselves condemned the *patronato* as "harder servitude than slavery itself," and by October 7, 1886, two years before the *patronato* was to terminate, a royal decree abolished slavery in Cuba.

commission that would discuss changes to be introduced in the island.

The Junta de Información, as the commission came to be known, was composed of Creole reformers and Peninsulars. To appease the fears of the conservative elements within Cuba, and to prevent the election of radical reformers, the Spanish government instructed the Cuban municipalities to set high property qualifications for voting. Yet to everyone's surprise, the reformers won a smashing victory in the elections. Of the sixteen Cuban commissioners, twelve were Creole reformers. Among them were some of the most prominent members in Cuban society, such as José Morales Lemus, Miguel Aldama, the count of Pozos Dulces, and José Antonio Saco. The results of this election clearly indicated the Cubans' desire for reform. They should by no means, however, be interpreted as a widespread Cuban desire for independence. It seems that a significant proportion of the white Creole population of the island still hoped, as late as the 1860s, for a modification of Spanish policy and the introduction of reforms that would permit them to continue within the Spanish empire.

The Junta met in Madrid in late 1866 and early 1867. It started its discussion in a pessimistic atmosphere, following the overthrow of a liberal Spanish government. Yet a number of political reforms were adopted, including representation in the Cortes, equality of access to civil employment, freedom from arbitrary arrest and search, and civil and criminal codes similar to those of the peninsula. On the question of emancipation, the Cuban commissioners, opposed to granting immediate freedom to the slaves, instead favored gradual emancipation. That many of the political and economic demands were adopted during the sessions and particularly that the Spanish government looked with sympathetic eyes to these possible reforms seemed to augur future success. On the last day of the conference, the colonial secretary, Alejandro de Castro, publicly congratulated the commissioners and called for a rapid implementation of their recommendations.

Yet, the hope for change was short-lived. It soon became clear that the colonial secretary was speaking for himself. The Narváez government, which had come to power as the Reform Commission began deliberations several months earlier, had decided to let the commission meet, but had no intention of implementing its recommendations. In early 1867 the Spanish government not only disbanded the Junta and dismissed all of its recommendations, but also imposed new and irritating taxes. Spain, furthermore, sent to Cuba Francisco Lersundi, a reactionary captain-general who prohibited public meetings and clamped a tight political censure over reformist literature.

The failure of the Junta de Información in particular and of reformism in general gave new impetus to the independence movement. Aware that Spain would not permit any significant changes and that the island's destiny as well as their own would best be served by an independent Cuba, Creoles began preparing for complete separation from Spain.

7

THE "EVER-FAITHFUL"
COLONY REBELS

WHILE remaining in the Spanish fold, the "ever-faithful" island, as Cuba became known, grew away from the metropolitan power. The interests and views of the Creoles and Peninsulars increasingly clashed. Reconciliation seemed difficult; those who clamored for violence became more numerous; finally war broke out. The wars for independence that followed lasted more than thirty years, from 1868 until the outbreak of the Spanish-American War, followed by the intervention of the United States in 1898. The wars were Cuba's belated reaction to the fight for independence throughout most of Latin America during the first quarter of the century.

This is not to say that there were no attempts made by Cubans to separate from Spain in the first part of the century. As early as 1809, at a time of turmoil and rebellion against Spanish power in Latin America, several Cubans led by a distinguished lawyer, Joaquín Infante, conspired to gain independence for Cuba. Infante even wrote a constitution that was to govern Cuba after independence. In the early 1820s the conspiracy of the Rayos y Soles de Bolívar, the most important of this period, sought to establish the Republic of Cubanacán. Led by José Francisco Lemus, a Cuban who had fought in the Colombian army, the Rayos y Soles organized into Masonic lodges throughout Cuba and received support from Colombia and

from Simón Bolívar, the South American "Liberator." Mexican revolutionaries also aided their Cuban brethren. A cell of the Gran Legión
del Águila Negra from Mexico was organized in Cuba to spread anti-
Spanish propaganda as well as to prepare an anti-Spanish rebellion
in Cuba. At a time when Spain was planning to reconquer her lost
colonies, Colombia and Mexico saw in the Cuban events an opportunity to weaken Spanish power by distracting its forces. They were,
therefore, eager to help the Cubans in their own struggle against
Spain.

Despite this outside aid, Cuban attempts of the early nineteenth
century failed to produce a strong movement for independence.
They were mostly sporadic and usually unconnected conspiracies
which declined toward the 1830s. Lacking widespread popular support, this early independence movement was weakened by several
factors. Among these were the growth of the sugar industry and of
wealth in general, the fear of a black rebellion, and the increase in
the feeling for annexation to the United States. Then, too, a number
of Spanish royalists and troops settled in Cuba following their defeat
in Latin America. Cuba became a heavily fortified garrison, the last
significant bastion of Spanish power in the New World.

The international picture was also not favorable to the Cuban
cause for independence. Fearful of European expansion into the New
World and particularly of English and French designs on Cuba, the
United States was quick to issue the Monroe Doctrine (1823), which
warned in part that the nation would not tolerate the transfer of
New World colonies from one European power to another. The
United States seemed to have preferred Cuba under a weak Spain
than under a mighty England. If anyone else was to have Cuba, some
U.S. politicians and business interests reasoned, it would be its
neighbor to the north.

The reasons for the war that broke out in 1868 were many and
complex. Throughout the nineteenth century Spain had experienced
increasing political instability, with liberal and reactionary governments alternating in power. Spanish policy changes were particularly reflected in the colony with such arbitrary and ruthless
captain-generals as Miguel Tacón (1834–1838) and Francisco Lersundi (1867–1869), sharing power with more moderate and understanding officials such as Domingo Dulce and Serrano. Tacón
conspired to prevent the Cuban deputies from being seated at the
revived Spanish Cortes, an insult the Cubans wouldn't forget. He

increased the powers of military tribunals and exiled several distinguished Cubans, among them José Antonio Saco. Lersundi suppressed political meetings and the reading of newspapers and books
in reading areas, particularly in tobacco workshops. Next to Tacón's,
Lersundi's iron despotism was the harshest brand of administration
experienced in the island. The Cubans became progressively alienated by and disillusioned with the Spanish policy and that country's
ability to govern Cuba.

The clash between Spanish economic measures and the desires of
the Creole sugar slavocracy also contributed to the mounting tension. Having grown throughout the nineteenth century into a powerful and vocal group who could control or at least decisively
influence the internal politics of the island, the planters now found
themselves with an imperial power whose protectionist policies
were challenging their status by attempting to curtail their prerogatives and reduce their mounting importance. Naturally they were
not about to relinquish their position without a fight.

Also throughout the century the Cubans progressively developed
a separate and distinct identity. While many thought of Cuba as
another province of Spain and demanded equal rights and representation, others longed for an independent nation. Writers, painters,
and poets looked inward portraying themes of their homeland, and
with their *"cuadros de costumbre,"* a type of writing representative of
the customs and way of life of a particular area, they helped develop
the roots of their nationality. Through their works they fostered not
only a pride in being a Cuban and a love for Cuban subjects but also
a sort of shame over the fact that the island still remained a Spanish
colony. While Spanish America with the exception of Puerto Rico
had successfully overthrown Spanish power, Cuba was still clinging
to its colonial ties.

The war broke out in 1868. It was organized and directed by radical Creole landowners in Oriente province together with a group of
lawyers and professionals. The bulk of the fighting, however, was
done by the peasants, with blacks and Chinese joining the rebel
ranks. The leadership of the movement was in the hands of the son
of a wealthy landowner from Oriente, Carlos Manuel de Céspedes.
Born in Bayamo, Oriente, on April 18, 1819, Céspedes attended secondary schools in Havana and later enrolled at the University of
Havana. He traveled to Spain to attend college and received a bache-

lor of law degree from the University of Barcelona and a doctorate of law from the University of Madrid.

In Spain Céspedes had his first taste of revolution. The Iberian nation was undergoing a period of political turmoil and Céspedes joined the conspiratorial activities of Army General D. Juan Prim against the regime of Baldomero Espartero. The failure of an anti-Espartero uprising in 1843 forced Céspedes to leave the country.

From Spain Céspedes traveled throughout Europe, finally returning to Cuba in 1844. The handsome, cultured, and energetic Céspedes opened a law practice and engaged in business in Bayamo. But law soon gave way to politics, as a strong anti-Spanish movement began to develop in Cuba. Narciso López's unsuccessful filibuster expeditions against Spanish power in Cuba and his subsequent execution in 1851 had an impact on the young Céspedes. Arrested because of his anti-Spanish statements and banished from Bayamo, Céspedes began to organize a war for independence in Oriente province. After the 1868 "Glorious Revolution" in Spain, he saw an opportunity for revolt in Cuba and called for immediate revolutionary action, claiming that "the power of Spain is decrepit and worm-eaten" and that if it still appeared great and powerful to Cubans it was because "for more than three centuries we have looked at it from our knees."

Céspedes and his group were determined to strike a blow at Spanish control of Cuba. When they learned that their conspiratorial activities had been discovered by the Spanish authorities they were forced to act. On October 10, 1868 Céspedes issued the historic "Grito de Yara" from his plantation, La Demajagua, proclaiming Cuba's independence. He soon freed his slaves and incorporated them into his disorganized and ill-armed force and made public a manifesto explaining the causes of the revolt. Issued by the newly organized Junta Revolucionaria de Cuba, the manifesto stated that the revolt was prompted by Spain's arbitrary government, excessive taxation, corruption, exclusions of Cubans from government employment, and deprivation of political and religious liberty, particularly the rights of assembly and petition. It called for complete independence from Spain, for the establishment of a republic with universal suffrage, and for the indemnified emancipation of slaves.

The manifesto was followed by the organization of a provisional government with Céspedes acting as commander-in-chief of the army and head of the government. Céspedes's almost absolute power as well as his failure to decree the immediate abolition of slavery soon caused opposition within the revolutionary ranks. Facing mounting pressure, Céspedes conceded some of his power and called for a constitutional convention to establish a more democratic provisional government.

Delegates from several eastern towns met at Guáimaro in April 1869 and adopted a constitution that provided for a republican-type government. Unhappy with Céspedes and fearful of concentrating too much power in the office of the president, a faction led by Camagüey's rebel chieftain, Ignacio Agramonte, obtained a large degree of authority for the House of Representatives, including legislative power and control over presidential decisions. This group, as long as it retained power, was also able to legalize the abolition of slavery by introducing Article 24 of the constitution which declared "all inhabitants of the Republic to be absolutely free." Céspedes was elected president of the new republic and Manuel Quesada was appointed commander-in-chief.

The war soon intensified in eastern Cuba. Céspedes decreed the destruction of cane fields and approved the revolutionary practice of urging the slaves to revolt and to join the *mambises,* as the Cuban rebels were then called. Numerous skirmishes occurred, but Cuban forces were unable to obtain a decisive victory against the Spanish army. Simultaneously, Céspedes made several unsuccessful attempts to obtain United States recognition of Cuban belligerency.

While Céspedes retained civilian leadership, the military aspects of the war were under the leadership of Dominican Máximo Gómez. Unhappy with the treatment Dominicans had received from Spain during Spanish occupation of his own country (1861–1865), and horrified by the exploitation of the black slaves, he started to conspire with the Cuban revolutionaries and joined Céspedes after the *Grito de Yara.* His experience in military strategy was invaluable to the revolutionary cause and he was soon promoted to the rank of general and later to commander of Oriente province. A master of guerrilla warfare, Gómez alternated training the Cubans in that type of struggle with commanding his forces in numerous battles. He organized the Cuban rebels into highly mobile small units that could operate independently, continuously harassing the Spanish troops.

The Cubans scored a few minor victories at the beginning, but the Spaniards soon gained the offensive. By 1871 the rebels had been pushed back to Oriente province and the rebellion was contained in that part of the island. In a meeting with rebel President Céspedes, Gómez argued for an invasion of the west. He pointed out that the rebellion should be made an unbearable economic burden for Spain and that this would be accomplished by an invasion that would emancipate all black slaves in the island and cripple the sugar industry. "If liberty is not given to the slaves," Gómez wrote in his campaign diary, "and if production of the great sugar plantations is not impeded, the revolution is destined to last much longer and rivers of blood will flow unfruitfully in the fields of the island."

Gómez's plan for an invasion of the west was fully supported by the mulatto leader Antonio Maceo. Under Gómez's direction Maceo had developed into one of the most daring fighters of the Cuban army. Showing extraordinary leadership and tactical capabilities, he won respect and admiration from his men as well as fear and scorn from the Spanish troops. He kept tight discipline in his encampment, constantly planning and organizing future battles. Maceo enjoyed outsmarting and outmaneuvering the Spanish generals and on successive occasions he inflicted heavy losses on them. His incursions into the eastern sugar zones not only helped to disrupt the sugar harvest but principally led to the freedom of the slaves who soon joined the ranks of the Cuban army.

By 1872 Maceo had achieved the rank of general. His prominent position among revolutionary leaders soon gave rise to intrigue and suspicion. Conservative elements who supported the war effort began to fear the possibility of the establishment of a Negro republic with Maceo at its head. The example of Haiti still loomed in the minds of many. Dissension in the revolutionary ranks and fears of the blacks were slowing down the revolutionary effort. After a prolonged silence, Maceo finally answered those who accused him of attempting to establish a black republic. "In planting these seeds of distrust and dissension," he wrote, "they do not seem to realize that it is the country that will suffer. . . . I must protest energetically that neither now nor at any other time am I to be regarded as an advocate of a Negro Republic. . . . This concept is a deadly thing to the democratic Republic which is founded on the basis of liberty and fraternity."

Landed groups strongly opposed Gómez's plan for an invasion. Although they supported the Cuban cause, they feared for their economic interests, and after much discussion the plan was finally rejected. The Dominican leader returned to the zone of Guantánamo where he continued to engage the Spanish forces victoriously. In 1872 Gómez again prevailed upon the government to accept his plan. But before it could be implemented, dissension within the revolutionary ranks prompted Céspedes to relieve him as commander of the Oriente province. Céspedes himself was deposed in 1873 and was later forced to seek refuge from the Spanish in San Lorenzo, a farm in Oriente province, where on February 27, 1874 he was killed after a brave, but futile struggle against a Spanish force that attacked the farm.

Gómez was restored to his position of command after Céspedes was deposed and he again began to set plans for the invasion into motion. It did not get underway, however, until 1875. When it did, opposition to Gómez and the invasion, particularly from landed and sugar interests, was so strong that it never got beyond Las Villas province in central Cuba. Resistance also came from within the ranks: some officers resented a Dominican in command; others were jealous of Gómez's position and actions. Furthermore, supplies, weapons, and money failed to arrive from exiles in the United States. Finally, in 1876 Gómez was forced to resign his military post. "I retired that same day," he wrote in his diary, "with my heart broken by so many deceptions."

The war dragged on with neither the Cubans nor the Spaniards able to win a decisive victory. Finally, on February 11, 1878 the Peace of Zanjón ended the Ten Years' War. Most of the generals of the Cuban army accepted the pact; Maceo, however, refused to capitulate and continued to fight with his now depleted army. He held a historic meeting, known as the "Protest of Baraguá," with the head of the Spanish forces, Marshal Arsenio Martínez Campos, requesting independence for Cuba and complete abolition of slavery. When these conditions were rejected, he again resumed fighting.

It was, however, a futile effort. Years of bloodshed and war had left the Cuban forces exhausted. Aid from exiles decreased and Maceo now faced the bulk of the Spanish forces alone. Realizing the hopeless situation, he left for Jamaica. From there he traveled to New York to raise money and weapons necessary to continue fighting. He soon joined the activities of Major-General Calixto García, then organizing a new rebellion. This uprising, known as "La Guerra Chiquita" (Little War, 1879–1880), was also to end in disaster. Maceo was sent to Cuba and García was captured soon after he landed in the island. Exhausted and disillusioned after the long, bitter struggle and faced with a powerful and determined Spain, the Cubans were in no mood to join this new and ill-prepared attempt.

After more than ten years of strife the Cubans were unable to overthrow Spanish power in the island. The reasons for this failure are to be found partially in internal dissension, regionalism, and petty jealousies among the leaders, and partially in the lack of internal organization and external support which resulted in chronic shortages of supplies and ammunitions. The odds against the Cubans were also almost insurmountable. They were fighting well-disciplined, organized, and equipped forces augmented steadily by reinforcements from Spain. The Spaniards also controlled the seas, preventing the smuggling of reinforcements and weapons from abroad. The Cubans were thus forced to carry on guerrilla operations in the hope of demoralizing the Spanish army or creating an international situation favorable to their cause.

The international scene, furthermore, remained unpropitious. The United States refused to recognize the rebels, perhaps in the hope that Spain would eventually be willing to sell the island. Under President Ulysses S. Grant, the United States reaffirmed its neutrality laws and asserted that it was not prepared to intervene in Cuba. These actions affected armed shipments to the rebels, facilitated Spanish espionage activities, and created disillusionment and frustration among exile groups. Great Britain's position was not much different. Interested primarily in maintaining close relations with the United States, Great Britain was not willing to oppose U.S. policies and seemed content to see Cuba remain under Spanish control. Against those odds it is a wonder that the rebels were able to keep their struggle alive for ten years!

The protracted war had a profound effect on the Cubans. Many Creoles fought in parts of the island they had never even seen before. Gradually, regionalism collapsed and a common cause emerged; the *"patria chica,"* with its stress on local loyalties, gave way to the fatherland. The war also forced many to take sides on issues, thus accelerating the process of popular participation and integration. Finally, the war provided numerous symbols that became part of Cuba's historical heritage. The national anthem and flag as well as the national weapon, the machete, came out of this war. In particular, the dedication of the *mambises* who abandoned position and comfort to fight Spanish power became for future generations an example of unselfish sacrifice for the fatherland.

The impact of the war was particularly felt in the economic realm. The destruction caused by the fighting did away with the fortunes of many Cuban families. Although the struggle concentrated in eastern Cuba and many sugar plantations escaped the ravages of war, the continuous development of a landed slavocracy in Cuba suffered a severe blow. Numerous participants and sympathizers with the Cuban cause lost their properties. Most Peninsulars sided with Spain and many estates passed from Creole to loyalist hands. Some Creole loyalists also profited from the losses of their brethren, as they had backed the Spanish cause. The growth and power of the Creole propertied class was to be further undermined in 1886 with the abolition of slavery.

American investment also grew in Cuba as a result of the war. Taking advantage of the bankruptcy of many Spanish and Cuban enterprises, U.S. capital acquired sugar estates and mining interests. The expansion of European beet sugar production closed this market for Cuban sugar thus making the United States the largest and most important buyer of the island's crop. The depressed world price of raw sugar ruined many Cuban producers and facilitated U.S. economic penetration. The McKinley Tariff of 1890, which placed raw sugar on the free list, led to an increase in Cuban-American trade and especially to the expansion of sugar production. Although by 1895 control of the economy was still largely in the hands of the Spaniards, American capital and influence, particularly in the sugar industry, was exerting a growing influence.

With the first major attempt at independence having ended in partial disaster, many Cubans turned to *autonomismo*. The movement, which advocated autonomous rule for Cuba under the Spanish monarchy, differed little from reformism. *Autonomismo* had its origins in the first half of the century but lost momentum during the periods of annexation and *reformismo*. Now, after the end of the Ten Years' War it coalesced into the Partido Liberal Autonomista. The founders of the party, former annexationists and reformists, called for a system of local self-government patterned on the English colonial model and requested numerous economic and political reforms but within the Spanish empire.

It soon became clear, however, that Spain still intended no radical changes in its policies. By 1892 the much promised and awaited reforms were not forthcoming. Disillusionment and frustration began to take hold of those who still hoped for a continuous association with Spain. The party warned that unless Spain stopped its policy of repression and persecution another rebellion would be inevitable. While the stage was being set for the decisive effort at independence, however, the forces that advocated independence were still racked by schism and indecision. The enthusiasm and prestige of the military leaders of the Ten Years' War were not sufficient to coordinate and direct the independence effort against Spain. This leadership vacuum came to be filled by a young poet and revolutionary: José Martí.

Born in Havana on January 28, 1853 of Spanish parents, Martí spent his early years as an eager student. At the age of fifteen he composed several poems, and at sixteen he published in Havana a newspaper, *La Patria Libre,* and wrote a dramatic poem, *Abdala.* His teachers aroused in him a devotion to the cause of freedom. He enrolled at the Instituto de Segunda Enseñanza de La Habana but was soon arrested for his anti-Spanish activities. After serving several months of hard labor, he was deported to Spain in January 1871. In Spain Martí published a political essay, *El presidio político en Cuba,* an indictment of Spanish oppression and conditions in Cuban jails.

Resuming his studies, the young revolutionary received a degree in philosophy and law from the University of Zaragoza in 1874. From Spain he traveled through Europe and in 1875 went to Mexico, where he worked as a journalist. After a short visit to Cuba in 1877, he settled in Guatemala, where he taught literature and philosophy. The same year, he married Carmen Zayas Bazán, daughter of a Cuban exile. Shortly afterward he published his first book, *Guatemala,* in which he recorded his impressions and described the beauty of that country. The book was a tribute to a young girl, María Granados, whom he secretly loved.

Unhappy with Guatemala's political conditions, Martí returned to Cuba in December 1878. The Peace of Zanjón had just been signed, and Martí felt that conditions in the island would be propitious for his return. Spanish authorities, however, soon discovered his continuing revolutionary activities and again deported him to Spain. He escaped to France and from there moved to the United States and then Venezuela. Finally, in 1881 he made New York the center of his activities, although he continued to travel and to write about the many problems of the Latin American nations. He wrote a regular column for *La Opinión Nacional* of Caracas, and for *La Nación* of Buenos Aires, gaining recognition throughout Latin America.

His poetry and prose as well as his journalistic articles became popular. Martí was a precursor of the modernistic movement in poetry. In 1882 his most significant poems, composed for his son, were published in a book called *Ismaelillo*. Martí's best known poems are his *Versos sencillos* (1891), which emphasize such themes as friendship, sincerity, love, justice, and freedom. His *Edad de Oro* (1889), a magazine especially devoted to children, won the hearts of many Latin American youngsters. Martí's greatest contribution to Spanish-American letters were his essays. Written in a highly personal style, they brought about an innovation in prose writing.

Martí realized very early that independence from Spain was the only solution for Cuba and that this could only be achieved through a fast war that would at the same time prevent U.S. intervention in Cuba. His fear of a military dictatorship after independence led in 1884 to a break with Máximo Gómez and Antonio Maceo, who were at the time engaged in conspiratorial activities. He withdrew from the movement temporarily, but by 1887 the three men were working together with Martí assuming political leadership. In 1892 he formed the Partido Revolucionario Cubano in the United States and directed his efforts toward organizing a new war against Spain.

Martí called for the suppression of the Spanish colonial system and for the establishment of a republican government in Cuba. The new order, generated through revolution, would enact laws according to the needs of society. He felt that after liberation from Spain, Cuba had to be liberated from Spanish customs and its legacy of social vices. This was to come about slowly through a process of political maturity and of education, which without hate would establish the foundation of a healthy republic. The new nation was to be based on the close collaboration of all social classes and not on the struggle of one class against another. It would be the fatherland where everyone could live in peace with freedom and justice, "a nation based on law, order, and the hard work of its inhabitants."

The task of the government, Martí believed, was to put an end to the injustices of society. Government was to act as the equilibrating force, active and ready to participate in the shaping of society. He wanted a government born out of and in accord with the needs of the country—"a government that, without creating dissatisfaction among the intellectual aristocracy, would allow for the development of the numerous and uneducated elements of the population."

Martí felt that to create a just society it was not enough to grant political liberty; it was also necessary to distribute the wealth. He did not advocate taking land away from the large landholders, but distributing the land the government possessed. He believed in nineteenth-century classical liberalism, but maintained that national wealth should flow from agriculture more than from industry. He emphasized that the greatness of nations was dependent on the economic independence of its citizens; therefore, it was necessary that everyone should possess and cultivate a piece of land. "The distribution of land," he explained, "if given to those who are working for low wages, would draw them away from low salary jobs." He hoped to end Cuba's dependence on sugar and called for diversification of agricultural exports to avoid the evils of monoculture.

Much has been written regarding Martí's attitude toward the United States. His writings have been taken out of context to show him as being strongly anti-Yankee, or to portray him as the advocate of a Latin America in the image of the United States. The truth lies, perhaps, somewhere between the two extremes. Martí admired the accomplishments of the United States, but at the same time he saw it as a society in which, according to him, man placed too much emphasis on material wealth and on his selfish interest. "The Cubans," he wrote, "admire this nation, the greatest ever built by freedom, but they distrust the evil conditions that, like worms in the blood, have begun their work of destruction in this mighty Republic. . . . They cannot honestly believe that excess individualism and reverence for wealth are preparing the United States to be the typical nation of liberty."

Martí was a firm believer in individual initiative, private property, and honest profit. He saw two evils in the United States capitalistic society: monopoly that limited the free flow of products in the national market; and protectionism, which caused the same result in international trade. For Martí, the injustices of capitalism were only temporary defects and abuses that could be remedied. He did not advocate the suppression of free enterprise, but his humanitarian approach to economics and his desire for justice for the poor and the working class forced him to criticize capitalism. "The rich capitalist," he wrote, "forces the worker to work for the lowest wages. . . . It is the duty of the State to put an end to unnecessary misery."

Understanding the influence that economics exerted on politics, Martí advocated that a nation should sell to many different nations and not become dependent on any one market. "Whoever says economic union," he wrote, "says political union. The people who buy command; the people who sell obey." Martí viewed with alarm the economic ties Cuba had established with the United States and realized the danger involved in any closer commercial relations with their neighbor to the north. Acknowledging the economic importance of the United States and Cuba's geographical situation, Martí advocated friendlier relations, but without any political or economic dependence. He also saw the impossibility of maintaining Cuban independence against the will of the United States. "We are firmly resolved," he said, "to deserve, request and obtain its [United States] sympathy, without which independence would be very difficult to obtain and maintain."

People devoted to the liberation of their country are often so absorbed in the task that they become narrow-minded and lose touch with events surrounding them. Not so Martí. He was a citizen of America. Like Bolívar, he thought in terms of a continent; he looked at events of his homeland, but never lost sight of America. He thought of himself as a son of America, and as such, he felt indebted to her. He considered it a magnificent spectacle to see a continent, made up of so many factors, emerging into compact nations. What was needed was the union of all the Latin Americans as well. "The spiritual union," he said, "is indispensable to the salvation and happiness of the peoples of America." He saw the Western Hemisphere divided into two peoples with different origins and customs, but felt that with mutual understanding and respect for the sovereignty of every nation the differences could be overcome.

Martí had seen the political chaos and confusion of the emerging Latin American nations and the ambitions of *caudillos,* who sacrificed the interest of the people in their desire to remain in power. He had witnessed the political confusion and foreseen the difficulties with which Cuba was to be faced. His writings served not as a mere rhetorical exercise, but a lively lesson for his contemporaries and future generations.

Martí's pilgrimage throughout the Americas in the 1880s and early 1890s helped to unite and organize the Cubans. With Gómez and Maceo he worked tirelessly toward the realization of Cuban independence. So well had they organized the anti-Spanish forces that their order for the uprising on February 24, 1895 assured the ultimate expulsion of Spain from the island. The war, however, was not the fast and decisive struggle Martí had sought. It took his own life early in 1895, dragged on for three more years, and eventually prompted the American intervention (1899–1902) that he had feared.

After Martí's death the leadership of the war fell to Gómez and Maceo, who were now ready to implement their plan to invade the western provinces. In repeated attacks they undermined and defeated the Spanish troops and carried the war to the sugar heart of the island. From January to March of 1896 Maceo waged a bitter but successful campaign against larger Spanish forces in the provinces of Pinar del Río and Havana. By mid-1896 the Spanish troops were on the retreat and the Cubans seemed victorious throughout the island. Then came a change in the Spanish command: the more conciliatory Marshal Arsenio Martínez Campos was replaced by General Valeriano Weyler, a tough and harsh disciplinarian. Weyler's policy of concentrating the rural population in garrisoned towns and increasing numbers of Spanish troops allowed the Spaniards to regain the initiative after Maceo's death on December 7, 1896, in a minor battle. Yet they were unable to defeat the Cuban rebels or even engage them in a major battle. Gómez retreated to the eastern provinces and from there carried on guerrilla operations. He rejected any compromise with Spain. In January 1898 when the Spanish monarchy introduced a plan that would have made Cuba a self-governing province within the Spanish empire, Gómez categorically opposed it.

This was the existing condition in Cuba when the United States declared war on Spain. The reasons for U.S. involvement were many. A growing and energetic nation, the United States was looking for new markets for its budding industrial establishment. U.S. investments in the island were now threatened by the devastating war carried on by the Cubans. National security also demanded the control of the Central American isthmus and of its maritime approaches. A strong navy as well as naval bases would be essential to protect the future Panama Canal. A few miles from the Florida coast, dominating the sea lanes to the isthmus, the rich Spanish colony was a growing heaven for investors and the dream of every expansionist in the

United States. It now seemed ripe to fall into the hands of its northern neighbor.

The ingredients for U.S. involvement were all there. All that was needed was the proper national mood and a good excuse to step in. The first was easily achieved. The American people wanted intervention. Aroused by stories of Spanish cruelty blown out of proportion by irresponsible "yellow journalists" and by a new sense of Anglo-Saxon "racial" responsibility toward the "inferior" people of the Latin world, large sectors of public opinion clamored for U.S. involvement and pressured President William McKinley to intervene. The excuse was provided by the explosion of the U.S. battleship *Maine* in Havana's harbor early in 1898.

The Spanish-American War was short, decisive, and popular. Such defenders of manifest destiny as Alfred T. Mahan, Theodore Roosevelt, and Henry Cabot Lodge seemed vindicated by an easy and relatively inexpensive war. American business interests saw new commercial and investment opportunities as a result of the capture of Cuba, Puerto Rico, and the Philippines. U.S. strategic interests were also assured by the final expulsion of Spain from the New World and the emergence of the United States as the dominant Caribbean power.

The defenders of imperialism, however, were not unchallenged. In the United States Congress, Senator Henry M. Teller had a resolution approved bearing his own name which pledged the United States to an independent Cuba. Catholic and labor leaders criticized the United States and called for the granting of complete independence to Cuba. Similarly, Cuban leaders complained that Cuba was not a part of the Treaty of Paris (1898) which ended the Spanish-American War, that their soldiers had been excluded from the cities by the American army, and that despite innumerable sacrifices, independence still loomed more as a hope than a reality. Manuel Sanguily, a staunch defender of Cuba's sovereignty, denounced the fact that the most reactionary Spanish elements had been permitted to remain in the island and retain their possessions; he complained that "the Cubans had been deprived of their healthy moment of historical revenge."

Those who criticized American policies, however, were voices crying in the wilderness. This was the finest hour for American expansionists and they were not about to give up Cuba completely. It was not until 1902, after two years of American occupation of the island, that the United States granted Cuba nominal independence, and only after Congress had defined the future relations of the United States and Cuba. On February 25, 1901 Senator Orville H. Platt introduced in Congress the famous amendment bearing his name. The Platt Amendment stipulated the following:

The President of the U.S. is hereby authorized to 'leave the government and control of the island of Cuba to its people' so soon as a government shall have been established in said island under a constitution which, either as a part thereof or in an ordinance appended thereto, shall define the future relations of the United States with Cuba, substantially as follows:

I. That the government of Cuba shall never enter into any treaty or other compact with any foreign power or powers which will impair or tend to impair the independence of Cuba, nor in any matter authorize or permit any foreign power or powers to obtain by colonization or for military or naval purposes or otherwise, lodgment in or control over any portion of said island.

II. That said government shall not assume or contract any public debt, to pay the interest upon which, and to make reasonable sinking fund provision for the ultimate discharge of which the ordinary revenues of the island, after defraying the current expenses of government, shall be inadequate.

III. That the government of Cuba consents that the United States may exercise the right to intervene for the preservation of Cuban independence, the maintenance of a government adequate for the protection of life, property, and individual liberty, and for discharging the obligations with respect to Cuba imposed by the Treaty of Paris on the United States, now to be assumed and undertaken by the government of Cuba.

IV. That all acts of the United States in Cuba during its military occupancy thereof are ratified and validated, and all lawful rights acquired thereunder shall be maintained and protected.

V. That the government of Cuba will execute, and, as far as necessary, extend, the plans already devised or other plans to be mutually agreed upon, for the sanitation of the cities of the island, to the end that a recurrence of epidemic and infectious diseases may be prevented, thereby assuring protection to the people and commerce of Cuba, as well as to the commerce of the southern ports of the United States and the people residing therein.

VI. That the Isle of Pines shall be omitted from the proposed constitutional boundaries of Cuba, the title thereto being left to future adjustment by treaty.

VII. That to enable the United States to maintain the independence of Cuba, and to protect the people thereof, as well as for its defense, the government of Cuba will sell or lease to the United States lands necessary for coaling or naval stations at certain specified points, to be agreed upon with the President of the United States.

On March 2 the bill became law, and on June 12 a constitutional convention meeting in Havana to draft a constitution adopted the amendment by a majority of one as an annex to the Cuban Constitution of 1901. The constitution also provided for universal suffrage, separation of church and state, a popularly elected but all-powerful president who could be reelected for a second term, and a weakened senate and a chamber of deputies.

The distinguished black general of the war against Spain, Juan Gualberto Gómez summarized the feelings of the more radical leaders: "The Platt Amendment has reduced the independence and sovereignty of the Cuban republic to a myth." Others, however, seemed to prefer this to a continuous U.S. occupation. Sanguily conceded: "Independence with some restrictions is better than a military regime." A few supported the actions of the United States.

In spite of the opposition it generated, the occupation did have a number of beneficial and generally supported results. The United States faced a difficult task indeed in governing Cuba. Famine and disease were rampant. Industrial and agricultural production were at a standstill. The treasury was empty. The Cuban revolutionary army was idle and impatient. With no experience in colonial affairs, the United States tackled the job. The military governors, Generals John Brooke (January 1899–December 1899) and Leonard Wood (December 1899–May 1902), supported by a variety of Cuban secretaries, were the supreme authority and under them were other American generals in charge of every province. These were soon replaced by Cuban governors. A method of food distribution was established that proved effective. A system of rural guards, initiated earlier by General Leonard Wood in Oriente, was soon extended to all the provinces, providing employment to many soldiers after the Cuban army was disbanded.

Under Wood's administration particular attention was given to health and education. Hospitals were built, sanitation and health conditions improved, and yellow fever was eradicated, primarily through the work of the Cuban scientist Carlos J. Finlay, who discovered the mosquito vector of yellow fever. A public school system was established, and the university was modernized. Wood recognized the judicial system, provided buildings and other facilities, and placed the judges on salary for the first time. In 1899 he proclaimed an electoral law that gave the franchise to adult males who were literate, owned property, or had served in the revolutionary army. Elections for municipal offices were held in June 1900, and in September, thirty-one delegates were elected to the Constitutional Convention that drafted the Constitution of 1901, mostly followers or representatives of the revolutionary army.

On May 20, 1902 the occupation ended. On that day General Wood turned over the presidency to Tomás Estrada Palma, first elected president of the new republic and former successor to Martí as head of the Cuban Revolutionary Party. It was a day of national happiness as the Cubans plunged into a new era of political freedom and republican government. Optimism, however, was tempered by the shadow of the United States hanging over the new nation. Looking into the future a few Cubans warned that the immediate task was to resist foreign encroachments. Many still remembered Martí's prophetic words: "Once the United States is in Cuba, who will get it out?"

III

THE SEEDS OF REVOLUTION

8

THE PLATT AMENDMENT
REPUBLIC

APPARENTLY highly favorable conditions accompanied Cuba's emergence into independence. There were no major social or political problems similar to the ones other Latin American nations had experienced after their break with Spain. There was no large unassimilated Indian population and although blacks represented a significant proportion of the total population there was no major racial conflict, the two groups having learned to live together since colonial times. There was also no strong regionalism and no powerful church to challenge the authority of the state. Furthermore, the liberal-conservative feud that plagued countries like Mexico during the nineteenth century was nonexistant in Cuba.

The economic situation was also favorable. The infusion of foreign capital, the increasing trade with the United States, and favorable sugar prices augured a prosperous future. Cuba and the United States signed a Commercial Treaty of Reciprocity in 1903 which assured Cuban sugar entering the United States a 20 percent tariff preference. In return, Cuba granted certain American products preferential treatment. The treaty reinforced the close commercial relations between the two countries, but it also made Cuba further dependent on a one-crop economy and on one all-powerful market.

In spite of the apparently favorable conditions, however, Martí's vision of a politically and economically independent nation failed to materialize in the post-independence years. Whether he would have been able to prevent the events that followed the War for Independence can only be conjectured. A process of centralization extended the great sugar estates of the colonial period, restraining the growth of a rural middle class and creating a landless agrarian proletariat of poor whites and mulattoes. Cuba became more and more commercially dependent on the United States, and the inclusion of the Platt Amendment into the Cuban Constitution of 1901 established United States supervision of political developments in Cuba.

Another problem was that Cuba had preserved the colonial Spanish attitude that public office was a source of personal profit. Electoral frauds became a standard practice. Politics became the means to social advancement, a contest between factions for the spoils of office. *Personalismo* was substituted for principle; allegiance to a man or a group was the only way to ensure survival in the political arena. The Spanish legacy of political and administrative malpractice increased in the new nation too suddenly to be checked by a people lacking experience in self-government. Although the United States' dissolution of Cuba's veteran army prevented a repetition of the typical nineteenth-century Spanish-American experience, where the army filled the political vacuum left by Spain, many veterans took an active part in politics, and their influence, sometimes not too beneficent, was felt in the years following the establishment of the republic in 1902.

As successor to Spain as the overseer of the island's affairs, the United States unwittingly perpetuated the Cubans' lack of political responsibility. Cubans enjoyed the assurance that the United States would intervene to protect them from foreign entanglement or to solve their domestic difficulties, but the situation only encouraged their irresponsible and indolent attitude toward their own affairs and was not conducive to responsible self-government. In the early decades of the republic, the Cubans developed what became known as a "Platt Amendment mentality," where they found it easy to rely upon the United States for guidance in their political decisions. "Tutelage," wrote Cuban intellectual Jorge Mañach, "favored the growth of general civic indolence, a tepid indifference to national dangers."

This civic indolence was not conducive to the growth of Cuban nationalism. Although the Cubans were enclosed in a geographic unit, shared a common language, religion, and background, they lacked national unity and purpose. The influence of the United States weakened the forces of nationalism in the early part of the century. As the century progressed, another force, *"españolismo,"* became an important factor in keeping the nationality divided. When Cuba became independent, Spaniards were guaranteed their property rights and were allowed to keep commerce and retail trade largely in their own hands. Immigration from Spain, furthermore, increased considerably and by 1934 there were an estimated 300,000 Spaniards in the island. This influx constantly strengthened Spanish traditions and customs. Many Spaniards themselves remained divided, retaining the ways of their own native provinces, hoping for an eventual return to Spain and thus failing to assimilate into the mainstream of Cuban society.

A dangerous tendency to solve differences through violence also permeated the political atmosphere. In 1906 President Estrada Palma called for U.S. intervention to offset the so-called Guerrita de Agosto. Organized by José Miguel Gómez and his liberal followers, this revolt aimed at preventing Estrada Palma's reelection to a second term in office. The United States sent in marines to end the conflict, initiating a new intervention which lasted from 1906 until 1909.

This second intervention differed significantly from the first. The United States had not been eager to embark on a new period of rule in Cuba and the provisional governor, Charles E. Magoon, turned to dispensing government sinecures or *botellas* to pacify the various quarrelling factions. Magoon also embarked on an extensive program of public works, gave Havana a new sewage system, and organized a modern army. These accomplishments, however, were partially overshadowed by extravagant spending, leaving a floating debt where there once had been a surplus. Magoon also drew up an organic body of law for the executive and the judiciary, and for provincial and municipal government. He also provided an electoral law, as well as laws for a civil service and for municipal taxation. Evidently, the U.S. government considered as one of the main purposes of the intervention the enactment of fair legislation that would prevent civil wars. Having pacified the country and introduced this new legislative apparatus, the United States called for municipal and national elections. The Liberals won a solid majority and elected their leader, José Miguel Gómez, to the presidency (1909–1913). The United States seemed willing to allow the democratic process to follow its course, and on January 28, 1909, the interventionist forces were withdrawn from the island.

The impact of this second intervention was far reaching in other, less positive ways. It removed any pretense of Cuban independence, strengthened the Platt Amendment mentality, and increased doubts about the Cubans' ability for self-government. Disillusionment took hold among many leaders, intellectuals, and writers, and this feeling was transmitted to the mass of the population. Cynicism and irresponsibility increased and so did the resort to violence to solve political differences. Even hitherto peaceful racial relations were affected.

Unhappy with the lack of political opportunities a group of radical blacks organized the Agrupación Independiente de Color (Independent Color Association). The group soon developed into a political party. But despite their appeal to the racial consciousness of the blacks, they had an extremely poor showing in the elections of 1908.

Their electoral fiasco increased their frustration. When the Cuban Senate passed a law prohibiting parties along racial lines, the Agrupación staged an uprising. Led by Evaristo Estenoz, a former soldier during the War for Independence, several bands of blacks roamed through the mountains of Oriente Province. The ill-organized rebellion met with much opposition and distinguished black leaders such as Senator Martín Morúa Delgado and Juan Gualberto Gómez criticized the rebels. The United States became alarmed over the uprising and, over the protests of President José Miguel Gómez, landed marines in several parts of the island. Trying to avert another full-fledged intervention, Gómez moved swiftly and harshly. Estenoz and most of the minor leaders were captured and executed and the rebellion was crushed. The Agrupación collapsed soon after these unfortunate events. It was to be the last time that a revolt along strictly racial lines was to develop in Cuba.

The tendency to resort to violence was displayed in two other instances at this time. In 1912 Veterans of the War for Independence demanded the ouster of pro-Spanish elements from bureaucratic positions and threatened to take up arms against the government of President Gómez. When the United States expressed "grave concern" over these events the veterans rapidly renounced their violent tactics. The second incident occurred again in 1917. This time the Liberal party rebelled to protest the fraudulent reelection of President Mario García Menocal (1913–1921). Led by former president Gómez the rebels took control of Oriente and Camagüey provinces.

But Menocal, supported by a warning from the United States that it would not recognize a government that came to power by unconstitutional means, moved troops into the areas controlled by the rebels and captured Gómez. The rebellion soon died out and although its leaders were arrested they were later pardoned.

Disregard for educational matters served to aggravate an already precarious situation. Critics who argued for an educational system in accord with the country's needs were ignored. The University of Havana, founded in 1728, was the only center of higher learning in Cuba. During the first United States intervention, and under the leadership of Secretary of Public Instruction Enrique José Varona, new professors were added, up-to-date scientific equipment was introduced, and the campus was moved from the Santo Domingo Convent to its present location. Varona's measures attracted new students, and the total university budget was increased.

Despite this relative progress, the university was far from fulfilling its important educational tasks. It lacked proper financial resources, a competent full-time faculty, and an up-to-date system of education and was, in addition, producing an overabundance of professionals. Writing almost thirty years later, University of Havana professor Pablo F. Lavín complained about Cuba's educational backwardness, the poor facilities of the university, the lack of professors, and the excessive number of professional men. He also criticized the verbalistic and memorizing method of learning being employed at the university. "There exists," he explained, "a divorce between education and the social and economic needs of the country."

Among the factors contributing to the divorce between education and the island's real needs was the perpetuation of the old Spanish attitude that favored intellectual over manual work. Many Cubans, particularly among the upper classes, extended a social stigma to business and commerce and left these endeavors largely to immigrant groups, especially Spaniards, Chinese, and Jews. With the larger businesses controlled or at least strongly influenced by United States corporations and with smaller enterprises dominated by immigrant groups, numerous Cubans turned to the professions. Law and medicine became the most popular, the first because of its importance as a stepping-stone for political prominence, and the second because of its associated social status. Although the Cuban countryside was in need of doctors, most of them remained in

Havana, attracted by the existing opportunities and cosmopolitan atmosphere of the capital.

The inability of Cuban society to absorb all university graduates accentuated the feelings of frustration in a generation that found itself with little opportunity to apply its acquired knowledge. The severe economic crisis with its accompanying financial chaos and social misery that affected Cuba in 1920 after a sharp drop in the price of sugar accelerated the desire for change, leading to a questioning of the existing order of society, not only among intellectuals and writers, but also among other groups who were barred from becoming productive members of society.

This economic crisis led in particular to a resurgence of economic nationalism. Several groups demanded protective legislation for Cuban interests and questioned the close economic ties between the United States and Cuba. The Platt Amendment as well as the repeated interventions of the United States government in Cuba's internal affairs came under attack. Anti-U.S. feeling, xenophobia, and the retrieval of the national wealth became the main themes of this blossoming nationalism. As the decade progressed, however, its scope was widened to include a call for social justice and for an end to political corruption and economic dependence on a single crop.

Alfredo Zayas, president of Cuba from 1921 to 1924, as corrupt as his administration was, managed to take advantage of this nationalism to reassert Cuba's sovereignty vis-à-vis the United States and its special envoy, Enoch Crowder. Crowder had been sent to Cuba as the personal representative of President Warren G. Harding. He was to supervise the peaceful settlement of political differences and to encourage the Cuban government to introduce several reforms, such as the modification of fraudulent electoral practices and a reduction in the budget. Crowder went so far as to impose the formation of an "Honest Cabinet" in 1922. The cabinet, composed of a number of distinguished Cubans, reduced the budget, trimmed the bureaucracy, and annulled several public works contracts that would have enriched a number of public servants.

Zayas at first cooperated, although half-heartedly, with the new cabinet, since he was negotiating a loan with the United States. Crowder's actions on the whole marked a less aggressive attitude on the part of the United States. Instead of the direct interference of the past, the U.S. government was encouraging a preventive policy, one of restrained involvement. Zayas, however, capitalizing on the steadily growing feeling against U.S. interference and aided by a $50 million loan from the J. P. Morgan firm, which strengthened his financial situation, was in a strong position to strike out. He disbanded the "Honest Cabinet" and curtailed Crowder's interference in Cuba's internal affairs. This met with the disapproval of the U.S. government, which reminded Zayas that he had promised to keep the cabinet "indefinitely." But the United States could do little as the flames of Cuban nationalism spread through newspapers and in the streets, abetted by Zayas and his government.

Despite the mismanagement of his administration, Zayas had retrieved his country's credit, averted intervention, and through later negotiations secured definite title to the Isle of Pines off the southern coast of Cuba after a two decades' delay imposed by the Platt Amendment. The graft and inefficiency of his administration overshadowed these achievements, however, and discontented groups attempted to reform Cuba's public life. A group of intellectuals founded the Cuban Council of Civic Renovation. In newspaper and magazine articles they criticized the Zayas administration and called for increased taxation of the wealthy, a new reciprocity treaty between Cuba and the United States, government control of sugar production, a national health system, the incorporation of women to public life, and the purification of the political system. Workers formed the Havana Federation of Workers and organized several strikes requesting better wages and working conditions. A number of war veterans sponsored a movement called the Association of Veterans and Patriots, whose actions finally led in 1924 to a short-lived revolt against the government.

The failure of even these groups to achieve the needed reforms thrust upon university students, supported and prodded by a group of Cuban intellectuals of the old generation, the leadership of the brewing revolution. Influenced by the Mexican and Russian revolutions, and particularly by the reformist ideas emanating from the Córdoba Reform Movement in Argentina, which sought to reform that country's universities, to make them more available to the less privileged sectors of society and to project them into the social, political, and economic life of the country, the students began searching for answers to Cuba's problems. Close supervision of Cuban affairs by the United States became the objective of their attacks, for most of the island's difficulties were blamed on the northern neighbor.

A variety of articles and books appeared in the early 1920s that nurtured a feeling of nationalism or *"Cubanismo"* among the population in general and the students in particular. Fernando Ortíz published several studies on Cuban folklore, Carlos M. Trelles wrote on the growth and decline of the Cuban nation, and Jorge Mañach complained about the still missing sense of nationality. Composer Amadeo Roldán began to successfully exploit Cuban themes in his music. Such influential magazines as *Revista Bimestre Cubana* and *Cuba Contemporánea* and later the *Revista de Avance* echoed the demands of the reformist groups. Articles appeared dealing with the ills of monoculture—that is, the dependence on one major export crop—, the decadence of the educational system, and the need for a purification of politics and for a less submissive role toward the United States.

Student effervescence increased when José Arce, rector of the University of Buenos Aires, visited the University of Havana late in 1922. Arce lectured at the campus on the accomplishments of the Cordoba Reform Movement and on the methods employed by the Argentinian students to obtain their demands. His words inspired his listeners and prompted the creation of the Directorio de la Federación de Estudiantes (Student Federation), the occupation of university buildings by the students, and the organization of short-lived student strikes.

This particular movement was directed at the university as an institution and at its cultural role in society. The students wanted a modern university more in accord with Cuba's needs—one which would be administered with their participation, sheltered from government interference, and more accessible to the less privileged sectors of society, particularly those who lived far away from Havana and were unable to attend the one university. The students obtained a series of academic and administrative reforms, larger government subsidies, and the establishment of a University Commission composed of professors, students, and alumni. The commission drew plans to reform the university and purged several professors accused of "senility and incompetence." The students were unsuccessful, however, in their demand for university autonomy. Perhaps aware that such a measure would create a sanctuary for political agitators, the government refused to relinquish its control of the university.

One of the principal leaders of the reform movement was Julio Antonio Mella, a young law student with strong anti-American feelings. Born out of wedlock in Havana in 1903, Mella was raised by his father, a tailor of Dominican ancestry, after his British mother had moved to New Orleans. During his school days Mella fell under the influence of one of his teachers, and exiled Mexican poet Salvador Díaz Mirón, whose narratives of the Mexican Revolution inspired his young listener with ideas of social justice and political reform. After an unsuccessful trip to Mexico and New Orleans in 1920 to study for the military profession, Mella entered the University of Havana.

A powerful speaker and a constant agitator, the handsome, dark complexioned, athletic Mella became the idol of university students. He participated in student demonstrations against President Zayas and United States Envoy Crowder, and became secretary general of the Student Federation. Mella spearheaded the university reform movement, organizing in 1923 the First Congress of Cuban Students. For him the university reform movement transcended the academic walls. Mella considered it part of a social struggle to better the conditions of the less privileged sectors of society, calling the movement "another battle of the class struggle." Inspired by Victor Raúl Haya de la Torre's "Popular University González Prada" in Lima, Mella founded in Havana the short-lived "Popular University José Martí," a leftist institution devoted to the education of the workers. In addition to editing two magazines, *Alma Mater* and *Juventud,* Mella also organized the Anti-Imperialist League and the Anti-Clerical Federation.

Through these activities Mella became associated with several Cuban Marxists. One of them, Carlos Baliño, a prestigious figure of Cuba's War of Independence and later founder of the Communist Association of Havana, collaborated closely with Mella in *Juventud* and eventually brought the young student into the association. Encouraged by the Mexican Communist Party, Baliño and Mella called a congress of all Communist groups in the island for August 1925. The number of militant Communists in Cuba was small, however, and of the nine Communist groups only four sent delegates.

From this 1925 congress emerged the Cuban Communist Party. José Miguel Pérez, a Spanish Communist, was appointed secretary general and the party soon became affiliated with the Communist International. Mella became one of its most important leaders, entrusted to propagandize the creation of the party, to edit its newspaper, *Lucha de Clases,* and to direct the education of new party members. Although the party was small and disorganized, the Communists soon formed a Youth League, using Mella and other student leaders to agitate and to gain followers within the university.

Mella and a small group of students were directing their attacks against President-elect Gerardo Machado. Although the regime enjoyed much support, Mella sensed Machado's authoritarian nature and labeled him a "tropical Mussolini." Mella's activities first clashed with university authorities, who expelled him temporarily, and then with Machado, who accused him of terrorist activity and had him jailed. Mella went on a nineteen-day hunger strike. Finally, the pressure of public opinion forced Machado to release him. After fleeing to Mexico, Mella traveled to Belgium and later to the Soviet Union to attend Communist meetings. His turbulent life ended mysteriously in 1929 allegedly at the hands of a Machado-paid assassin in Mexico, shortly after breaking up with the Communists and being expelled from the Mexican Communist party.

It is indeed difficult to determine what motivated a student leader such as Mella. His paternal grandfather's prominent role in the Dominican Republic's independence movement may have inspired within him a desire to fight against oppression. His ancestry of mixed nationality enhanced his search for identity and for recognition. The shame of illegitimacy haunted him, increasing his bitterness and frustration. Mella embraced communism and found in it a reason for his existence. For him, communism offered an ideology that promised to bring justice to Cuba's economic and social system, creating order out of the existing chaos. But of more importance, it offered him a cause for which to fight and an escape valve for his tormented personality.

Mella can be considered only partially representative of his student generation. He shared with his university colleagues a desire to improve the educational and political conditions of Cuba and to oppose United States supervision of Cuban affairs. He differed from them, however, in that he renounced his generation's romantic nationalism and vague ideological conceptions to embrace an international movement devoted to the overthrow of the existing order and to the establishment of a proletarian dictatorship.

9

THE UNFINISHED
REVOLUTION

THE university reform movement, which had started as a crusade
for academic reform, soon developed political overtones. Machado's
decision to remain in power for another term was the spark that
ignited student opposition. Claiming that his economic program
could not be completed within his four-year term and that only he
could carry it out, Machado announced his decision to reelect himself. In April 1928 a packed constitutional convention granted
Machado a new six-year period of power without reelection and
abolished the vice-presidency. Through a fake election in November
in which he was the only candidate, Machado was given a new term,
to run from May 20, 1929 to May 20, 1935.

Whereas a similar attempt by Estrada Palma to remain in power
had resulted in rebellion, Machado's decision only brought about a
wave of national indignation against the invalidation of suffrage.
The regime still enjoyed the support of the business and conservative
sectors of society. Increased revenues had brought prosperity, and
Machado's improved administration, especially in the field of public
works, had gained him a strong following. The Cuban armed forces,
organized two decades earlier during Gómez's administration, also
strongly backed the regime. Machado had successfully won over the
military through bribes and threats and had purged disloyal officers.

He used the military in a variety of civilian posts both at the national and local level, thus increasingly militarizing society. The few officers that were discontent with Machado's reelection seemed powerless and ineffective to oppose the regime. In the midst of growing domestic and international problems, the United States looked with indifference at events in Cuba and seemed unwilling to become involved in Cuban affairs as long as the Machado administration maintained order and stability and a friendly posture toward Washington. Machado, furthermore, prevented the growth of political opposition by winning control of the Conservative party and aligning it both with his own Liberal party and with the small Popular party. Through bribes and threats Machado was able also to subordinate Congress and the judiciary to the executive's will.

Machado's decision to extend his presidency met with stern student opposition. Riots and demonstrations occurred in several towns throughout the island. Machado took immediate measures to prevent further opposition from that quarter. He temporarily closed the university, dissolved the Student Federation, and abolished the University Reform Commission. He also tightened political control. Several Spanish and European labor leaders were expelled from the country as undesirable aliens. Antigovernment newspapers were closed down and the military took an increasingly growing role in surveillance and policing the population. Machado warned sternly that he would keep order and peace at any cost.

These measures, however, failed to control the students completely. A small but active group organized the Directorio Estudiantil Universitario (University Student Directorate) in mid-1927 to oppose the regime. The Directorio issued a manifesto defending the right of university students to discuss politics and attacking Machado's reelection attempts. Students demonstrated in front of the university, shouting anti-Machado slogans and tearing down government posters. Machado rapidly retaliated. Following his orders, the University Council, composed of faculty and administrative officials, formed disciplinary tribunals and expelled most of the Directorio leaders from the university.

The expulsion of the rebellious youths brought only temporary peace. Machado's unopposed reelection in November 1928 provided new ammunition for student protests while Mella's assassination furnished the martyr whose memory spurred student hatred. Throughout 1929 the expelled leaders of the Directorio renewed their contacts with university students. In September 1930 they established a second Directorio, agreed to issue a manifesto condemning the regime, and planned a massive demonstration for September 30.

The demonstration ended in disaster. When police attempted to break up the gathering, a riot developed and a policeman fatally wounded Directorio leader Rafael Trejo. Several other students and policemen were also wounded. Numerous students were arrested. Trejo's death unloosed a wave of anti-Machado feeling. The government responded this time by closing many high schools as well as the University of Havana, which remained closed until 1933. Forbidden by police to hold open meetings, the students developed what they called *tánganas* (impromptu protest gatherings). The *tánganas* led first to clashes with the police and later to organized violence and terrorism.

Trejo's death was the turning point in the struggle against the regime. From that time on many Cubans viewed the courageous student generation that battled Machado's police with admiration and respect. For some, "the generation of 1930," as these students were later known in Cuban history, seemed irresponsible and undisciplined, but for others it became the best exponent of disinterested idealism. Embattled by the first shock waves of the world depression and oppressed by an increasingly ruthless dictator, many Cubans, especially among the less privileged sectors of society, turned in hope toward these youngsters. They placed their faith in a generation that, although inexperienced and immature, seemed incorruptible and willing to bring morality to Cuba's public life.

The members of the generation of 1930 were generally very young. Most of the student leaders were in their early twenties. A majority came from middle-class backgrounds. Several were descendants of veterans of the wars of independence. Their ancestors' participation in public affairs seemed to have been an inspiration for their own active political roles. Many came from areas outside of the capital city. Living apart from families and parental discipline and exposed to the loneliness of a new environment, these students gravitated toward the campus and were perhaps more prone to political involvement than the average city student. Coming from smaller towns where social and economic stratification was accentuated, they contrasted life in the provinces and the capital. While some soon forgot their background and became "assimilated," others found the contrast shocking and attempted to bridge the gap between the two areas. They called for a more egalitarian society in the city and the modernization of the countryside, with better health and education facilities for the rural population.

Student and government confrontation gained momentum with the closing of the university. Unable to attend classes, many students joined the anti-Machado ranks. As time passed they became convinced that only armed action would force Machado to relinquish power. Urban violence, a hitherto almost unknown phenomenon in Cuba's political history, flourished.

The regime responded to each demonstration with harsher measures. But for every student beaten or arrested by police, new students emerged to pick up the banner of revolt. On January 3, 1931 police arrested twenty-two students on charges of plotting against the government. The next month eighty-five University of Havana professors, almost the entire faculty, were indicted on charges of sedition and conspiracy to overthrow the regime. Among those arrested was Dr. Ramón Grau San Martín, a distinguished physiology professor and later president of Cuba. The professors were released pending investigation, but Machado refused to release the rebellious youngsters. Late in 1931 student leaders conspired with some army officers who were discontented with Machado's increasingly ruthless administration to take over Camp Columbia in Havana and depose Machado. The government discovered the plot and arrested the principal conspirators. The *porra* (Machado's secret police) murdered two of the plotters.

While the principal leaders of the Directorio were in jail in 1931, a small group formed a splinter organization, the Ala Izquierda Estudiantil (Student Left Wing). The reasons for the split were varied. First, the two groups differed in economic background: most of the Ala Izquierda leaders came from poorer homes; those of the Directorio were primarily from middle-class ones. Also there were ideological differences. Strongly influenced by Marxist ideas and more radical in their outlook, Ala Izquierda members opposed the relations Directorio leaders maintained with Cuba's political parties and politicians. Many of the Ala Izquierda leaders embraced communism.

During the anti-Machado insurrectionary period, the Ala Izquierda became merely a tool of the Cuban Communist party. The party, led by Rubén Martínez Villena, a popular poet and intellectual, directed the organization's activities and used it to influence the student movement. Raúl Roa, one of its members (later Castro's minister of foreign relations), explained that "the Ala, as well as the Anti-Imperialist League became parallel organizations of the Cuban Communist party."

Throughout most of his regime, the Communists opposed Machado and advocated, as the only correct strategy to overthrow his government, the mobilization of the proletariat, culminating in a general strike. They insisted that only the proletariat constituted a truly revolutionary class; its hegemony would guarantee the victory of all the oppressed classes and the ultimate social revolution, which would end all class conflicts. The Caribbean Bureau of the Communist International urged the party in those days to cooperate with the anti-Machado forces with the specific objective of gaining leadership of the revolutionary movement. This did not mean, however, the creation of united fronts, but rather taking control of the anti-Machado movement by emphasizing the idea of class struggle and by appealing to the soldiers and workers to join the Communist cause. The Cuban Communists were ordered, furthermore, to split the anti-Machado movement by denouncing non-Communist leaders as "outs" who were only interested in power.

The Directorio and the Ala Izquierda were not the only groups opposing Machado. The Union Nacionalista, headed by a War of Independence colonel, Carlos Mendieta, also condemned the regime in newspapers and in public demonstrations. In 1931 Mendieta and former president Menocal organized a short-lived uprising in Pinar del Río Province. That same year, a group led by engineer Carlos Hevia and newspaperman Sergio Carbó equipped an expedition in the United States and landed in Oriente Province, only to be crushed by Machado's army. In New York representatives of several anti-Machado organizations united and formed a revolutionary junta.

Most prominent, perhaps, of these anti-Machado groups was the ABC, a clandestine organization composed of intellectuals, students, and the middle sectors of society. Led by several Cuban intellectuals who were Harvard graduates, the ABC undermined Machado's position through sabotage and terroristic actions, and in December 1932 published a manifesto in Havana criticizing the underlying structure of Cuban society and outlining a detailed program of economic and political reforms. Although the means to achieve their political and economic program were not clear, the ABC called for the elimination of large landholdings, nationalization of public services, limitations on land acquisitions by U.S. companies, and producers' cooperatives as well as political liberty and social justice.

Late in 1932 the ABC drew up a two-phase plan to eliminate Machado. The first phase consisted in assassinating a prominent government official, and the second in blowing up, with buried explosives, the Havana cemetery during the official's funeral, thus killing all top government leaders, including Machado. The first part of the plan was completed on September 28, 1932, when ABC members shot and killed Senate President Clemente Vázquez Bello near Havana's Country Club suburb. The second part, however, failed when the government, unaware of the plot, ordered Vázquez Bello's funeral to take place in Santa Clara, his hometown in Las Villas Province, and a gardener working at the Havana cemetery accidentally discovered the buried explosives.

Vázquez Bello's assassination cost Machado's opposition dearly. Police raided secret meeting places, arresting students and ABC leaders, whom they tortured and killed under the *ley de fuga* (law of escape), the name applied to Machado's police method of killing prisoners while "trying to escape." Those students and opposition leaders not captured or driven into exile lived in a continuous state of terror. They were persecuted and, in many instances, were finally hunted down in their various hiding places and assassinated by Machado's *porra*.

This was the existing condition in the island when the United States, attempting to find a peaceful solution to Cuba's political situation, sent Ambassador Benjamin Sumner Welles in 1933 to act as mediator between government and opposition. By then U.S. interests in Cuba had grown significantly. Investment concentrated in land and in the sugar industry, but also extended into transportation, natural resources, utilities, and the banking system. World War I had accelerated this trend, making Cuba more and more dependent on its neighbor to the north. As economic dependence increased, so did political dependence. A new crop of Cuban businessmen, technocrats, and, naturally, politicians developed who identified with their counterparts in the United States and sought political guidance from Washington and Wall Street. This "Platt Amendment complex" permeated large sectors of Cuban society, with the exception, perhaps, of some writers, intellectuals, and students who saw the dangers of the close relationship for the development of a Cuban nationality and identified the *patria* with the workers, the poor, and the blacks.

Their ranks were small, however, and economic prosperity drowned their voices. The fear of, or the desire for, U.S. involvement in Cuban affairs was the dominating theme and many Cubans were willing to use the threat of or even actual intervention by the United States to further their narrow political and economic objectives.

Sumner Welles's mediation was supported by most political factions and leaders, with the exception of the Conservative followers of former president Menocal, the Directorio, and a few Cuban leaders. Menocal declared that the mediation had led to the dissolution of the Revolutionary Junta functioning in New York, thus destroying the unity of the anti-Machado opposition. "It is impossible for the Machado government," he asserted, "to give life to a succeeding government without branding it with its own vices." The Directorio also opposed the United States' action. The leaders of the generation of 1930 saw themselves as representatives of the national will and heirs to Martí's legacy; their mission was to carry on the revolution that the United States had frustrated in 1898. Finding inspiration and guidance in Martí's teachings and his vision of a just society in a politically and economically independent nation, they opposed American supervision of Cuban affairs and the humiliating Platt Amendment. Stressing that the student movement aimed not only at Machado's overthrow but also "toward promoting a thorough cleansing of the system," the Directorio denounced the mediation as "tacitly implying an intervention by the coercive powers of the American government."

Sumner Welles's mediation efforts culminated in a general strike, in dissension within the armed forces, and in several small army revolts which forced Machado to resign and leave the country on August 12, 1933. It is interesting to note that this general strike deepened the schism between the Cuban Communist party and the anti-Machado groups. Although the party played an important role in promoting the strike, it reversed itself just prior to Machado's fall and issued a back-to-work order, fearing that the general strike might provoke United States intervention or the establishment of a pro-United States government. This was accomplished when Communist party leader César Vilar visited Machado and reached an agreement with the dictator, obtaining concessions for the party in return for calling off the strike.

Few workers obeyed the Communists' back-to-work order, however. The party's lack of organization prevented the order from filtering down to the lower ranks, and the increasing excitement precluded the following of such a radical turn. The pact with Machado discredited the Communists, especially among the students who found it hard to condone their shifting tactics. From that time on, the party, alienated from progressive and revolutionary forces within the country, found it easier to reach agreements and work with traditional conservative political parties and governments, even with military presidents.

Carlos Manuel de Céspedes was appointed by Sumner Welles and the army to succeed Machado. The son of Cuba's first president during the rebellion against Spain in the 1860s, and a prestigious although uninspiring figure, Céspedes soon received United States support and the backing of most anti-Machado groups. He annulled Machado's constitutional amendments of 1928, restored the 1901 Constitution, and prepared to bring the country back to normalcy.

Returning Cuba to normalcy seemed an almost impossible task at the time. Cuba appears not to have escaped the worldwide chaos of the early 1930s. The deepening economic depression had worsened the people's misery, and Machado's overthrow had released a wave of uncontrolled anger and anxiety. Looting and disorder were widespread in Havana, where armed bands sought out and executed Machado's henchmen. In rural areas, discontented peasants took over sugar mills and threatened wealthy landowners.

Machado's overthrow, however, did mark the beginning of an era of reform. The revolutionary wave that swept away the dictatorship had begun to acquire the characteristics of a major revolution. Although it lacked defined ideology, this revolution was clearly aimed at transforming all phases of national life. The leaders of the generation of 1930 were the best exponents of this reformist zeal. Espousing usual Communist propaganda issues, such as anti-Americanism and nonintervention, and advocating measures of social and economic significance for the less privileged sectors of society, the students monopolized the rhetoric of revolution. To them the Céspedes regime represented an attempt to slow down the reformist process that had been gaining momentum since the 1920s. Considering the regime a product of the mediation and a tool of the United States, the Directorio and several minor groups manifested their relentless opposition to Céspedes rule. Céspedes's refusal to abrogate the 1901 Constitution, which was regarded as too closely modeled after the United States Constitution and ill-adapted to

Cuba's cultural milieu, created a crisis. The Directorio, furthermore, linked Céspedes to the deposed dictator, pointing to his serving in Machado's first cabinet and living abroad as a diplomat. The students accused the regime of "softness with *porristas*" and of failing to confiscate the huge fortunes of the dictator's followers.

In September 1933 the unrest in Cuba's political picture again came to a head. Unhappy with both a proposed reduction in pay and an order restricting their promotions, the lower echelons of the army, led by Sergeant-stenographer Fulgencio Batista, invited the Directorio to meet with them at Camp Columbia in Havana on September 4. Batista's contact with Directorio leaders dated back to the anti-Machado struggle when he had served as stenographer during some of the students' trials. By the time the students arrived at Camp Columbia, army discipline had collapsed. Sergeants were in command and had arrested numerous army officers. After consulting with Batista and the army, the Directorio agreed to Céspedes's overthrow and named five men to form a pentarchy (a five-member civilian executive commission) to head a provisional government. That same night Céspedes handed over the presidency to the five-member commission who formally took possession of the presidential palace.

September 4, 1933 was a turning point in Cuba's history. It marked the army's entrance as an organized force into the running of government and Batista's emergence as self-appointed chief of the armed forces and the arbiter of Cuba's destiny for years to come. On that date the students and the military, two armed groups accustomed to violence, united to rule Cuba. The marriage, however, was short-lived. A contest soon began between students and military for supremacy. Very few expected the students to win.

The Pentarchy's inability to rule the country became evident at once. The group lacked not only the support of the various political parties and groups, but also of the United States. The Roosevelt administration, surprised and confused by events in the island, refused to recognize the five-man government and rushed naval vessels to Cuban waters. When one member of the Pentarchy promoted Sergeant Batista to the rank of colonel without the required approval of the other four, another member resigned and the regime collapsed. In a meeting with Batista and the army on September 10, 1933, the Directorio appointed Dr. Ramón Grau San Martín as provisional president.

The new president had no political experience to qualify him for the job at such a crucial time. He had won the admiration of the students when in 1928 he allowed the expelled Directorio leaders to read their manifesto to his class. At a time when other professors refused the students' request, Grau's gesture gained for him a following at the university. While he was in jail in 1931, Grau and students met again and cemented their relationship. When the Pentarchy collapsed, their old professor was the students' first choice. A witty and intelligent man, Grau projected a controversial image. He appeared indecisive and powerless, yet he was actually cunning and determined. Effeminate in looks and gesture, he is reputed to have been quite a ladies' man.

With Grau, the generation of 1930 was catapulted into power. The students held Cuba's destiny in their hands. It was a unique spectacle indeed. Amidst thunder from the left and the right, and opposition from most political parties and personalities, the Directorio held daily meetings to shape governmental policy. An American newspaperman attending one of these meetings reported that the students regarded their government "as a non-Communist leftist dictatorship."

Originally the Directorio leaders had no program beyond eliminating Machado. Machado's removal was considered the panacea that would cure all of Cuba's ills. As time went on, however, several factors heightened both their convictions and political sophistication. Some students who spent their exile in the United States returned to Cuba with ideas suggested by Franklin Delano Roosevelt's New Deal. The American evolutionary experiment in social justice with freedom exerted strong influence. Others became impregnated with the ABC ideology. Still others who lived in Europe came in contact with communist or fascist ideology, or with the social and economic ideas of the Spanish Republic. Students told a United States correspondent visiting Havana in September 1933 that their movement "compared most closely with the new revolutionary Spanish Republic." They read a variety of authors, including Argentina's José Ingenieros, Uruguay's José E. Rodó, Mexico's José Vasconcelos, Cuba's José Martí and Enrique José Varona, and Spain's Francisco Giner de los Ríos, Miguel de Unamuno, and José Ortega y Gasset. The Cuban students were strongly influenced by the Spanish generation of 1898, with its humane, spiritual, and tolerant ideas.

The Directorio leaders advocated several reforms. Now that Machado had been overthrown, they wanted to wipe out all vestiges of his regime, including corrupt pro-Machado army officers, politicians, office holders, and university professors. They called for a complete reorganization of Cuba's economic structure, including revision of the foreign debt, tax reforms, and a national banking and currency system removing Cuba from monetary and financial dependence upon the United States. Aware that the Platt Amendment would only allow for continuous United States interference, they wanted its removal. The students also demanded agrarian reform and eventual nationalization of the sugar and mining industries. Finally, they wanted an autonomous university, sheltered from political interference.

Grau's regime was the high-water mark of the revolutionary process and of the intense nationalism of the generation of 1930. Nationalist sentiment rather than radical doctrines dominated the regime's consideration of economic questions. The government was pro-labor and opposed the predominance of foreign capital. Soon after coming to power, Grau abrogated the 1901 Constitution and promulgated provisional statutes to govern Cuba, and called for a constitutional convention with elections subsequently set for April 1, 1934. He also demanded the abrogation of the Platt Amendment. Grau took immediate action to eliminate Machado's followers from government positions and appointed commissioners to "purge" government offices. Since the dictatorship had utilized the machinery of the old political parties, Grau issued a decree dissolving them. The government also complied with one of the oldest demands of the university reform movement by granting the University of Havana its autonomy from government control.

With the island riding a mounting wave of strikes and social unrest, Grau implemented a popular and reformist program. On September 20 he issued a decree establishing a maximum working day of eight hours. On November 7 the government issued a decree on labor organization which sought to "Cubanize" the labor movement and restrict Communist influences by limiting the role of foreign leaders. It required Cuban citizenship of all union officials, and all labor organizations were ordered to register with the Labor Department. On the following day Grau signed the Nationalization of Labor Decree, popularly known as the "50 Percent Law." This law required that at least half the total working force of all industrial, commercial, and agricultural enterprises be comprised of native Cubans (except for managers and technicians, who could not be supplanted by natives), and that half the total payroll be allotted to Cubans. While these two decrees gained much labor support for the government and diminished Communist influence in the unions, they also alienated the many Spaniards and other foreign minority groups living in the island.

Grau's measures also aroused American hostility. The United States viewed the unrest in Cuba with much concern. The over-throw of the United States–backed Céspedes regime was undoubt-edly a defeat for Roosevelt's policy toward Cuba in general and for Ambassador Sumner Welles's mediation efforts in particular. Grau's seizure of two American-owned sugar mills which had been closed down because of labor troubles, and his temporary take-over of the Cuban Electric Company because of rate disputes and additional labor problems, increased Washington's apprehension.

The United States' refusal to recognize Grau complicated the many problems facing him, since U.S. recognition was considered by Cuban political leaders as a key factor for the existence of any Cuban government. United States policy condemned the Grau regime and encouraged opposition groups and rebellious army offi-cers. Opposition was strongest from the Communists, the displaced army officers, and the ABC. Student leader Eduardo Chibás bitterly complained that while the Directorio never used terrorism against the ABC-backed Céspedes regime, the ABC used it to combat Grau's government. The ABC seemed unhappy over their inability to obtain a share of power and feared that the consolidation of the Grau regime might exclude them from future political participation. A Communist-supported demonstration honoring Mella on September 29 led to a clash with the army in which six persons were killed and many others wounded. The army retaliated by raiding the headquar-ters of the National Confederation of Labor and the Anti-Imperialist League, burning furniture and Communist literature.

This military attack on the Communists was followed by a con-frontation with army officers and the ABC. Former army officers had taken refuge in the Hotel Nacional—where Ambassador Sumner Welles resided—and prepared to fight against the regime. On Octo-ber 2 the army began to bombard the hotel. By that time Sumner Welles had moved out. The battle of the National Hotel lasted sev-eral hours, until finally the officers surrendered. As the officers were being removed from the hotel, an unexpected shot precipitated panic among the soldiers and several officers were slaughtered. On November 8 rebel forces backed by the ABC and recruited from the army, police, and civilians seized Atarés Fortress and various other strongholds in Havana. The revolt was also crushed, but only after a two-day battle. Although these victories temporarily consolidated the government, they also strengthened Batista's and the army's influence.

Inner conflict in the government contributed to its instability. A faction led by student leader and Interior Minister Antonio Guiteras advocated a continuation of the program of social reform. Strongly nationalistic and sincerely motivated, Guiteras initiated much of the regime's legislation, and many considered him the real brains behind Grau. Another faction controlled by Batista and the army wanted a conservative program that would bring about United States recognition. Grau seemed to have been caught in the middle of these conflicting forces. On November 6 the Directorio, feeling that its mandate had expired, declared itself dissolved, announcing, however, that its members would continue to support President Grau.

By January it became evident that the regime would soon collapse. Student support was rapidly waning. The military conspired to take power. Washington refused to recognize a regime that threatened its vested interests in the island. Industrial and commercial leaders opposed Grau's legislation. Fearing that the government's program would attract labor support, the Communists violently attacked Grau. A national teachers' strike for better wages further aggravated the already unstable situation. On January 14, 1934 Army Chief Fulgencio Batista forced President Grau to resign. After a two-day rule by engineer Carlos Hevia, Batista appointed Carlos Mendieta as Cuba's Provisional President. Within five days after Mendieta's accession to power, the United States recognized Cuba's new government.

To the United States and to its ambassadors in Cuba, Sumner Welles and his successor, Jefferson Caffrey, Batista represented order and progress under friendly rule. Welles had been persistently hostile to Grau, distrusting his personality as well as his ideas and programs. He was fearful of the social and economic revolution Grau was attempting to enact and the damage this might cause to U.S. interests in the island. Caffrey, who replaced Welles in Havana in December, reported that he agreed with Welles "as to the inefficiency, ineptitude, and unpopularity with all the better classes in the country of the *de facto* government. It is supported only by the army and ignorant masses who have been misled by utopian promises."

Both Welles and Caffrey looked toward Batista as the one leader capable of maintaining order while guaranteeing a friendly posture toward the United States and its corporate interests in Cuba. Two days after the battle of the Hotel Nacional, Welles and Batista had a long meeting during which the ambassador told Batista that he was "the only individual in Cuba today who represented authority." Evidently Caffrey felt the same way, for on January 10, when Batista asked him what the United States "wanted done for recognition," the ambassador replied: "I will lay down no specific terms; the matter of your government is a Cuban matter and it is for you to decide what you will do about it." Naturally, this type of statement to Batista, head of the army, with all his power, can only be interpreted as an invitation to him to pursue a course which would serve his own interests. Within a week Batista had come to terms with Mendieta, the distinguished opposition leader most likely to gain recognition from Washington, and had forced Grau's resignation.

From exile Grau bitterly criticized Batista and the United States. "The deciding factor which led to my final resignation," he wrote, "aside from the perturbing influence of illegitimate interests and the handiwork of Mr. Caffrey, was my refusal to grant an extension of military jurisdiction repeatedly requested by the head of the army [Batista], which would have prevented ordinary courts of justice from judging common crimes committed by members of the armed forces."

10

THE FAILURE OF
REFORMISM

In spite of its short duration, the revolutionary process of 1933 had
a profound impact on subsequent Cuban developments and events.
It gave university students a taste of power and catapulted them
into the mainstream of politics, and created an awareness among the
students and the population at large of the need, as well as the possibility, for rapid and drastic change. It weakened foreign domination
of the economy, and opened new opportunities for several national
sectors hitherto prevented from obtaining a bigger share of the
national wealth because of Spanish and American presence and control. Furthermore, the state's involvement in the management of the
economy was accelerated and new impetus given to the rise of organized labor. But the failure of the revolution also convinced many
that it would be almost impossible to bring profound structural
changes to Cuba while remaining friendly toward the United States.
For the more radical elements emerging out of the 1933 process, it
became clear that only an anti-U.S. revolution that would destroy
the Batista military could be successful in Cuba.

In the years following Grau's overthrow, the generation of 1930
experienced the harsh facts of Cuba's power politics. The students
thought that Machado's overthrow would signal the beginning of a
new era of morality and change. They learned better. Dominated by

the army, Cuba's political life returned to the corruption and old ways of the past. To govern Cuba, Batista chose as allies many of the old politicians expelled from power with Machado. Opportunistic and unscrupulous individuals assumed important government positions, corruption continued, repression and terrorism flourished. The years of struggle and suffering seemed in vain.

Students felt disillusioned and frustrated. Most abandoned their earlier idealism and found comfort in professional and business ventures. Some departed for foreign lands, never to return to their tragic island. Others accepted radical ideologies such as communism or fascism. Several, however, broke with their past and shared in the spoils of office. Desiring to continue fighting for their frustrated revolution, many organized or joined the Partido Revolucionario Cubano (Auténtico) in February of 1934.

Taking their name from Martí's Partido Revolucionario Cubano of 1892, this group became the repository of revolutionary virtue. Directorio leaders joined the new party and Grau San Martín, then living in Mexican exile, was appointed president. The party's program called for economic and political nationalism, social justice, and civil liberties, and emphasized the right of Cubans to share more fully in the country's economic resources. Although the party was silent on the question of peaceful or forceful methods of achieving power, Grau seemed at first to favor peaceful opposition to Mendieta and Batista.

The opposition of some to the use of violence split the generation of 1930. Believing that violence was the best strategy to fight Batista, Grau's former interior minister, Antonio Guiteras, founded the Jóven Cuba, a clandestine revolutionary organization. Batista's most militant opponents joined the organization. Jóven Cuba continued those tactics of urban violence employed so successfully against Machado. Terrorism flared; bombs exploded daily and sabotage crippled electric power. The violence of the Machado days reappeared with unabated strength.

Students were particularly active against the Mendieta government. Early in 1934 the University of Havana was reopened after three years of suspended classes. Demonstrations soon followed. With autonomy as a sheltering device and with almost total control of university affairs, the students displayed increasing hostility toward Mendieta and Batista, announcing their determination to combat the regime with every means at their disposal. Their demands included full reestablishment of all constitutional guarantees; subjection of the military to civil authority; repeal of the constitutional provision prohibiting the confiscation of property from Machado's followers; and, finally, withdrawal of all troops from educational institutions.

Labor unrest and Auténtico opposition added a grim note to an already unstable situation. In 1934 and early 1935 approximately one hundred strikes occurred throughout the island. Discontent in the sugar mills was widespread. The Auténticos repeatedly condemned the regime. In a public manifesto they requested elections, pointing out that the most important development of the year had been "the tremendous growth in military influence."

Opposition to the government culminated in a general strike in March 1935. Begun as a protest of elementary school teachers against the government's neglect of education, the strike quickly spread to other sectors of society throughout the country, acquiring a political character. University students organized a strike committee, appealing to the people to join the movement. Criticizing the government's inability to restore social and political peace, the university faculty soon voted to support the students. Labor followed suit and joined the strikers. One factor precipitating the strike was the breakup of the coalition supporting Mendieta. First the Menocalistas left the government. Next was the ABC, which complained it had not received its promised share of authority. Then prominent cabinet members, unhappy with increasing military control, repression, and graft, resigned, weakening the people's confidence in the regime. This confidence reached a low ebb when the government's finance minister was accused of embezzling public funds.

Mendieta bitterly criticized the strike, claiming that it was directed against wealth and property, peace and order, and even the Cuban family. Fearing that the movement might topple the regime, Batista threw the army's full weight against the strikers. Students and labor leaders were persecuted, imprisoned, or assassinated. Unions were dissolved. The university was closed and occupied by the military. After several days of struggle, the backbone of the strike was broken.

Repression, however, continued. On May 8 Batista eliminated his most bitter opponent, Antonio Guiteras. While waiting in Matanzas Province for a boat to escape to the United States, the founder of the Jóven Cuba was betrayed by one of his associates and killed in an encounter with government forces. The previous months witnessed the first time in the history of the Cuban republic that military firing squads executed civilians—the two victims, Jaime Greinstein and José Castiello, were accused by the government of terrorism, but their only crime had been to oppose Batista.

The failure of the strike consolidated the regime. In the years that followed, Cuba's political life was all but dominated by Batista and the army. Until 1940, when he officially assumed the chief executive office, securing his election through a coalition of political parties that included the Communists, Batista maintained tight political control, ruling through puppet presidents: Mendieta (1934–1935), José A. Barnet (1935–1936), Miguel Mariano Gómez (1936), and Federico Laredo Brú (1936–1940). Desiring to win popular support and to rival the Auténticos, he imitated his Mexican counterpart, General Lázaro Cárdenas, by sponsoring an impressive body of welfare legislation. Public administration, health, sanitation, education, and public works improved. Workers were allowed to unionize and organize the Confederation of Cuban Workers. Legislation to provide pensions, insurance, limited working hours, and minimum wages largely satisfied the workers' demands.

Batista also made a serious effort to bring education and better living conditions to the countryside. Under his ambitious "civic-rural" program numerous schools were built. Where teachers were lacking, he sent army personnel to fill their places. The "Civic-Military Institute" which he established provided for the housing and education of the orphans of workers, soldiers, and peasants. In 1936 he issued the "Sugar Coordination Law," which protected the tenants of small sugar plantations against eviction. Although Batista and his associates continued the practice of pocketing some of the funds earmarked for these projects, they nevertheless made a sincere attempt to improve the health and educational level of the rural population.

Meanwhile, student political involvement had ground almost to a halt. Even after the university reopened in 1937, there was little student activism. With most of the leaders of the generation of 1930 in exile and therefore unable to provide needed leadership, and with the regime clamping down on opposition, students followed a less militant path. Batista's and the army's method of dosing rebellious students with castor oil also seemed to dampen student ardor.

Other factors were important in containing student activism in the late 1930s. The disillusionment that followed the "frustrated revolution" promoted among the students a more cynical attitude toward politics. The early idealism of the generation of 1930 was less evident now among new student leaders. Furthermore, the more conciliatory policy followed by President-elect Gómez and by his vice-president and successor, Laredo Brú, generated a cordial climate. Laredo Brú allowed for the return of political exiles, avoided repressive measures against students, and called for the drafting of a new constitution. With elections for a constitutional convention and for a new president in sight, politics took a more normal course. Grau himself, aware that violence would not bring him to power, returned from exile and engaged in electoral practices, thus legitimizing the Batista-supported regimes.

With only 57 percent of the eligible voters participating in the election for the constitutional convention, government parties won 558,000 votes, but only thirty-five delegates; the opposition parties won 551,000 votes and placed forty-one delegates. Several leaders of the generation of 1930, including Eduardo Chibás and Carlos Prío Socarrás, were elected as delegates. When the convention convened in Havana in early 1940, Grau San Martín was chosen president of the assembly. Despite pressure from both right and left, work went smoothly, with Batista and Grau competing for popular support. But when Batista and former President Menocal signed a political pact that left oppositionist groups in a minority position in the assembly, Grau resigned. In spite of this, there was an unusual degree of cooperation among the various political groups, and the constitution was soon completed and proclaimed that same year.

The constitution was in many respects the embodiment of the aspirations of the generation of 1930. The president was to serve only one term of four years, though he might be reelected after eight years out of office. Many civil liberties and social welfare provisions were defined at great length. The state was to play a strong role in economic and social development. Workers were guaranteed paid vacations, minimum wages, and job tenure. Cuban nationals were to be favored over foreigners in the establishment of new industries. The University of Havana's autonomy received constitutional sanction in Article 53. The convention thus fulfilled one of the oldest demands of the students.

Batista was the first president elected under the new constitution. Supported by a coalition of political parties, and by the Communists, he defeated his old rival Grau San Martín. His administration coincided with World War II, during which Cuba collaborated closely with the United States, declaring war on the Axis powers in 1941. The United States, in turn, increased aid and trade relations with Cuba. It granted Batista credits for agricultural development and for public works in Havana. Batista allowed for the establishment of a variety of U.S. military facilities on Cuban territory; the Export-Import Bank lent Cuba $11 million to ensure an increased sugar crop; and in early 1941 Batista concluded a sugar deal with the United States authorizing the sale of the whole harvest at $.0265 per pound. Many Cubans complained that the low price imposed an excessive sacrifice for Cuba. This burden, added to a series of war taxes that Batista had earlier imposed and also shortages of finished goods and some food, incurred much unhappiness among the population.

Although Batista enjoyed wartime powers, his administration was short of dictatorial. He enjoyed the backing of the propertied classes and he cultivated labor support. He also catered to the left, allowing the Communists complete freedom of operation. On the first anniversary of Batista's assumption to the presidency, the Communist party president, Juan Marinello, eulogized his accomplishments. After Germany attacked the Soviet Union in 1941, the Cuban Communists ended their denunciation of the United States as an imperialist power and began defending President Roosevelt as a "great statesman," and the war against Germany as a "just war."

Batista rewarded his loyal allies. In 1942 Marinello entered the cabinet as minister without portfolio, and afterwards a young Communist theoretician, Carlos Rafael Rodríguez, joined the cabinet. Of bourgeois origin, Rodríguez joined the Communist party at an early age, after having been a Directorio leader in Cienfuegos. He participated in the 1935 strike and graduated from the university in 1939. A writer, an economist, and a dedicated Marxist, Rodríguez's entry into the government was the high point of Communist collaboration with Batista. Two decades later, Rodríguez's was to become one of Castro's closest collaborators and the liaison man with the Soviet and other Communist leaders. In 1944, the Communists changed the name of their party from Union Revolucionaria Comunista to Partido Socialista Popular and issued a mild political program that called for racial equality and rights for women, but failed to attack the United States or even to request agrarian reform or large-scale nationalization of foreign properties in Cuba.

By this time signs of a social phenomenon appeared that later permeated Cuban politics. Whereas prior to Machado's rule uprisings in
the countryside and guerrilla fighting had been common, during the
anti-Machado insurrection urban terrorism and violence had been
successfully employed. The pattern of violence, evident then at the
national level, reappeared now at the local level, with groups
employing violence not only to mobilize political power and influence governmental policies, but for other purposes as well. These
ranged considerably, from punishing Machado's supporters who had
escaped "revolutionary justice" to obtaining government privileges
and subsidies, influencing the appointment of personnel, and securing university degrees with little or no study. Rivalries among gangs
led to frequent street fighting and vendettas.

Batista's tight political control and the events of World War II prevented the growth of these groups. Some incidents of violence, however, occurred in the late 1930s and early 1940s. The most notorious,
perhaps, were two unsuccessful assassination attempts, one on the
life of Chibás in November 1939, and another on Orestes Ferrara in
March 1943. Ferrara was an old Machado supporter and had been
elected to the 1940 constitutional convention.

At the end of World War II, as Grau and the Auténticos came to
power, organized use of violence took on an unprecedented dimension. The relative calm of the war years suddenly ended, giving way
to a violent and materialistic era. Urban violence reappeared now
with tragic proportions. Although part of the generation that
emerged out of World War II retained a redemptionist fanaticism and
a desire to fulfill the aspirations of "the frustrated revolution," a still
larger part evidenced an insatiable appetite for power and wealth,
and a determination to obtain both regardless of obstacles. Violence-
prone refugees of the Spanish Civil War also extended their activism
and rivalries to Cuba.

Elected to the presidency in 1944, Grau followed a conciliatory
policy toward these groups and permitted their proliferation, in
many instances placing their leaders on government payrolls. There
were various reasons for his acquiescence. First, several of the gang
leaders had participated in the anti-Machado struggle and had maintained close contact with the Auténticos. Grau was unwilling now
to confront his old friends, the "boys," as he used to call them.
Unable to count on the support of the Batista-oriented military,
Grau's appointees had organized their own private armies to protect

their areas of graft and privilege. These armies, furthermore, helped to implement Auténtico decrees and to expel the Communists from control in the labor unions. Fearing the power of these gangs and their troublemaking capabilities if employed against the government, Grau allowed them almost complete freedom of action. When in September 1946 a militant gang assassinated the son of a government minister, an outraged Grau complained that he had done everything possible to establish a tolerant government. "In the Ministry of Education," he added cynically, "there is a payroll devoted especially to support these gangsters. But I cannot permit one of my collaborators to be attacked in this manner." This situation continued under the presidency of Grau's protégé, Carlos Prío Socarrás. Elected in 1948, the former Directorio leader also avoided confronting his old friends and continued his predecessor's mild policies.

The three most prominent urban groups operating in Cuba at this time were the ARG (Acción Revolucionaria Guiteras), the MSR (Movimiento Socialista Revolucionario), and the UIR (Unión Insurreccional Revolucionaria). Some members of these organizations belonged to the generation of 1930, and several had participated in the Spanish Civil War or World War II. ARG activists were originally linked to the Grau revolutionary government of 1933 and to Guiteras' Jóven Cuba. One of the MSR leaders, Rolando Masferrer, fought on the Communist side during the Spanish Civil War. After returning to Cuba, he broke with the Communists, was elected to Congress on the Liberal party ticket, and helped organize the MSR. The UIR leader, Emilio Tró, fought with the United States forces in the Pacific and after he returned to Cuba, Grau appointed him director of the National Police Academy. This job put him in a position of strength and provided the necessary protection for his activities. Not only Tró, but also other leaders of action groups, such as Mario Salabarría, head of the rival MSR, were appointed to important posts within the police department.

These *pistoleros* found sanctuary and allies at the University of Havana. The university's autonomy, which inhibited police from entering the campus, afforded a safe emplacement for their activities. Although most of the *pistoleros* were nonstudents, some student leaders joined the gangs. Others acted on their own, using their influence and toughness in student politics. Still others sold their services to the highest bidder. The prestige associated with being a student leader was used by unscrupulous individuals to further their political aspirations and obtain government positions for friends and relatives. Within the university a position of leadership allowed such a student to pass courses with little or no studying. Faculty and administrators fell prey to this elite of campus politicians, professional students, and gangsters. Respect and order reached a low ebb. An interesting example of university life was afforded by the president of the Student Association of the School of Agronomical Engineering. This student moved his wife and children to a university cottage at the school's botanical gardens, brought to the campus a cow and several goats, and lived in full comfort.

Organized use of force became one of the main characteristics of student politics. Rivalries between the UIR and MSR were particularly strong. In February 1948 MSR leader Manolo Castro was assassinated in Havana. His death led to the assassination of two students. In April Justo Fuentes, vice-president of the Federation of University Students (FEU), was shot and killed in Havana. Violating the university's autonomy, police stormed the campus in September, confiscated a large cache of arms that included machine guns and thousands of bullets, and arrested several students. On September 20 Gustavo Mejías, president of the Student Association of the School of Sciences and an opponent of the *bonches* (as the student armed bands were called), was shot to death at the university's swimming club. The widespread activities of the *bonches* led the Cuban daily *El Mundo* to declare editorially:

> violence holds sway at the University. Professors and students are nothing but the evident prisoners of a few groups of desperados who impose their will and pass their examinations at pistol point. The University Council itself has declared its inability to repress these gangs for lack of coercive powers.

Student politics was only a microcosm of Cuba's political life. An entire system of nepotism, favoritism, and gangsterism predominated. Despite numerous accomplishments, the Auténticos failed to provide the country with an honest government or to diversify Cuba's one-crop economy. The reformist zeal evident during Grau's first administration had diminished considerably in the intervening decade. Grau himself seemed softened after years of exile and frustration. He faced, furthermore, determined opposition in Congress and from conservative elements that had joined his party. Not only

Grau, but many of the old student leaders of the generation of 1930 shared in the spoils of office. When confronted with the reality of Cuban politics, their early idealism and reformism gave way to materialism and opportunism.

For many, the Auténticos had failed to fulfill the aspirations of the anti-Machado revolution, especially in the area of administrative honesty. Perhaps the Cubans expected too much too soon. The rapid reforms implemented during Grau's first administration were still remembered and the people expected their continuation.

Grau's failure to bring honesty and order to Cuba's public life and the presidential aspirations of Auténtico Congressman Eduardo Chibás produced a rift in the party. Chibás and other Auténtico leaders formed the Partido del Pueblo Cubano (Ortodoxo) in 1947. Led by Chibás, a former student leader of the generation of 1930, this party became the repository of the ideals of the "frustrated revolution" and the refuge of a new generation, determined to transform those ideals into reality.

By 1950 the Ortodoxos had become a formidable political force. Though lacking a well-defined platform, the party's nationalistic program of economic independence, political liberty, social justice, and honest government, and its insistence upon remaining free from political pacts, had won for it a considerable following, especially among University of Havana students. With the slogan *"vergüenza contra dinero"* (honor vs. money) Chibás, now an elected senator, pounded on the consciences of the Cubans in his Sunday radio programs and sought to awaken their minds to the corruption of the Auténtico administrations. Chibás monopolized the rhetoric of revolution, becoming the exponent of the frustrated old generation and the leader of a new generation bent on bringing morality and honesty to Cuban public life. It was he more than anyone else who, with his constant exhortations, calls for reform, and attacks on Cuba's political leadership, paved the way for the revolution that followed.

Many students shared this redemptionist fanaticism, a readiness to sacrifice everything for Cuba's political salvation. In the university, more than anywhere else, the nation's problems were evoked and debated. Theories of all sorts vigorously flourished. The authoritarian ideas of fascism and communism, offering ready formulas to bring order out of Cuba's chaos, were widely discussed. Although the Communists had attracted several intellectuals and some students embraced Marxism, the past history of opportunism and political accommodations of the Cuban Communist party had discredited it in the eyes of the Cuban people, particuarly among the students. In this atmosphere it was, above all, the nationalistic program of the Ortodoxo party—economic independence, political liberty, social justice, and an end to corruption—that captured the imagination of Cuban youth. Chibás became the idol of university students.

One of those later captivated by the Chibás mystique was Fidel Castro. As a student at the Jesuit Belén High School in Havana in the early 1940s, Castro fell under the particular influence of two of his teachers, the Spaniard Father Amando Llorente and Father Alberto de Castro. Admirers of Franco's Spain and the falangist ideology, both transmitted to their young disciple their enthusiasm for their cause and for Hispanidad, a movement initiated by Ramiro de Maetzu, then much in vogue in Spain. In his course on the history of Latin America, de Castro expounded on some of the ideas of Hispanidad. He explained that the independence of Latin America had been frustrated because of lack of social reforms and lamented that Anglo-Saxon values had supplanted Spanish cultural domination. He called for closer identity among the Latin American nations and with Spain and emphasized that the new Spain had been liberated from both Marxism-Leninism and Anglo-Saxon materialism. He, furthermore, criticized liberal democracy as "decadent," and proclaimed the supremacy of spiritual over material values. De Castro asserted that those having the truth "which is revealed by God" had the duty to defend it against all errors. He rejected compromise and called for the purification of society. Fidel seemed to have been captivated by the teachings of his professors and especially by de Castro's ideas. Fidel read all the works of José Antonio Primo de Rivera who, in 1933, founded the Falange Española, a Spanish brand of fascism; he was fascinated by Primo de Rivera's speeches and by the idea of a rich man who left everything and went to fight for what he believed in.

This is not to say that Fidel Castro was a fascist or that he admired the fascist powers by the time he left Belén. But his stay at the school and the ideas of his teachers left an impact on his young mind. One of his schoolmates at Belén, José Luis Alemán, told the author that there was little regard for democratic ideas at the school during this period while fascist and falangist ideas were very strong. "Fidel," explains Alemán, "was especially impressed by falangist ideas." Castro had thus been exposed to a variety of ideologies and had become acquainted at a young age with a totalitarian model for the organization of society.

Once he left Belén and entered the university, Fidel fell under the spell of Chibás's charisma. He later was to run as the party's candidate for the House of Representatives in the 1952 elections. In his Moncada manifesto, which was to be read after the successful capture of that military barracks, Castro explained that his anti-Batista revolution is inspired "in the ideas of José Martí and adopts as its own the revolutionary programs of Jóven Cuba, of the radical ABC and of the Party of the Cuban People [Ortodoxo]."

While studying law at the University of Havana in the late 1940s, Fidel participated in the activities of student gangs and associated closely with UIR leaders. Although police files implicated him in the murder of rival student leader Manolo Castro in 1948 and in other violent actions, nothing was proved. Fidel soon acquired a reputation for personal ambition, forcefulness, and fine oratory. Yet, he never became a prominent student leader. On several occasions he was defeated in student elections or prevented from winning by the nature of student politics. Perhaps his unhappy experiences at the university created in him the dislike for elections he evidenced after coming to power.

In 1947 Fidel enrolled in an abortive expedition against the Dominican Republic dictator Rafael Leónidas Trujillo. The expeditionary force was allegedly financed by the Grau government and supported by the FEU. Manolo Castro, Rolando Masferrer, and other MSR members were deeply involved. A Dominican general, backed by exiled Dominican leader Juan Bosch, commanded the forces. Training was held at Cayo Confites in eastern Cuba. Desiring to participate in the venture, Fidel contacted FEU President Enrique Ovares. In a training camp where his political rivals were in charge, Fidel feared for his life and wanted Ovares to negotiate a truce with the MSR leaders. Fidel was allowed to join, but soon the Cuban government, pressured by several Latin American nations and the United States, called off the expedition. While the expeditionaries were being taken back to Nuevitas Bay in a Cuban navy frigate, Fidel jumped overboard and swam ashore. "Castro," says Ovares, "was afraid that Masferrer would try to kill him now that the truce was over. His action, furthermore, made for good publicity."

One of the most controversial episodes of Fidel Castro's student life was his participation in the "Bogotazo"—the riots in Bogotá,

Colombia following the assassination of Liberal party leader Jorge Eliecer Gaitán in April 1948. Following a schism within the International Union of Students (UIE), the FEU began organizing a Latin American Union of Students, financed by Juan D. Perón. The Argentinian dictator favored the establishment of an anticolonialist, antiimperialist Latin American Student Union under his control. Opposing the Ninth Inter-American Conference scheduled to meet in Bogotá, Perón suggested that the FEU have a preliminary meeting of Latin American students in Bogotá to coincide with the conference. Not only Perón, but also the Communists were bent on disrupting the Inter-American Conference.

Enrique Ovares, Fidel Castro, Rafael del Pino, and Alfredo Guevara represented the Cuban students. Ovares explained to the author that Fidel had to leave Cuba earlier, for the MSR had accused him of being involved in Manolo Castro's assassination. After traveling to Venezuela, Fidel met his colleagues in Bogotá. Ovares recalls that Fidel, claiming that it would be good for his political future, asked to preside over the student meeting. But despite Castro's pleadings, Ovares insisted on presiding himself. The two students attempted to visit Gaitán and to ask him to deliver the closing speech at their meeting.

Gaitán, however, did not live to deliver the speech. Shortly before his meeting with the Cuban students, he was assassinated. His death unleashed a wave of anger against the Conservative regime of President Mariano Ospina Pérez. Riots and chaos followed. Fidel was caught up in the violence that rocked Colombian society. Picking up a rifle from a police station, he joined the mobs and roamed through the streets distributing anti-United States propaganda and inciting the populace to revolt. Ovares is still puzzled by Castro's conduct. "When I found him several hours later carrying the rifle," says Ovares, "I asked him what he was doing. Fidel only responded that it was his duty." For some, Castro's actions evidenced his link with international communism, while for others it was just a coincidence. Ovares emphatically denies that Fidel was a Communist agent. "It was," he claims, "a hysteric, ambitious, and uncontrollable Fidel who acted in those events." Pursued by the Colombian government for their participation in the riots, the students sought asylum in the Cuban Embassy and were later flown back to Havana.

Castro returned to Cuba to resume his activities in the Ortodoxo party. But before engaging once more in politics, he took time out in October 1948 to marry Mirta Díaz Balart, the sister of a friend in the law faculty at the university. A year later their son, Fidelito, was born. Castro later divorced his wife during the Batista dictatorship. Castro, as did many Cubans, followed Chibás with enthusiasm, regarding him as the only hope Cuba had of redeeming its political institutions and defending its sovereignty. Several years later, in discussing his own 26th of July Movement, Castro reiterated his allegiance to the ideas of Chibás: "For the Chibás masses, the 26 of July Movement is not different from the Orthodox Party; it is the Ortodoxia. . . . To Eduardo Chibás we offer thus the only homage worthy of life and his holocaust: the liberty of his people."

The "holocaust" to which Castro referred marked one of the most bizarre episodes of Cuban political history, an event that was once more to thwart the hopes of the Cuban people. In August 1951, at the end of what started out to be one of his routine weekly radio appeals, Chibás shot himself. Unaware that his radio program was over, Chibás continued speaking. "Cuban people, awake!" were his last words as he pulled a revolver and shot himself in the stomach. Chibás's "last knock on the conscience of the Cubans" and his death several days later produced a feeling of shock and sadness among the emotional masses. His body was taken to the University of Havana, where the Cuban people and the students could mourn him. Chibás's death created a leadership vacuum, produced a rift in the Ortodoxo Party, and facilitated Batista's coup d'état of March 10, 1952.

A number of reasons have been adduced to explain Chibás's suicide. Some claim that after being unable to prove an allegation of graft he had made against a Prío minister he had no choice but to kill himself. Others blame his suicide on a poll taken before the presidential elections scheduled for 1952. To his surprise the poll showed his popularity waning. Still others pointed to his unstable personality as the principal cause of his taking his own life. A few even claimed that he did not really intend to kill himself but merely to injure himself, thus playing on the sympathy of the Cuban people. A combination of factors undoubtedly had converged on this man's life to provoke such a drastic decision. Foremost among these must have been perhaps the frustration of years of struggle with little apparent results. Despite devoting his life to promoting the ideals of the 1933 revolution, he found that at the end of his long journey he had accomplished little. The evils he had combatted were more prevalent at the time of his death than ever before. Maybe he felt that his death might produce what his life had not—the revolution Martí had envisioned.

By the time of Chibás's death, Cuba's political life was a sad spectacle. Although Prío had introduced a number of reforms, and gangsterism had diminished within the University of Havana, his administration resembled that of his predecessor. Politics came to be regarded by the Cuban people with disrespect. To become a politician was to enter into an elite, a new class apart from the interests of the people. The elected politicians did not owe allegiance to their constituents, not even to their nation, but only to themselves and their unsatisfied appetites for power and fortune. Political figures, furthermore, were the objects of popular mockery. In particular, the image of the presidency was ridiculed and abused. Chibás's criticism, furthermore, helped to undermine not only the authority of the Auténticos, destroying completely what little prestige they still enjoyed, but the stability of Cuba's already fragile political institutions as well. The breakdown in morale, respect, and values was aggravated by Batista's interruption of constitutional government in 1952. What Cubans believed would never happen again—the return to military rule—became a reality.

11

BACKGROUND TO REVOLUTION

Convinced that he could not win the elections scheduled for June 1952, Batista overthrew President Carlos Prío's regime in a bloodless and masterfully executed coup d'etat on March 10. The coup was almost entirely dependent on army backing and caught the Cuban population, as well as Prío and his followers, by surprise. Batista quickly consolidated his position by replacing dissenting army officers with his own loyal men, exiling or arresting key Prío supporters, and taking temporary control over the mass media. Prío himself sought asylum in the Mexican embassy and later left the country.

Batista justified his move by claiming that Prío intended to perpetuate his own rule and that the tendency toward violence evident in the country required the order or authority that only he could provide. Yet, other reasons perhaps better explain his actions. Batista was surrounded by a small and intimate group of ambitious and unscrupulous politicians who had been excluded from the political process by the two preceding Auténtico administrations. Batista himself longed for the power he once held and hoped his move would win him the popularity he always coveted but never achieved. His weak position as the elections approached, and the maneuverings of President Prío, who bribed a number of Batista's allies into shifting their support, thus minimizing his political possibilities, convinced the old general that the only road to power was through violence.

The ease with which Batista took over underscored the weakness of Cuba's political institutions and the tendency toward violence that pervaded the political process. The legislative branch was weak and permeated by corruption. Even the judiciary had lost prestige because of its subservient role to the executive branch. The Ortodoxos were leaderless and largely ineffectual since Chibas's death. The Auténticos' corruption and inability to bring profound structural changes to the Cuban economy had cost them a good deal of support and discredited them in the eyes of many Cubans. The failure of this democratic reformist party was perhaps the single most important factor contributing to the 1952 coup and the events that followed.

The Cubans reacted skeptically to the new situation. Had it not been for the depressed status of the political life, as evidenced by the lack of respect for political figures, gangsterism, and graft that prevailed during the previous administrations, perhaps the Cubans would have reacted more vigorously. Batista's performance in 1944, when he allowed free elections, and his promises now for honest and impartial elections in November 1953 contributed to the people's acquiescence. The swiftness of the coup and the display of military power by Batista also did much to contain whatever outbursts of opposition that did occur. Interested in stability and economic development, business groups, both local and foreign, welcomed to a large extent a regime that would impose order.

The importance and power of the business community had grown significantly, helped in part by the rapid economic growth experienced by the island in the 1940s. World War II had paralyzed sugar production in many areas of Europe and Asia, making possible the further expansion of Cuba's sugar industry. At the same time the deterioration of international trade during the war years gave Cuba an extraordinary amount of foreign exchange that would otherwise have gone toward the purchase of agricultural and industrial import items. All of this served to accelerate the diversification process in Cuba's economic development. Domestic production flourished, and other new productive activities were established. This circumstance was put to good use by Cuban entrepreneurs, who began to occupy relatively important positions in the development of the island's economy.

Several other factors helped to accelerate Cuba's economic growth in the postwar years. The moderate nationalistic policy in the international economic field, adopted during the administrations of Grau and Prío, achieved important tariff concessions. Cuba's commercial banking institutions expanded and the credit facilities offered by these institutions permeated all private economic activities. After 1950, the year in which the National Bank of Cuba began to operate, Cuba counted, for the first time in its republican life, with an official and central bank. The official banking system was expanded a short time later with the establishment of the BANFAIC (Agricultural and Industrial Development Bank). With the assistance of the commercial banks, the system could now coordinate the credit system required by the pace of economic development of the nonsugar productive sectors.

In the postwar years national entrepreneurs intensified the process of "Cubanizing" the sugar industry, which had begun in the 1930s. In 1939 Cuban capital owned 54 sugar mills, which produced 22 percent of the total sugar production of the island. In 1952 there were 113 Cuban-owned sugar mills, which accounted for 55 percent of the total sugar production, excluding those sugar mills operated by foreign sugar companies in which Cuban capital participated to the point that in many cases Cubans owned the majority of the capital stock issued. Cuban entrepreneurs, who had become an important factor in the commercial, sugar, and financial sectors, demonstrated great ability in developing new production, and in taking advantage of the combination of favorable circumstances.

Batista encouraged the growth of Cuban capital and his return to power stimulated foreign investment. The mining sector, helped by sizable investments of U.S. capital, expanded its production of nickel, cobalt, and other minerals. The government helped develop new tourist centers and the tourist industry became one of the island's most important sources of revenue. Public works projects neglected or left incomplete by the Grau and Prío administrations, were financed and completed with the concomitant graft. Low-cost housing was made available through government credits, and a badly needed water system was built for Havana. The cattle industry expanded to the point where it ranked high compared to the rest of

Latin America. By the end of Batista's rule, Cuba's economy was well into what Walter Rostow has characterized as the take-off stage.

Yet despite this process, the Cuban economy suffered from certain structural weaknesses which prevented any sustained period of rapid economic growth. Chief among these was an excessive concentration on sugar production and foreign trade; a critical dependency on one major buyer-supplier; substantial unemployment and underemployment; and inequalities between urban and rural living standards.

Cuba was a one-commodity, foreign-trade-oriented sugar enclave. The crop dominated the economy and powerfully influenced policy making. From 1949 to 1958 about 30 percent of the gross national product was generated by the sugar sector. Sugar also accounted for 85 percent of exports, which in turn represented over one-third of the gross national product. Thus Cuba was highly vulnerable to the effects of price fluctuations in the international sugar market. The preferential treatment accorded Cuban sugar in the U.S. market was subject to quotas and prices set by the U.S. Congress. It was evident by the 1950s that sugar had long ceased to be a growth industry and thus could not provide an impetus for development.

Closely tied to its role of sugar supplier was Cuba's excessive dependence on the United States for trade relations. The advantageous position of Cuban sugar in the United States was bought with fairly sizable Cuban tariff concessions which limited the growth of domestic industry and favored imports of U.S. manufactured goods. In the 1950s about 75 percent of Cuban imports came from the northern neighbor, while some 65 percent of Cuban exports found their way to U.S. markets. Most investment funds came also from U.S. financial centers, although domestic banking showed remarkable growth after the creation of the National Bank.

Unemployment and underemployment were widespread. A 1956–1957 study found that about 17 percent of the labor force was unemployed with another 13 percent classified as underemployed. Even during the sugar harvest months some 200,000 persons were without jobs, and this figure jumped to 457,000 during the "dead season." The high proportion of workers engaged in service occupations (36 percent in 1957) was a clear indication of vast underemployment.

Living conditions differed greatly between urban and rural areas. Outside major urban centers, livable housing and educational and health services were scarce and of poor quality. For example, the rural illiteracy rate was almost four times that of the urban area.

Most new housing in the 1950s consisted of multiple-dwelling units and suburban residences in and around Havana. At the same time rural immigrants poured into make-shift neighborhoods occupying any vacant urban land. With few employment opportunities available, these neighborhoods became centers of indigency, crime, or, at best, underemployment.

Despite these weaknesses, the economic progress of the mid-1950s and the elimination of the gang violence so prevalent during the Auténtico administrations gained for Batista the support of the business sectors not intimately linked with the opposition groups. Batista also moved to gain labor and peasant support. He continued the pro-labor policies initiated by the preceding administrations, and through bribery, flattery, and intimidation, won the support of key labor leaders. Yet Batista was unable to build up a labor movement completely loyal to him. Controlled by Eusebio Mujal, Cuba's labor czar, the Cuban Confederation of Labor cooperated as an independent ally of the regime, but with Mujal retaining an autonomous hold on the confederation. Batista also introduced numerous decrees extending to small tenant farmers the right of permanency already enjoyed by sugar-growing tenant planters, and expanding his base of support in the rural areas.

Despite the apparent support of business, labor, and peasant groups, however, Batista failed to develop an active base of political backing. Political loyalties were often the result of intimidation or expediency and for that reason were often short-lived in Cuba. Batista's actual political base was now narrower than in the 1930s. Even within the armed forces, and particularly in the middle and lower echelons of the officers' corps, there were numerous disgruntled Ortodoxo and Auténtico officers who engaged in conspiratorial activities against the regime.

The establishment of the Batista dictatorship had a profound impact on the content and tone of literature. Writers decried the moral decomposition of the republic and even questioned the ability of the Cubans to govern themselves. Although themes like nationalism, reformism, and anti-Americanism were still present in the literature after 1952, they were now impregnated with pessimism and sadness over the future and over the retrogression that the return of a military dictatorship meant for Cuba's political development. Writers pointed out that there was a feeling of general guilt over the Cubans' inability to live up to the principles and examples of the founding fathers. They insisted that the Cubans rejected their individual responsibilities by claiming that society as a whole was not fulfilling its collective responsibilities, and came to believe that they never deserved men like Martí, Maceo, or Gómez.

The idolization of Martí grew even stronger after 1952. Two events, the half-century commemoration of the birth of the republic in 1952 and the one-hundredth celebration of Martí's birth in 1953, gave rise to a literature attempting to assess the development and status of Cuba at such significant junctures. A variety of books and articles appeared on Martí's life and on the epic struggle for Cuba's independence. In them, and especially in numerous speeches, Martí's teachings were contrasted with the conditions in which the dictatorship had submerged Cuba. Old revolutionaries, idealistic youngsters, intellectuals, journalists, and crooked politicians as well, invoked Martí. They all seemed to find shelter and comfort by repeating his words and bathing in the baptismal stream of his thought.

Writings and speeches soon gave way to violence, however. The imposition of strict censorship by the Batista regime silenced all criticism. Opposition leaders were either jailed or exiled. Repression increased. The voices that clamored for a peaceful solution to the interruption of Cuba's constitutional process were soon drowned by voices clamoring for violence. Cuba again was submerged in terrorism and violence, a violence that finally culminated in a major revolution.

Opposition developed from various sectors. Numerous Ortodoxos, a faction of the Auténtico Party under Grau, and most of Cuba's politicians peacefully opposed Batista, hoping for an honest election. Another faction of the Auténticos, together with several Ortodoxo leaders, went underground and began plotting insurrectionary activities.

The active banner of rebellion, however, was to be carried by university students. Students laid their rivalries aside, directing all their efforts against the new regime. Militant anti-Batista student leaders emerged with effective political power, not only in the student community, but nationally as well. During the first three years of Batista's rule, student opposition was limited to sporadic riots, demonstrations, and protests. Although at the time these unorganized acts may have seemed unimportant, they did help awaken the minds of Cubans to the growingly oppressive nature of Batista's regime and thus paved the way for the insurrection that followed.

Several factors enhanced the importance of University of Havana students during the 1950s. First, the more than 17,000 students attending the university were represented by only one organization, the Federation of University Students, giving that body concentration and strength. Second, the location of the university in the heart of the capital city exposed the students to the continuous shock waves of Cuba's political turmoil, placing them in an ideal situation for making their political views known. The inadequate student recreational and library facilities and a staff of part-time teachers, who lacked a sense of pedagogic responsibility, diminished still further the campus's educational atmosphere. Finally, the university's autonomy—originally a sheltering device against government encroachment—had converted it into a sanctuary for political agitators. Because police forces refrained in most instances from entering the campus, the students had a safe emplacement from which to carry on activities against the government.

During the first few years of Batista's regime, political parties exerted considerable influence upon the students in Havana. The Ortodoxos were particularly popular and influential because of the party's uncompromising attitude toward Batista, the mystique of its martyred leader, Eduardo Chibás, and the fact that its more prominent members included several professors at the University of Havana. The National Revolutionary Movement, an offshoot of the Ortodoxo party, also commanded strong student support. Led by a university professor, Rafael García Bárcena, this group recruited a number of students for an attack on the military camp that had given Batista command of the army. Bárcena, also a professor at the War College, a school for army officers, had maintained close contact with the military and expected his attack to coincide with a military coup. Bárcena invited Fidel Castro to participate in the attack, but Castro refused, perhaps considering it a suicidal attack, or perhaps wanting to direct his own movement. Batista's intelligence service averted the plot and arrested Bárcena and several fellow conspirators in April 1953. They were brutally beaten by the police, tried, and sentenced to prison.

A small faction within the Ortodoxos also advocated violence as the correct tactic to combat Batista. Fidel Castro belonged to this group. After receiving his doctorate of law from the University of Havana in 1950, he joined the party and was nominated to run as an Ortodoxo candidate to the House of Representatives in the aborted

1952 election. Batista's coup thwarted Castro's ambitions for a parliamentary career, and he began organizing a small group of followers for his ill-fated attack on the Moncada military barracks in Oriente Province on July 26, 1953.

Although Fidel stored armaments and trained activists within the shelter of the university campus, he was able to recruit only a few students for his venture. His failure to obtain a large following among students requires some explanation. First, Batista had been in power just a short time and was promising elections and a quick return to constitutional government. His performance in 1944, when he allowed honest elections, must have convinced many who would have otherwise followed a violent road to wait a bit longer before resorting to violence. At the time the population had barely recovered from the shock of the coup, the opposition was divided and powerless, and the army, purged of anti-Batista officers, was solidly behind the regime. Violence seemed premature and ill-advised. Second, Castro was not the only one involved in conspiratorial activities within the university. Other groups more influential among the students, such as Bárcenas's, had been planning the violent overthrow of Batista's regime. Finally, Castro was unable to count on the support of his UIR allies. The professional gunmen in this group refused to accept the leadership of a man of action of lesser stature, such as Castro was then.

Castro's Moncada attack was set to coincide with the Santiago carnival in eastern Cuba. This carnival, held in July, is actually a three-day Afro-religious festival. Although Catholicism is Cuba's official religion, Santería, a syncretic cult in which the Catholic saints are equated with African deities, is widely practiced, particularly among the poorer elements of the population, black and white, but also among the white upper class. In Santiago the carnival was a time of festival honoring the African deities with continuous drinking and wild dancing in the streets to the sound of African tribal instruments.

Expecting army discipline to be low at this time, Castro and his group planned a surprise attack to capture the Moncada barracks. This would coincide with a vigorous publicity campaign projecting the movement as an Ortodoxo uprising supported by pro-Ortodoxo army officers. Castro hoped that this would cause sufficient confusion to paralyze the army and thus prevent it from reacting against the rebels. Batista would then be forced to resign and the Ortodoxos would be catapulted into power with Castro now as the party's undisputed leader. In reality, the party was not consulted and its leaders were informed of Castro's plans only the day before the Moncada assault.

Castro's attack ended in disaster. The garrison's discipline was not relaxed and the army fought back the attack. Some of the attackers failed even to enter the military barracks. Those who did were massacred. Castro himself escaped to the mountains, only to be captured and sentenced to years in prison. The attack had failed, yet it gave Castro and his movement national prestige. It showed, furthermore, Castro's awareness of insurrection as psychological warfare and the importance he attributed to publicity and the mass media as tools in the struggle against Batista. Later on, while in jail, he redrafted his famous address before the tribunal that sentenced him, his brother, and other conspirators to jail. The manuscript of the pamphlet, *History Will Absolve Me,* was smuggled out of jail and several thousand copies were distributed throughout Cuba. The pamphlet, however, had little impact, as most of the population remained unaware of its existence or considered Castro's attack a suicidal and futile attempt against the regime.

In *History Will Absolve Me,* Castro outlined his political program. He associated his movement with the ideals of Martí and Chibás, and called for reforms that were within the mainstream of Cuba's political tradition. Similarly, in the Moncada manifesto that was to be read if the military barrack was captured, Castro emphasized that his revolution "is inspired on the ideas of Martí and adopts as its own the revolutionary programs of Jóven Cuba, of the Radical ABC and of the Ortodoxos."

At no time during his struggle against Batista did Castro outline a program that departed from Cuba's political tradition. Although the most radical elements of the revolutionary leadership thought that Cuba needed profound structural economic changes that would cure the ills of monoculture, unemployment and underemployment, and dependence, most of the oppositionist leaders to Batista wanted political changes. None of these groups, including Castro or his 26th of July Movement, offered a program along Marxist lines. The great majority of the Cuban people who supported the anti-Batista struggle were hoping for a return to the Constitution of 1940, honesty in government, and an end to violence.

Cuba's small Partido Socialista Popular also opposed Batista, but through peaceful means. The Communists had worked closely with Batista during his first administration and had been alienated from the more progressive groups in Cuba since the 1930s when they supported the Machado dictatorship. Since then, the party had lost prestige and membership and was a weak, ineffectual contender in the political process. Now, due to the international situation, particularly the pressure of the United States, the Communists were unable to arrive at a *modus vivendi* with Batista. The Communists advocated a "national democratic front government arrived at by the action of the masses." The party criticized terroristic attempts and other *"petit bourgeois"* forms of action, such as Castro's Moncada venture, labeling them "putschism" and "crazy adventures sometimes hatched out on the university campus." Not until very late in the anti-Batista struggle did the Communists join the revolutionary forces, and even then their participation contributed little to the final overthrow of the regime.

The mock elections of November 1954, from which Batista, running unopposed, emerged victorious, placed Cuba at a dangerous crossroads. The opposition wanted new elections, while Batista insisted on remaining in power until his new term expired in 1958. Government officials and oppositionist leaders met throughout 1955 in an attempt to find a compromise. The failure to reach an agreement forced the Cuban people reluctantly onto a road leading to civil war, chaos, and revolution.

A final attempt to compromise occurred late in 1955 with the emergence of the Sociedad de Amigos de la República (SAR), a nonpartisan organization headed by Colonel Cosme de la Torriente. A distinguished eighty-three-year-old jurist and diplomat and a surviving veteran of the Cuban War of Independence, Cosme de la Torriente sought an interview with Batista in which he hoped to influence the government to hold new elections. Batista, however, refused the interview, alleging Cosme de la Torriente to be simply the leader of another political faction.

Batista's refusal catapulted Cosme de la Torriente into national prominence. Political parties and student leaders rallied to his support. The SAR held a public meeting, one of the largest in Cuban history, to show mass support for the oppositionist cause and thus perhaps compel the government into allowing new elections.

Sensing the mounting dissatisfaction with his regime and the significance of the SAR's defiance, Batista changed his initial attitude and started lengthy negotiations that came to be known as *"El diá-logo cívico"* (the civic dialogue). These were a series of meetings whereby Cosme de la Torriente, heading a committee of opposition leaders, tried to work out with a similar group of government leaders, a compromise formula. It soon became evident that the "diá-logo" was doomed to failure. When in March 1956 Batista's group refused to consider a proposal calling for elections that same year, the negotiations ended.

The students reacted violently to the failure of political groups to find a peaceful solution. At the end of 1955 a series of riots shocked the country. On November 27 the FEU organized a ceremony to honor the memory of eight students shot by Spanish authorities in 1871. When the meeting turned into an anti-Batista rally, police arrested several student leaders and caused others to be hospitalized as a consequence of their brutal methods. Similar events occurred in Santiago, where police ruthlessly beat students who tried to observe the November 27 commemoration. In protest the FEU called a student strike, which quickly spread throughout the country. All universities, colleges, and secondary schools closed down. For three weeks daily sorties were made against the police all over the country.

On December 2 students attempting a march from the University of Havana were stopped and beaten by the police. FEU President José A. Echeverría had to be hospitalized. On December 4, during a baseball game, a group of fifteen students ran onto the field displaying banners condemning the regime. Several dozen policemen who had been waiting for the demonstrators surrounded them and beat them brutally in front of thousands of astonished television viewers.

Clashes with the police continued unabated during the following weeks. On December 10 a popular Ortodoxo youth leader died from wounds sustained three days earlier in his hometown of Ciego de Ávila, Camagüey Province. Instantly he became a new martyr whose funeral was made into a gigantic symbol of political protest. Thousands attended from all over Cuba, including a delegation from the FEU. In a gesture of protest the FEU asked labor and the public to join it on December 14 in a five-minute nationwide work stoppage. The stoppage was widespread despite lack of support from the Batista-oriented hierarchy of Cuban labor.

A month had scarcely gone by when new riots erupted in Havana. The anniversaries of the birth of Martí on January 28 and of the death of a student killed during an anti-Batista demonstration on

February 13 were used by the FEU to challenge the government. On February 24 new demonstrations throughout the island commemorated *"El Grito de Baire,"* which began the War of Independence against Spain in 1895.

On April 19 a group of students attempted to enter a courtroom in Santiago de Cuba to hear the trials of schoolmates accused of participating in riots and illegal possession of arms. Barred from the court, they began demonstrating in the street, but were dispersed when fired upon by police and army troops. Two students were wounded fatally, and many were hurt during this encounter. Public indignation in Santiago mounted; retaliations took the lives of two soldiers, one policeman, and two civilians. Most schools throughout Cuba closed, signifying their sympathy with the students of Santiago. Normal school students attempting to hold a meeting in a public park in the City of Guantánamo were discouraged by the authorities; four students were wounded and seven arrested.

Rioting quickly spread to Havana. A group of university students stoned a TV station where a government-sponsored youth program was being televised on April 21. Several participants were wounded. A police cordon was thrown around the grounds of the University of Havana and, on the pretext of searching for hidden arms, government forces entered the university, demolishing the rector's office and destroying documents, scientific equipment, and furnishings. Batista replied to the moral indignation of university authorities and students by declaring that the autonomy of the university was limited to educational, administrative, and internal affairs; when subversive political elements were entrenched within the university, the government must enforce law and order.

Instead of seeking to discourage rebellion by moderation, the regime encouraged it by meeting terrorism with a counter-terrorism that defeated its own ends. No better method could have been devised to increase the bitterness and opposition of the people. Each murder produced another martyr and new adherents to the struggle against Batista. By the end of 1955 the leaders of the FEU realized that the efforts of nonpartisan organizations to reconcile government and opposition were futile. They proposed the creation of an insurrectionary movement to lead the struggle against Batista. As the FEU proposal found little response among the electorally oriented politicians, the students formed their own clandestine organization—the Revolutionary Directorate. In a secret meeting at the university, Echeverría announced its creation with himself as the head.

Whereas students from earlier generations had been able to find national leaders such as Grau or Chibás to embody their aspirations and ideals, students in the mid-1950s were unable to find a comparable charismatic leader. Some of the old leaders of the generation of 1930 seemed to have renounced their early idealism. Others were disillusioned and frustrated. Chibás was dead. National reformist leadership seemed to be either lacking or ineffective. Although the students still identified with some Ortodoxo leaders, they were now unwilling to place their faith too readily in members of the older generation. A generation break stronger perhaps than any other one in Cuban history was taking place in the 1950s—a break that thrust the leadership of the anti-Batista movement upon the young. The students were still willing to follow a leader, but one from their own ranks. Echeverría thus emerged as the representative of Martí's and Chibás's ideals. He, more than anyone else, commanded the admiration of the students and, as time went by, of the Cuban people.

While these riots and demonstrations were going on, other Cubans not connected with student activities were plotting to unseat Batista. A group known as Montecristi plotted with army officers to overthrow the regime, but Batista uncovered the conspiracy and arrested its principal instigators in April 1956. That same month another group, belonging to Prío's Organización Auténtica, unsuccessfully attacked the Goicuría army barracks in Matanzas province.

Castro, in the meantime, was released from jail and traveled to the United States seeking funds for the revolutionary cause and organizing his followers into the 26th of July Movement, an organization named after his ill-fated Moncada attack. In 1956 Echeverría traveled to Mexico and met with Castro. The two joined in a common strategy against Batista and the students agreed to support Castro's planned landing with riots and diversionary actions in Havana. Echeverría soon sneaked back into Cuba to alert his group. Late that year, Castro and a group of over eighty young revolutionaries, including his brother Raúl, and an Argentine physician, Ernesto Che Guevara, left from Mexico in the small yacht *Granma,* and landed in Oriente Province. There underground commando groups attacked several military installations, touching off a wave of sabotage throughout the province. Terrorism flared, bombs exploded. Underground cells derailed trains and sabotaged power lines, blacking out entire towns.

In Havana student leaders watched the Oriente developments anxiously. By the time Castro landed on December 2, however, the uprising was well on its way to being crushed and most of the leaders of Castro's 26th of July Movement were either dead or in jail. Batista suspended constitutional guarantees and established tighter censorship of news. The dreaded military police patrolled the streets of Havana day and night, rounding up suspected revolutionary elements. Castro's action was not supported by the general public, the army, or regular opposition parties. Castro and about a dozen survivors found refuge in the Sierra Maestra mountains and from there began waging guerrilla warfare against the regime.

The events in Oriente prompted the university faculty and administrators to suspend classes temporarily on November 30, 1956. Terrorism and violence continued, however, and the university remained closed until early 1959.

For more than four years the students had been a thorn in Batista's side. The government expected the closing of the university to neutralize student opposition, but instead the act threw almost 18,000 students into the vortex of national politics. As time went on and the university remained closed, the impatience of the students grew and many began joining insurrectionary organizations. Like their predecessors in the successful struggle against Machado in the 1930s, the students narrowed their focus to a single immediate goal: ending the dictatorship.

Despite the instability of the late 1930s, the fall of Machado had ushered in almost two decades of political freedom and constitutional government. The students, and the Cuban people in general, saw Batista's regime as only a temporary interruption of Cuba's democratic political development, as the consequence of Batista's own ambitions for power and Prío's corrupt rule rather than a symptom of more profound national problems. The reduced importance of political institutions at the local level, the reliance on *personalismo*, the economy's continuing dependence on a single crop, widespread administrative corruption—these conditions were not given the recognition they deserved. The elimination of Batista's dictatorship became the panacea to cure all of Cuba's ills. This simplistic thinking served Fidel Castro's purposes well during his stay in the Sierra Maestra. Lacking a well-defined ideology, Castro proclaimed the overthrow of the regime as the nation's sole, overriding task, advocating only the most obviously popular reforms.

The Revolutionary Directorate, together with several Auténtico leaders, planned to overthrow the government by assassinating Batista. Student leaders reasoned that such fast, decisive action would cause the regime to crumble and prevent unnecessary loss of life in a possible civil war. On March 13, in one of the boldest actions of the anti-Batista rebellion, a group of forty men stormed the presidential palace in the center of Havana and almost succeeded in killing Batista. A rapid flight to one of the upper floors of the palace and opportune reinforcements saved his life.

Despite the audacity of the assault, the strong palace defense held out. The poor quality of the attackers' weapons, and the failure of a second group to arrive turned possible victory into costly defeat. According to the official government report, twenty were killed, including five members of the palace guard. That figure, however, did not include the many conspirators whom the police hunted down and killed after the event.

While the palace attack was going on, a group led by Echeverría stormed a Havana radio station. Unaware of the failure at the palace, the students broadcast an announcement that Batista had been killed and his regime brought down. Their joy was short-lived. Minutes later, the police shot and killed Echeverría and wounded several other students.

Fidel Castro, from his hideout in the mountains, criticized the students' attack. In a taped interview shown in the United States in May, Castro called it "a useless waste of blood. The life of the dictator is of no importance. . . . Here in the Sierra Maestra is where to fight." Throughout his stay in the mountains, Castro opposed a military coup, the assassination of Batista, or any other violent act by a group not directly under the control of his 26th of July Movement.

Another group that spoke against the attack on the Presidential Palace, and against Castro's landing in Oriente as well, was the Partido Socialista Popular. The head of the PSP, Juan Marinello, wrote to United States journalist Herbert L. Matthews on March 17, 1957, explaining the official party line: "In these days, and with reference to the assaults on barracks and expeditions from abroad—taking place without relying on popular support—our position is very clear: we are against these methods." The Communists advocated, as the correct strategy against Batista, a mass struggle based primarily on the mobilization of the proletariat and leading toward national elections. They called for the creation of a Democratic Front of National Liberation to form a government representing the workers, peasants, urban petite bourgeoisie, and national bourgeoisie, all under the leadership of the proletariat.

The PSP leaders, however, were following a dual strategy. While publicly advocating peaceful opposition to Batista, they were secretly making overtures to the insurrectionary groups for closer collaboration. They apparently believed they could eventually dominate the FEU and neutralize the Revolutionary Directorate. But no union emerged out of the Communist contacts with the students. Echeverría and other student leaders were not ready for an alliance with the Communists and went ahead with their plans.

Throughout most of Batista's rule, the Communists had enjoyed virtually complete liberty; several of them even held minor posts in the government. Batista took certain measures against the PSP, principally to appease the United States government. These were few, however, compared to the persecution suffered by the non-Communist opposition. The PSP consistently sought to undermine, infiltrate, and control the groups combating Batista. The importance of the Directorate as a dangerous rival for power and the militant anti-Communism of several of its leaders were constantly present in the minds of the top members of the PSP.

The defeat suffered at the palace and the death of Echeverría, at the time perhaps the most popular figure opposing Batista, left the Directorate leaderless and disorganized. Almost a year went by before the organization recovered from the blow, and even then it never regained the prestige and importance it had enjoyed prior to the palace assault. While the Directorate declined, Castro, unchallenged in the mountains, grew in prestige, strength, and following. He gained adherents in the cities and won to his side many discontented elements who, whatever differences they might have had with his 26th of July Movement, found no other insurrectionary organization to join.

From that time on, the guerrilla movement gained in strength and importance. Highly dependent on the local population for intelligence and supplies, they remained in the mountains, concentrating on preserving and expanding their recruits and hoping for a general strike or a mass uprising that failed to develop. The primary military tactic was to ambush small military outposts to capture weapons and ammunition.

Following the murder of Frank País, the 26th of July Movement's national underground coordinator, by Batista's police on July 30, 1957, a spontaneous strike broke out in the three easternmost provinces of Cuba. This strengthened Castro's conviction that a general strike could topple the regime. When the underground of the 26th of July Movement did finally organize a general strike on April 9, 1958, it failed, but this increased the importance and also the prestige of the guerrilla movement in the anti-Batista struggle. From then on, Castro changed strategy and emphasized full-scale warfare, including hit-and-run raids, sabotage, and attacks on military installations. The main objective of the rebels was to isolate government outposts and reduce economic activity in the eastern half of the island.

Corroded by disaffection, corruption, and internal disputes, the army was unable to defeat the guerrillas. This inability increased the guerrillas' prestige and contributed to the internal demoralization of the armed forces. The guerrillas had certain other advantages over the army. For years the peasantry in the Sierra Maestra had been terrified by Batista's Rural Guard and welcomed the protection and promises offered by Castro and his group. The knowledge of the terrain and the intelligence provided by these allies proved invaluable. Then, the guerrillas operated in extremely mobile units in a vast and rugged terrain. The Cuban army was not trained in guerrilla tactics and lacked, in addition, the military leadership capable of carrying on this type of warfare against highly motivated guerrilla fighters. For many of the urban youth that joined Castro in the mountains, there was a sort of mystique in being a guerrilla, fighting for a just cause against an oppressive regime, and living in a rural environment. Finally, the guerrillas were supported by an urban network that supplied manpower, weapons, money, and other necessary aid.

Guerrilla warfare in the rural areas was accompanied by increased sabotage and terror in the cities. A large and loosely related urban resistance movement developed throughout the island. Underground cells of the 26th of July Movement, of the closely allied Civic Resistance Movement, of the Revolutionary Directorate, and of the Auténticos conducted bombings, sabotage, and kidnappings as well as distributed propaganda which undermined the foundations of the government and helped to create a somber atmosphere of civil war.

This urban underground developed into the backbone of the anti-

Batista struggle. It was the work of the urban underground more than anything else that brought about the downfall of the regime. The action of these groups provoked Batista and his repressive forces into such extreme retaliatory measures that the Cuban population became almost totally alienated from the regime. Batista's police tortured and murdered real and suspected revolutionaries. Bullet-ridden bodies of young men appeared in the principal streets of the capital with bombs tied to their bodies as reminders of the punishment revolutionaries would receive. A wave of national revulsion against such methods and against a dictatorship that obstinately insisted on remaining in power developed. Loyalties were weakened, even within the armed forces, and this hastened to the downfall of the regime. A military offensive was launched against the rebels in mid-1958, but it failed miserably.

U.S. policy also contributed somewhat to the growing demoralization within the military. Prior to 1958 the United States had supported the Batista regime, and U.S. ambassadors to Cuba showed more than the customary cordial attitude toward Batista. In the fall of 1957, however, the U.S. government began holding up shipments of weapons and munitions. An arms embargo was publicly announced in March 1958. Although these arms shipments were small and from Batista's point of view not decisive in the struggle against Castro, they did represent a sign of continuous backing for his administration. Thus, when the embargo was declared, many Cubans saw it as a change in Washington's policy, indicating disapproval and withdrawal of support for the regime. U.S. actions were undoubtedly a strong blow to the declining morale of the Batista regime and of the armed forces in particular.

The regime was further weakened when several institutions and sectors of Cuban society began a progressive withdrawal of their support. The church, professional and business groups, and the press exerted pressure on the government to allow a peaceful solution. At first they advocated free elections with absolute guarantees for all political parties, but the rigged elections of November 1958, in which Batista's hand-picked candidate won the presidency for a new four-year term, convinced many that violence would be the only method to eliminate Batista's rule. The army's refusal at the end of 1958 to continue fighting dealt the final blow to a crumbling regime.

IV

CASTRO IN COMMAND

12

CASTRO'S REVOLUTION

WHEN Batista and his closest allies escaped to the Dominican Republic in the early hours of January 1, 1959, power lay in the streets. Of the several groups that fought the Batista regime, the 26th of July Movement had an almost undisputed claim to fill the vacuum left by the dictator. Castro's charisma and his revolutionary prestige made him, in the eyes of the Cuban people, the logical occupant of Batista's vacant chair; he was the man of the hour, the new messiah. The other insurrectionary organizations lacked the mystique, the widespread support, and the organized cadres of Castro's movement. The Civic Resistance Movement, formed by prominent professional and university professors, was an amorphous group that followed Castro's orientation. The PSP had accepted Castro's leadership and seemed willing to cooperate with the *"petit bourgeois"* revolutionary. The regular army was leaderless and demoralized. Castro's bid for power was unchallenged.

Castro had unquestionable qualities of leadership. Endowed with an extraordinary gift of oratory and an exceptional memory, he would speak extemporaneously for hours. Like Martí had done years earlier, Castro lectured to the Cubans on the evils of their society and the need for profound and rapid changes. The overwhelming majority of the Cubans accepted his leadership enthusiastically. The atmosphere of gloom that prevailed during the Batista era was now converted into euphoria and hope for the future. Even those who had failed to participate in the anti-Batista struggle fervently joined the revolutionary ranks with a guilt feeling for their past behavior.

During the first few weeks in power, Castro assumed no official position except commander of the armed forces. His hand-picked president, former Judge Manuel Urrutia, organized a government, appointing a civilian cabinet composed mainly of prominent anti-Batista political figures. Urrutia then proceeded to tear down Batista's governmental structure. In a series of decrees he dissolved Congress; removed from office all congressmen, provincial governors, mayors, and municipal councilmen; abolished all of Batista's censorship and martial law restrictions; and began a clean sweep of Batista supporters in the bureaucracy.

It soon became clear, however, that real power rested with Fidel and his youthful rebel army officers. In public addresses Castro announced major public policies without consultation with the Urrutia cabinet and complained of the slowness of reforms. In mid-February Prime Minister Miró-Cardona resigned in favor of Castro, and by October Castro forced Urrutia to resign and appointed Oswaldo Dorticós, an obscure lawyer and former PSP member, as Cuba's president.

Castro's formal assumption of power initiated a period of increased radicalization. Some of Batista's more prominent military and civilian leaders were publicly brought to trial before revolutionary tribunals and the proceedings were televised; hundreds were executed summarily. Faced with mounting criticism, the regime ended these public trials but continued them in private, while also confiscating property of Batista supporters or collaborators.

On May 17, 1959 the first Agrarian Reform Law was passed. It established a National Institute for Agrarian Reform (INRA), and called for a maximum limit on landholdings with the remaining land being expropriated by the government. Large and medium agricultural estates were taken over, but little land was distributed among the peasantry; most of these lands were eventually converted into state farms with peasants living and working on them and receiving a salary and a small share of the profits.

The Agrarian Reform Law, together with a sharp reduction in urban rents, marked the beginning of the rapid confiscatory and redistributive phase of the revolution, which lasted until the formal establishment of the socialist economy in April 1961 when Castro proclaimed that the revolution was socialist. In order to destroy the structural imbalances that had plagued the Cuban economy, the revolutionary leadership aimed at agricultural diversification and industrialization, thus hoping to lessen dependence upon sugar. They also sought to weaken U.S. economic presence and influence in Cuba and to reduce the glaring inequalities between urban and rural standards. This was to be accomplished partially by nationalizing foreign and domestic enterprises. Natural resources, utility companies, the credit system, and most large and medium industries fell into the hands of the government. A gradual takeover of the mass communication media and the educational system also took place, and both became powerful tools of the state apparatus. The government initiated a program of low-income housing and a massive literacy campaign which, according to official claims, has wiped out the 30 percent illiteracy rate that existed prior to the revolution. Unemployment receded and unskilled urban workers received increases in real income through higher salaries, although skilled workers suffered substantial losses. The upper classes were wiped out, and middle-class families lost most of their income-producing property. Many migrated, particularly to the United States, or were absorbed into the larger proletariat created by the revolution.

Meanwhile, Castro insisted on a high standard of morality for the Cuban population, and for the government bureaucracy in particular. Immorality, as existed in the old Cuba, was associated with capitalism, and capitalism, with all its evil consequences, had to be destroyed. The pressures for economic survival, furthermore, made it necessary to end idleness, laziness, and other vices. The Castro regime thus assumed a puritanical attitude, prohibiting prostitution, gambling, and even such traditional and popular Cuban institutions as the lottery and cockfighting.

The most important moral reform occurred in connection with the administration of public funds. Stealing from the government was made a capital offense and the system of sinecures was ended. Although political integrity has not been achieved completely and new forms of privilege and sinecure have appeared, the widespread administrative corruption of the past was reduced.

The regime had made an all-out effort to provide a new and more militant role for women. Since the revolution, over half a million women have joined the labor force, and a Federation of Cuban Women under the leadership of Vilma Espín, Raúl Castro's wife, has been organized. Women fill a variety of jobs in and out of the government bureaucracy, and many work overnight on armed-guard duty. Although some of this work is voluntary, there is a great amount of direct and indirect coercion. The former takes the form of directives by the party, the Federation and other organizations to engage women voluntarily in tasks such as cane-cutting. The latter is more subtle. The more militant exert a sort of social pressure on the less militant to participate. Also, since political and even economic advancement in Cuba is reserved for those who sacrifice harder for the revolution, voluntary work is a way of showing your devotion and loyalty to the party and the revolutionary cause. There is also a greater interest and participation in politics and sports, and many more women than before the revolution are university-educated. Although it is difficult to assess the depth of change in the values and attitudes of women, as well as the reaction of men to these changes, unquestionably, the old feeling that a woman's place was in the home has collapsed completely, and women have found a new, more politicized and involved role in Castro's Cuba.

The new opportunities offered to women have also had the effect of undermining the family, one of the most important conservers of the old order. Relations between husband and wife have been undermined and the family has largely lost control of the children. Large numbers of children attend free boarding schools and see their parents for only short periods of time during the year. There is, therefore, not only frequent separation of husband and wife due to the work demands of the revolution, but also separation of parents from children. The regime has systematically encouraged these developments, perhaps aware that the only way to develop Cuba's new socialist man is through the destruction of the culture-transmitting institutions, such as the family and the church.

In February 1960 the regime created a Central Planning Board to plan and direct the country's economic development. Organizational models of East European countries were usually adopted, and the Ministry of Industry, under Che Guevara, took over and administered major industrial installations. The transformation of Cuba's private enterprise system into a centralized state-controlled economy resulted in growing inflation, disorganization, and bureaucratic chaos and inefficiency. Agricultural production declined sharply, partly as a result of neglect and Castro's plan for industrialization, and by 1961 food rationing was introduced for the first time in the island's history. Cuba is still suffering acutely from many of these problems.

The growing radicalization of the regime was accompanied by the destruction of possible opposition and by the growth in influence of the PSP. Political parties were not permitted to function, with the exception of the PSP, which later merged with Castro's own 26th of July Movement to form the Cuban Communist party, the country's ruling party. Many older political leaders became alienated from the regime; several went into exile, some joined the revolutionary ranks. Most of the leaders and groups of the anti-Batista struggle were coopted into the revolution and later fused with the Castroites, although an increasing number of former Castro allies became disenchanted with the revolution, feeling that Castro had betrayed the ideals he espoused while in the mountains. Abetted by Castro, Communists progressively occupied important positions in the government, gaining in prestige and influence.

Evidently, Castro saw significant advantages in using the PSP. The party provided the trained, disciplined, and organized cadres that Castro's movement lacked. But more importantly, the party had Moscow's ear, and therefore could serve as the bridge for any possible Cuban–Soviet rapprochement. Castro knew well that in any conflict with the United States, only the protective umbrella of the Soviet Union could defend him against possible U.S. pressures or attack. No other power, Castro reasoned, could or would confront the United States over Cuba. The experience of Guatemala in 1954, when a U.S.-sponsored coup overthrew the Communist-leaning regime of Jacobo Arbenz, was a clear warning to Fidel and particularly to his trusted adviser, Che Guevara, who had been a minor official in the Guatemalan government at the time of Arbenz's overthrow, that a profound revolution that would affect U.S. interests in Cuba would be a difficult task.

Ideologically, Castro was far from being a Marxist. He belonged to Cuba's vague populist political tradition. Martí and Chibás had called for an end to political corruption, destruction of Cuba's dependence on monoculture and one foreign buyer, and development of a unique and nationalistic identity. Although strongly influenced by falangist and fascist ideas while a high school student, and by Marxist ideas while at the University of Havana, Castro embraced none of these and was instead more a product of the Martí-Chibás tradition, although he broke with it in several fundamental aspects. While

Martí and Chibás had envisioned reforms in a democratic framework in a nation politically and economically independent from the United States, they both advocated friendly relations with the "northern colossus." Castro did not. He was anti-U.S. since his student days when he distributed anti-U.S. propaganda in Bogotá. As Castro and part of the Cuban revolutionary leadership perceived it, the possibility of a repetition of earlier U.S. interventionist policies in Cuba was a major deterrent to achieving profound socioeconomic changes in the island and the consolidation of Castro's personal rule—and Castro was committed to both of these goals. Perhaps because of his anti-Americanism, and particularly his conviction that a major revolution with himself in absolute control could not be undertaken within Cuba's political framework and in harmony with the United States, he broke with the Martí-Chibás tradition and led a totalitarian and anti-American revolution.

In the early months of his revolution, Castro reasserted his independence from the United States but maintained normal relations. During his visit to the United States in April 1959, he turned down tentative offers of aid, but insisted that Cuba stood with the West in the Cold War. He also met with several U.S. government officials, including then Vice-President Richard Nixon. Yet, as time went on, Castro increased his inflammatory denunciations of the United States. He accused the northern neighbor of every exile raid perpetrated against his country and blamed it for Cuba's economic and political ills.

Initially, the United States followed a "wait and see" policy. The Eisenhower Administration seemed to have been caught by surprise over events in Cuba and failed to grasp the magnitude of the changes going on or the nature of the leader sponsoring those changes. Differences arose between those who, feeling that Castro was a Marxist, advocated a hard line toward Cuba and those who counseled patience with the bearded leader.

Although tensions arose in connection with the public trials and executions of Batista supporters, serious differences grew after the Agrarian Reform Law was promulgated. The United States protested, to no avail, the expropriations initiated under the law. Agricultural expropriations were followed by further attacks on foreign investments, notably in the mining and petroleum industry. Complicating the relations between the two countries were arrests of U.S. citizens, Castro's refusal to meet with U.S. Ambassador

Philip W. Bonsal in late 1959, and the sabotage and raids carried out by Cuban exiles from U.S. territory.

Castro's militant Caribbean activities also increased Washington's apprehension. During the first year of the revolution, Cuban filibusters, joined by exiles from various Caribbean nations, launched a series of abortive expeditions in an attempt to raise the standard of revolt in several neighboring countries. The relationship of Castro to these expeditions has never been clearly defined. Many of these exiles had contributed to Castro's victory and now saw an opportunity to develop an international movement to dislodge dictators from the area. On several occasions Castro openly condemned some of the attempts and halted vessels loaded with weapons and men. Although it seems likely that at this early period Castro was unconnected with these attempts, the fact remains that expeditions were launched from Cuba against Panama, the Dominican Republic, and Haiti.

Whether or not the Cuban regime supported these attempts, Castro, Guevara, and Raúl believed that the political, social, and economic conditions which had produced their revolution in Cuba existed in other parts of Latin America and that revolutions would occur throughout the continent. From 1960 onward Cuban agents and diplomatic representatives established contact with revolutionary groups in the area and began distributing propaganda and aid. Several Cuban diplomats were expelled for interfering in the internal affairs of the countries to which they were accredited. As tensions mounted with the United States, Castro's assertion of the international character of his revolution increased, as did his involvement in promoting violence in Latin America. By July 1960 Castro was boasting that he would convert "the Cordillera of the Andes into the Sierra Maestra of Latin America," and money, propaganda, men, and weapons began to flow from Havana in increasing quantities to foment the "anti-imperialist" revolution.

The radicalization of the revolution and the deterioration of relations with the United States grew apace with Cuban-Soviet rapprochement. In February 1960, following the visit to Havana of Soviet Deputy Premier Anastas Mikoyan, Cuba signed a major trade agreement with the Soviet Union. The agreement provided that Cuba would receive, among other products, Soviet oil in exchange for sugar. But in June United States- and English-owned refineries in Cuba refused to process Soviet oil. Also, the U.S. House of Representatives approved a bill granting the president authority to cut foreign sugar

quotas at his discretion. Castro retaliated, and on June 28 he national-
ized the oil companies. In July the United States deleted the remaining tonnage of that year's Cuban sugar quota. In the following
months Castro confiscated the remaining U.S. properties together
with most major Cuban-owned businesses. In October the United
States announced an embargo on most exports to Cuba, and when
Castro restricted the staff of the U.S. embassy to eleven persons, the
United States severed diplomatic relations and withdrew its ambassador with the following statement: "There is a limit to what the U.S.
in self-respect can endure. That limit has now been reached."

By then the United States had embarked on a more aggressive policy toward the Castro regime. Groups of Cuban exiles were being
trained under the supervision of U.S. officials in Central American
camps for an attack on Cuba. The internal situation in the island
then seemed propitious for an attempt to overthrow the Cuban
regime. Although Castro still counted on significant popular support, that support had progressively decreased. His own 26th of July
Movement was badly split on the issue of communism. Also, a substantial urban guerrilla movement existed throughout the island,
composed of former Castro allies, Batista supporters, Catholic
groups, and other elements that had been affected by the revolution,
and significant unrest was evident within the armed forces.

The urban underground saw the landing of the U.S.-sponsored
invasion force as the culminating event to follow a series of uprisings
and acts of sabotage they hoped would split Castro's army throughout the island and weaken the regime's hold over the people. This
would coincide with Castro's assassination and with a coordinated
sabotage plan. In the weeks prior to the invasion, violence increased,
bombs exploded, shops were burnt.

Yet the planners in exile were not counting on the forces inside
Cuba. They placed an unjustified faith in the invasion's success, and
feared that the underground might be infiltrated by the regime. Arms
that were to be shipped into Cuba never arrived, and communications between the exiles and underground forces were sporadic and
confused. The underground was not alerted to the date of the invasion until April 17, the very day of the landing, when it could only
watch the Bay of Pigs disaster in confusion and frustration.

The whole affair was a tragedy of errors. Although the Cuban government did not know the date or the exact place where the exile
forces would land, the fact that an invasion was in the offing was

known in and out of Cuba. The weapons and ammunitions that were to be used by the invading force were all placed in one ship, which was sunk the first day of the invasion. The site for the invasion was sparsely populated, surrounded by swamps, and offered little access to nearby mountains where guerrilla operations could be carried out if the invasion failed. The invading forces could, therefore, all but discount any help from the nearby population.

Some of the air raids by Cuban exiles that were intended to cripple Castro's air force were cancelled at the last minute by a confused and indecisive President John F. Kennedy. Perhaps trying to reassert his authority over the CIA-sponsored invasion, to stymie possible world reaction, or to appease the Soviets, Kennedy ordered no further U.S. involvement. Castro's Sea Furys and T33s could, therefore, shoot down the exiles' B26s and maintain control of the air. While the invasion was in progress, Khrushchev threatened Kennedy: "The government of the U.S. can still prevent the flames of war from spreading into a conflagration which it will be impossible to cope with. . . . The world political situation now is such that any so-called 'small war' can produce a chain reaction in all parts of the world."

The failure of the invasion and the brutal repression that followed smashed the entire Cuban underground. On the first day of the invasion, the regime arrested thousands of real and suspected oppositionists. The resistance never recovered from that blow. His regime strengthened and consolidated, Castro emerged victorious and boasted of having defeated a "Yankee-sponsored invasion." The disillusionment and frustration caused by the Bay of Pigs fiasco among anti-Castro forces, both inside and out of Cuba, prevented the growth of significant organized opposition. Meanwhile, U.S. prestige in Latin America and throughout the world sank to a low point.

Following the Bay of Pigs fiasco, the United States turned to other methods of dealing with Castro. It pursued a vigorous, although only partially successful policy to isolate the Cuban regime and strangle it economically. The nation pressured its allies throughout the world to reduce their commerce with Cuba. In the Organization of American States, the United States forced the suspension of Cuba by a slim majority in January 1962, and several countries broke diplomatic relations with the Castro regime at this time. In 1964, after Castro had increased subversive activities in Latin America and had moved fully into the socialist camp, the OAS voted to suspend trade and diplomatic relations with Cuba; all countries that had not already done so severed relations, except Mexico, who strongly supported the principle of self-determination and refused to bow to U.S. pressures.

As Cuban-U.S. relations deteriorated, closer ties with the Soviet Union developed. Initially, Moscow maintained a cautious stand toward Castro. The Cuban "petite bourgeois" leader seemed impotent to defy the "northern colossus," and the ability of an anti-U.S. regime to survive so close to the U.S. shores seemed remote, particularly in light of the 1954 Guatemala experience. The Soviets, furthermore, were not greatly interested in far-away, raw-material producing Latin America, an area which they considered the backyard of the United States. Khrushchev's attempts at a detente with the United States and his desire to extract concessions from Washington over Berlin were important considerations in limiting Soviet involvement in Cuba lest they provoke a strain in U.S.-Soviet relations. Also, the Soviets recognized that Castro's attempts to identify with the Soviet camp, such as his April 1, 1961 speech declaring the Cuban revolution to be socialist, or his December 1961 speech in which he declared himself a Marxist-Leninist, were designed to involve the Soviet Union in Cuba's defense against possible hostile actions by the United States.

Other considerations were also limiting Soviet involvement in Cuba. Soviet experience with regimes that gained power without Soviet support had shown that these regimes pursued policy lines independent from the Soviets and were difficult to control. As it turned out, the Castro regime proved difficult and at times impossible to influence. Although Castro endorsed half-heartedly the Soviet doctrine of "peaceful coexistence" and the peaceful road to power, he also insisted that the Cuban model of violent revolution was the only valid one for Latin America, and that Cuba should exercise the leadership of the antiimperialist movement in the area. Naturally, this brought Castro into conflict with Moscow and with the pro-Soviet popular front-oriented Communist parties of Latin America, which were not now about to abandon their comfortable and peaceful position in the Latin American political arena to follow Castro's violent path.

Internal developments in the island also worried the Soviets. During the first two years in power, Castro accepted the principle of "collective leadership" and permitted the PSP to increase its prestige and to gain positions of importance in the ORI (Integrated Revolutionary Organizations), a merger of the PSP, the 26th of July Movement, and other groups which occurred in July 1961. By 1962, however, feeling his position threatened, Castro moved swiftly to curb the power of the "old guard" Communists and purged Aníbal Escalante, a PSP leader and ORI secretary, exiling him to the Soviet Union. This was the first of several attacks to be suffered by the PSP, which was effectively destroyed as an organization as it became an instrument of Castro's policies.

In spite of these difficulties and apprehensions, the Soviets gradually came to accept the bearded leader. The growing nationalism of Latin America and the enormous popularity of the Cuban revolution in the area were factors limiting the ability of the United States to carry on hostile actions against Castro during the first two years of his regime and encouraging the Soviets' hopes for the survivability of the revolution. Castro's radicalization and his expanding conflict with the United States also increased Moscow's interest. The Soviets saw in Cuban-U.S. tensions an opportunity to offset their failures to obtain U.S. concessions over Berlin. The embarrassment that the "loss" of Cuba could mean for the United States was an added incentive for the Soviets, who were still suffering from the scars left by the rebellion of its own Eastern European satellites. The growing Sino-Soviet dispute was also an important factor pressuring the Soviets into a more militant policy in support of antiimperialist revolutions in developing countries.

The single most important event encouraging and accelerating Soviet involvement in Cuba was the Bay of Pigs fiasco. The failure of the United States to act decisively against Castro gave the Soviets some illusions about U.S. determination and interest in the island. The Kremlin leaders now perceived that further economic and even military involvement in Cuba would not entail any danger to the Soviet Union itself and would not seriously jeopardize U.S.-Soviet relations. This view was further reinforced by President Kennedy's apologetic attitude concerning the Bay of Pigs invasion and his generally weak performance during his summit meeting with Khrushchev in Vienna in June 1961.

The Soviets moved swiftly. New trade and cultural agreements were signed and increased economic and technical aid was sent to Cuba. By mid-1962 the Soviets embarked on a dangerous gamble by surreptitiously introducing missiles and bombers into the island. Through these actions Khrushchev and the Kremlin leadership hoped to alter the balance of power and force the United States to accept a settlement of the German issue. A secondary and perhaps less important motivation was to extend to Cuba the Soviet nuclear umbrella and thus protect Castro from any further hostile actions by the United States.

On October 22 President Kennedy publicly reacted to the Soviet challenge, instituting a blockade of the island and demanding the withdrawal of all offensive weapons from Cuba. For the next several days the world teetered on the brink of nuclear holocaust. On October 26 a hysterical Khrushchev wrote to Kennedy:

> I think you will understand me correctly if you are really concerned about the welfare of the world. Everyone needs peace: both capitalists, if they have not lost their reason, and still more, communists. . . . I see, Mr. President, that you too are not devoid of a sense of anxiety for the fate of the world, of understanding, and of what war entails. What would a war give you? You are threatening us with war. But you well know that the very least which you would receive in reply would be that you would experience the same consequences as those which you sent us. . . . We, however, want to live and do not at all want to destroy your country. We want something quite different: to compete with your country on a peaceful basis. We quarrel with you, we have differences on ideological questions. But our view of the world consists in this, that ideological questions, as well as economic problems, should be solved not by military means, they must be solved on the basis of peaceful competition. . . .*

Finally, after an exchange of hectic correspondence, Premier Khrushchev agreed to remove the missiles and bombers, and to allow UN-supervised inspection of the removal in exchange for the United States' pledge not to invade Cuba. Although Castro refused to allow a UN inspection, the missiles and bombers were removed under U.S. aerial surveillance and the crisis ended. The United States has never publicly acknowledged that it pledged not to invade Cuba, but subsequent U.S. policies indicate that a U.S.-Soviet understanding was reached over Cuba which included a U.S. "hands off" policy toward the island.

The missile crisis had a significant impact on the countries involved. While it led to a thaw in U.S.-Soviet relations, it signifi-

---

*The complete text of this secret letter was released by the United States Department of State, which provided the author with a copy.

cantly strained Cuban-Soviet relations. Castro was not consulted throughout the Kennedy-Khrushchev negotiations and the unilateral Soviet withdrawal of the missiles and bombers wounded Castro's pride and prestige. It was a humiliating experience for the Cuban leader, who was relegated throughout the crisis to a mere pawn in the chess board of international politics. Castro defiantly rejected the U.S.-Soviet understanding and publicly questioned the Soviet willingness and determination to defend his revolution.

It is ironic that the crisis, hailed at the time as a U.S. victory, was nothing more than an ephemeral triumph. In return for the removal of offensive weapons from the island, the United States was satisfied to accept a Communist regime only a few miles from its shores. Even the withdrawal of nuclear weapons proved to be only temporary. As later events showed, the Soviets brought more sophisticated weapons to Cuba, but in a different form, using the island as a strategically important base for its nuclear submarines. The real victor, in spite of the humiliation he suffered, was Castro. His regime consolidated and his survivability guaranteed, he could now embark on an aggressive policy to export his brand of revolution throughout Latin America. The Soviet Union, furthermore, went to considerable lengths to appease their Caribbean ally, increasing aid and welcoming him as a hero during his extended trip to the Soviet Union in April–May 1963.

Despite Soviet attempts to appease Castro, Cuban-Soviet relations were still marred by a number of difficulties. After the missile crisis Castro increased contacts with Communist China, exploiting the Sino-Soviet dispute and proclaiming his intention to remain neutral and maintain fraternal relations with all socialist states. Cuba signed various trade and cultural agreements with Peking and Castro grew increasingly friendly toward the Chinese, praising their more militant revolutionary posture. He also defied the Soviets, as he joined the Chinese in refusing to sign the Nuclear Test Ban Treaty (1963). All of these maneuverings increased somewhat Castro's leverage with the Soviets and gained him more assistance.

The Chinese honeymoon was short-lived, however. In 1966 Castro blasted the Chinese for reducing rice shipments to Cuba below the quantities that Castro alleged had been agreed upon between the two countries. He described Mao's ideological statements as lightweight, called for the creation of a "council of elders" to prevent aged leaders from "putting their whims into effect when senility has taken hold of them," and threatened to handle Chinese diplomats the same way "we handle the American Embassy." By then, Castro had also become disappointed with China's attitude toward Vietnam and by its propaganda efforts to sway Cubans to its side in the Sino-Soviet conflict. Castro's insistence on absolute control of the revolutionary movement in Latin America and his awareness of China's limitations in supplying Cuba's economic need were further key factors in the cooling of the friendship between the two nations. Since the collapse of the Soviet Union, Cuban-Chinese relations have improved significantly.

The principal area of Soviet-Cuban conflict was Castro's revolutionary ventures in Latin America. In 1963 Castro embarked on major attempts to subvert and overthrow the Venezuelan government. Cuban personnel, as well as aid and money, went to finance the campaign of urban terrorism that Venezuela suffered in the subsequent years. With its vast coastline and its position as the gateway to South America, Venezuela was, from Cuba's point of view, an ideal target for the continental revolution. Venezuela's vast reserves of petroleum would solve the problems faced by an oil-poor Cuba dependent on the distant and unreliable Soviets for its oil needs. That the Venezuelan oil bonanza would fall into Communist hands and away from the United States was a pleasing prospect for Castro and perhaps for the Soviets too. The overthrow of the leftist João Goulart regime in Brazil in 1964 and the defeat of Salvador Allende, the Popular Front candidate in the 1964 Chilean elections, weakened the Soviet's "peaceful road" to power policy toward Latin America and reinforced Castro's position that violence was the best tactic.

Despite a short period of harmonious Soviet-Cuban relations following Khrushchev's ouster, differences again arose, this time directly involving the Communist parties of Latin America. Castro quarreled bitterly with the leadership of these parties for not supporting guerrilla movements and denounced the Kremlin for seeking to establish diplomatic and commercial relations with "reactionary" regimes hostile to the Cuban revolution. Castro proclaimed that the duty of every revolutionary was to make revolution and rejected the Communist doctrine that the Communist party should play the "leading role" in the national liberation struggle. In a small book entitled *Revolution within the Revolution?* by Regis Debray, the young French Marxist, Castro's new line was elaborated. Not only are Communist theory and leadership—which insists on the guiding role of the party and diminishes the possibility of struggle in the countryside—a hindrance to the liberation movement, but parties and ideology are unnecessary in the initial states of the struggle. Debray explains that the decisive contribution of Castroism to the international revolutionary experience is that "under certain conditions the political and the military are not separate but form one organic whole, consisting of the people's army, where the nucleus is the guerrilla army. The vanguard party can exist in the form of the guerrilla *foco* itself. The guerrilla force is the party in embryo." At the Tricontinental Conference in Havana (1966), attended by revolutionary leaders throughout the world, Castro insisted on his independent line, seeking to gain the undisputed leadership of a continent-wide guerrilla struggle and offering to provide the institutional means to promote his line.

His attempts at revolution all ended in disaster, however. The Venezuelan venture proved a real fiasco, with the majority of the Venezuelan people rejecting Cuba's interference in their internal affairs. The other major effort, led by Che Guevara to open a guerrilla front in Bolivia, ended in his capture and death in 1967. Neither another Cuba nor "many Vietnams," as Castro had prophesied earlier, erupted in Latin America.

Castro's failures in the area weakened his leverage with the Soviets, increased Soviet influence within Cuba, and forced Castro to look inward to improve his faltering economy. By the late 1960s the Cuban economy was plagued by low productivity, mismanagement, poor planning, and shortages of almost every item. Structural shortcomings seemed more entrenched than ever. The ills of the past were still there, with renewed vengeance. Long-term trade agreements with the Soviets were perpetuating Cuba's role as sugar producer, forcing her to abandon indefinitely any plans for significant diversification and industrialization. Trade continued with one large industrialized nation whose commercial policies reminded Castro of those pursued by its previous trading partner. Cuba's foreign debt also reached alarming proportions without significant improvements in the island's ability to save foreign exchange. The unemployment of the pre-Castro era gave way to a new type of unemployment in the form of poor labor productivity, absenteeism, and ineffective and overstaffed bureaucracy. The regime resorted to coercive methods to ensure a labor supply for critical agricultural tasks. The living standard deteriorated, perhaps more rapidly in urban areas, as high capital accumulation was given first priority over consumer goods.

13

THE DECADE OF
INSTITUTIONALIZATION

IN its second decade, the Cuban revolution faced critical problems. Internally, mounting economic difficulties inspired a new frenzy of planning activity and greater regimentation in the hope of stimulating productivity. One result was the expanded influence of the military in society, and its increasingly important role in both economic and political life. The party, which had remained weak and ineffective throughout the 1960s, was enlarged and strengthened in its efforts to spread its influence throughout society. Meanwhile, the regime continued to pursue its aim of transforming Cuba in accordance with a new set of values and with the ultimate end of creating a new socialist man. Externally, the Cuban leadership attempted to break out of its isolation in Latin America, became selective in its support of revolutionary movements in the area, moved even closer to the Soviet Union, increased its influence on the non-aligned movement, and embarked on a series of successful military interventions, primarily on the African continent.

Although past Cuban-Soviet relations had been punctuated by frequent instances of Castro's insubordination and attempts to assert his independence, in mid-1968 relations entered a period of close collaboration and friendliness. A turning point occurred in August 1968, when Castro supported the Soviet invasion of Czechoslovakia, a response dictated primarily by political and economic considerations. First, he came to believe that Cuba would enjoy greater protection by ensuring its continued membership in the Soviet bloc than by espousing the principle of sovereignty for small countries. Second, poor sugar harvests in 1967 and 1968 increased the need for more Soviet economic aid and highlighted the extent to which Cuba's future development was dependent on outside assistance. Third, the failure of Castro's guerrilla activities, particularly the Bolivian fiasco, removed an important irritant in the Soviet-Cuban relationship. A guerrilla movement brewing in Latin America would have hindered Havana's rapprochement with Moscow. After Che Guevara failed, Castro could more easily accept Soviet ideas on the peaceful road to power in Latin America. Fourth, Castro's distrust of President Richard Nixon and his policies also influenced his decision to move closer to the Soviet Union. He perceived Nixon as the same man who had helped hatch plans, in 1960, for the U.S. support of armed intervention in Cuba and feared that, as the war in Vietnam came to an end, Nixon might turn against Cuba. Finally, Castro's ideas contrasted markedly with those of the Dubcek group in Czechoslovakia. The Cuban leader considered himself to the left of both the Soviets and the Czechs, and therefore could not sympathize with the liberalization taking place in Prague. For internal reasons also, he could not logically support liberalization abroad while maintaining orthodoxy at home.

In the months following his Czech stand, Castro's accommodation with the USSR became increasingly manifest. In November 1968 he welcomed a delegation from the East German Communist party with great ceremony and signed a joint communiqué on the "Necessity of Fighting against All Forms of Revisionism and Opportunism." In his yearly Anniversary of the Revolution speech on January 2, 1969, he drew up a balance sheet of ten years of revolution and concluded by expressing deep gratitude to the socialist camp and particularly to the Soviet Union for their aid and solidarity.

In other ways the Cubans went out of their way to demonstrate their new spirit of collaboration with the Soviets. In June 1969 Castro reversed one of the rare collective decisions by the Central Committee of Cuba's Communist party—namely, that Cuba would not participate in the World Conference of Communist Parties convened by the Soviet Union. According to the new line, he sent as an "observer" to the Moscow conference Carlos Rafael Rodríguez, the most steadfast theoretician of the former Partido Socialista Popular and a member of the secretariat of the ruling Communist party of Cuba. Rodríguez delivered a speech unstinting in its praise of the Soviet Union, which closed with this pledge: "We declare from this tribune that in any decisive confrontation, whether it be an act by the Soviet Union to avert threat of dislocation or provocation to the socialist system, or an act of aggression by anyone against the Soviet people, Cuba will stand unflinchingly by the USSR."

This show of solidarity had wide implications. Several other ruling Communist parties, including those of China, Vietnam, and Korea, had refused to attend the conference, precisely because its main objective was to enlist support for a crusade against Peking. Cuba's attendance and Rodríguez's statement showed support for the Soviet position—Castro was casting his lot with the USSR. This was followed by calls of the Soviet navy at Cuban ports and by the visits of Soviet Defense Minister Marshal Grechko and Prime Minister Alexei Kosygin. In turn, Fidel and Raúl visited Eastern Europe and the Soviet Union for extended periods of time.

In the early 1970s Soviet military and economic aid increased substantially and Cuba moved closer to the Soviet Union, becoming in 1972 a member of the Eastern European Council for Mutual Economic Assistance (CMEA). The result was greater direct Soviet influence in the island. Soviet technicians became extensively involved in managerial and planning activities at the national level. The total number of Soviet military and technical advisers increased considerably, and numerous economic advisers arrived. These were particularly influential in the Ministry of the Sugar Industry and the Ministry of the Armed Forces, where a joint Soviet-Cuban Advisory Commission was organized. Of special significance were long-term agreements between Cuba and the USSR that geared the Cuban economy into the Soviet Economic Plans. A new Inter-Governmental Coordinating Committee was also established, giving the Kremlin considerable leverage over Cuban developments. The Soviet Union's influence and its presence became more extensive than at any other time, with the possible exception of the period immediately preceding the 1962 missile crisis. Castro exchanged the pervasive influence of the United States for a new, more complete dependence on the Soviet Union and Eastern Europe, dependence that lasted until the collapse of the Soviet Union.

As a result of his own economic problems as well as mounting

Soviet influence, Castro began to turn inward. The Soviets had long been pressuring the Cubans to curb their activities in Latin America and to concentrate on revitalizing their sagging economy. Quite significant in this connection, an article in *Pravda* on October 2, 1970, bluntly asserted that "the Cuban people and the Cuban Communists realize that Cuba's main contribution to the world socialist system and the general revolutionary process now lies in economic building and creating a developed socialist society on this base."

In the early 1970s Castro's speeches downplayed the notion of Latin American revolutions or his continuous support for terrorists and anti-American groups. They concentrated instead on domestic, political, and economic issues. Official Cuban media routinely called for revolutionary action, but without declaring, as was customary, that armed struggle is the only road to power. An August 1972 publication of the Cuban-engineered Continental Organization of Latin American Students (OCLAE) urged Latin American students to devote themselves to the struggle "to its final consequences." It proposed "new forms of organization to confront imperialist violence," but it strikingly omitted any reference to the once standard demands for guerrilla warfare.

Prior to 1968 Castro had been the foremost proponent of violent revolution. Latin American revolutionaries and terrorists received training in Cuba and were sent back to their native countries to lead insurgencies, and Cuba had been channeling funds, arms, and propaganda to rebel groups in various Latin American nations. Even areas where conditions did not seem propitious for violence were considered targets. Castro advocated reliance on groups of vanguard guerrilla fighters rather than on mass movements and believed that guerrilla campaigns could create the conditions necessary for revolution.

The implementation of these ideas brought Castro into conflict with Moscow and the Communist parties of Latin America. For several years the Soviets called for the formation of popular fronts and mass movements. They criticized Castro's emphasis on armed struggle as "left wing opportunism which leads the masses to adventuristic actions." In the Soviets' view it could jeopardize their economic offensive in Latin America as well as their attempts to increase political influence in the area. They perhaps were also afraid of being drawn into involvements and confrontations with the United States not of their own choosing.

Most of the traditional Communist parties in Latin America followed the Soviet lead. They particularly resented Castro's claim to supremacy over the revolutionary movement and disliked his branding of Communists who opposed armed struggle as "traitorous, rightist, and deviationist." Having achieved a secure and comfortable position in most Latin American countries, the Communist parties and their middle-aged leaders feared that a call to violence would lead to failure, persecution, and exile. They were working toward creating "the necessary conditions for revolution" through propaganda, infiltration, popular fronts, and even elections, but in most countries they showed little inclination to plunge into armed struggle.

Castro came to recognize that there were "different roads to power." While not completely renouncing his original goal of exporting his own brand of communism, he became more selective in furnishing Cuban support.

The electoral failure of the Popular Front in Uruguay and more importantly the overthrow of the Allende regime in Chile in 1973, however, marked a turning point for the Cuban-inspired revolutionary struggle in Latin America. The Cuban leadership examined its strategy and tactics in the area and concluded that the way to power in Latin America was not through ballots but through bullets. Beginning in the mid-1970s, Castro increased his support to select groups, particularly in Central America, providing them with propaganda material, training, advisers, financial help, and ultimately weapons. An acceleration of the revolutionary armed struggle in the area followed.

Castro also became involved with African-Americans in the U.S. and with the Macheteros, a Puerto Rican terrorist group. Cuba focused particular attention on the black struggle in the United States, providing aid and training to the Black Panthers and the Black Liberation Army, as well as a safe haven on the island for black leaders. Castro continuously promoted the independence of Puerto Rico and supported the Macheteros who committed terrorist acts and bank robberies in the United States. Several still live in Cuba.

Cuban military and intelligence personnel aided Middle Eastern groups and regimes in the struggle against Israel, and Cuban troops fought on the side of Arab states, particularly Syria, during the Yom Kippur War. Castro sent military instructors and advisers into Palestinian bases; cooperated with Libya in the founding of World Mathaba, a terrorist movement; and established close military cooperation and exchanges with Iraq, Libya, southern Yemen, the Polisario Front for the Liberation of Western Sahara, the PLO, and others in the Middle East.

This coincided with the U.S. debacle in Vietnam and the Watergate scandal. The inability of American administrations to respond swiftly and decisively to conditions in Central America, as well as in other parts of the world, and to the Soviet-Cuban challenge in Africa, emboldened the Cuban leader. More than 40,000 Cuban troops supported by Soviet equipment were transferred to Africa in order to bring to power communist regimes in Angola and Ethiopia.

Cuba's commitment to revolution in Africa dated from the mid-1960s, when Che Guevara visited the area to promote violent anti-colonialist resistance. In particular, the Popular Movement for the Liberation of Angola (MPLA) and its Marxist leader, Aghostino Neto, were supported by Castro, the Portuguese Communists, and the Soviets. The possible defeat of Neto's group, one of the three and perhaps the weakest of those fighting for power, produced a convergence of Soviet and Cuban policies in Angola in the mid-1970s. Cuban involvement enhanced Castro's international prestige and influence, encouraged the creation of Marxist regimes friendly to Cuba, and showed Cuban solidarity with Moscow's interests in the area as well as tested the combat readiness of Cuban troops.

Emboldened by Cuban-Soviet victories in Angola and Ethiopia, the Castro regime focused its attention on the rapidly deteriorating conditions in Nicaragua. There, archaic and unjust social, political, and economic structures dominated by an oppressive, corrupt, and inefficient dynasty began to crumble when faced with increasing popular discontent. Cuba jointly with Panama and Venezuela increased support to the *Frente Sandinista de Liberación Nacional* the principal guerrilla group opposing the Somoza regime and led by Castro's longtime friend Marxist leader Tomás Borge, among others. In July 1979, Somoza fled to the United States and the *Frente* rode victorious into Managua.

The Sandinista victory in Nicaragua stands as an imposing monument to Cuban strategy and ambitions in the hemisphere. The overthrow of Somoza gave the Castro line its most important boost in two decades. It vindicated, although belatedly, Castro's ideological insistence on the value of violence and guerrilla warfare as the correct strategy to attain power in Latin America. Castro's long-held belief that the political, social, and economic conditions that had produced his revolution in Cuba existed or could be created in other parts of Latin America and that revolution would occur throughout the continent seemed at last justified. Jesús Montané Oropesa, member of the Cuban Communist Party Central Committee, emphasized that the revolutionary victories in Nicaragua and Grenada were the most important events in Latin America since 1959. "The triumph in Nicaragua," explained Montané, "verified the effectiveness of armed struggle as a decisive means of taking power."*

From that time on, the tempo of Cuban-supported violence accelerated in Central America. Aided by an extensive network of intelligence, military forces, and a sophisticated propaganda machinery, the Cuban government increased its support to various groups in the area. In cooperation with Sandinista leaders, Cuba aided insurgent groups in El Salvador, Guatemala, and Colombia. Castro's commitment to revolutionary violence was reinforced once again, showing convincingly that the Cuban leadership is willing to seize opportunities and take risks to expand its influence and power.

The beginning of the 1970s saw the economic scene riddled with many problems. Castro highlighted these in a speech on July 26, 1970. After acknowledging that Cuba had failed to reach its goal of a 10 million-ton sugar crop and that total production for the year would be only 8.5 million tons, he used the failure as a point of departure for deep soul-searching with regard to the whole range of past economic policies and practices. Noting that the effort invested in the sugar crop had been detrimental to most of the other sectors of the economy, he cited low productivity of such vital items as milk, bread, vegetables, and clothing, and explained that industrial production was badly lagging behind established goals. The lack of spare parts, failures in the transportation system, and decreasing productivity throughout the consumer sector were plaguing the economy. "Insufficient production in the face of increasing expenditures," he said, "has resulted in growing difficulties." While worker absenteeism had aggravated the situation, a small workforce was also a factor.

Castro in his speech laid the blame for the economic failures on "the bureaucracy" as well as on himself. In a calculated gesture, he told the Cubans that "we have a certain underdevelopment in leadership" and that the people could change leaders "right now, at any

---

*Radio Havana, October 21, 1980.

moment they wish." He acknowledged Cuba's deepening dependence on the USSR, admitting "that we have had large imbalances in our foreign trade, particularly with the Soviet Union." In conclusion, he warned Cubans that "the next years will be hard ones," with little hope of immediate prosperity.

Castro's exhortations and admonitions were echoed by other government officials. Labor Minister Jorge Risquet attributed the country's mounting economic problems principally to "widespread passive resistance" by workers. Discussing the reasons for labor inefficiency, Risquet complained that there was no rapport between Cuban workers and their superiors, among them, the state administrators and Communist party and labor union officials. He reported that productivity among sugar workers was so low that the cost of the 1970 sugar harvest was three times higher than the crop's value on the world market.

Because of these difficulties Cuba's leadership reexamined economic policies in an effort to devise more workable economic plans. Production goals were reduced and tailored to the realities of the situation. The regime encouraged decentralized implementation of centrally determined policies and programs and showed an increasing preoccupation with economic—as opposed to social—objectives. Castro himself admitted that in the period of socialist construction certain economic incentives still had to be employed, thus signaling a partial departure from the emphasis on moral incentives. In a speech on July 26, 1973, Castro explained that "along with the moral stimulus, we also have to use the material stimulus, without abusing one another. The first would lead us to idealism, the second would lead us to develop individual selfishness." While some reliance on moral incentives continues, primarily because of Castro's commitment to this policy and because of the Soviet Union's inability or unwillingness to deliver large quantities of consumer goods, a reorientation began toward the production of more consumer goods in an attempt to motivate the labor force.

To stimulate productivity and forestall any further slackening of revolutionary momentum, Castro's July 26 speech was followed by an increased regimentation and militarization of society. The standard holidays (traditionally of great significance in Cuban life) were deemphasized. Military officers were appointed to important civilian posts, and the armed forces became a super-agency supplying administrators for both central and local organizations dealing with political, economic, and educational matters. Development organizations, at both the national and the local level, came under the aegis of the military. In line with this trend, the army established special centers to train low-level cadres for jobs in various national and local organizations. Under the control of Raúl Castro, the Ministry of the Revolutionary Armed Forces became one of the most powerful and influential Cuban institutions.

On the ideological front, greater emphasis was placed on the need for sacrifice: the building of socialism demands high investment rates coupled with maximum technical and scientific knowledge and minimum consumption. The regime argued that worker's goodwill was not enough and that in certain circumstances coercion was unavoidable in the interest of "building a socialist society." A variety of austerity measures were instituted, including further reductions in sugar and coffee rations and cutbacks in consumer goods and imports from Western countries.

Unhappy with Castro's management of the economy and with Cuba's repeated failures to meet its production goals and international obligations, the Kremlin pressured the Cubans to adopt more orthodox Soviet policies. Castro acknowledged Soviet displeasure when, in an interview published in the Soviet magazine *Ogonek* in 1970, he confessed that "previously we did not fulfill many pledges and accordingly—very naturally and justifiably—a certain skepticism developed concerning our economic plans." President Dorticós also recognized the arduous path in building a "genuine Communist society," pointing out that Cuba still needed to develop the foundations of socialism through the use of Soviet economic methods, including the use of material incentives.

These confessions highlighted a limited return to economic rationality. Instead of continuing with their plans to phase out the use of money, the leadership acknowledged the need for monetary transactions and for applying economic criteria—efficiency, productivity, cost accounting, and growth. In an attempt to increase labor productivity, they further deemphasized moral incentives and egalitarian wage-distribution policies and introduced greater decentralization and managerial discretion as well as a larger role for market forces.

These policies resulted in a modest improvement during the first half of the decade. Industrial production expanded, and more consumer goods became available. The economy was aided significantly by the world rise in sugar prices as well as massive infusions of Soviet equipment and aid. In addition to providing several billion dollars' worth of free military equipment, the Kremlin postponed repayment of the principal and interest due on Cuba's debt to the Soviet Union, granted some interest-free credits, and linked the prices of petroleum and sugar to prevent a deterioration in the Cuban terms of trade. By selling petroleum to Cuba below OPEC prices, the Soviets, further-more, sheltered the Cuban economy from the shock of higher oil prices affecting the Western economies.

In spite of this recovery, the economy remained plagued by major problems. Low productivity, mismanagement, inefficiency, under-employment, and overambitious goals were the more persistent ones. Sugar prices collapsed from $.65 per pound in 1974 to as low as $.08 in 1977. Foreign exchange dwindled, and imports decreased. The impact would have been far more significant if it were not for the fact that the Soviets, who purchased half of Cuba's annual sugar production, subsidized the economy by paying a price for sugar well above the world market.

Unexpected problems also hurt the economy. A blue mold fungus destroyed most of the tobacco crop in 1979–1980 while other dis-eases affected the sugar and cattle-raising industries. The slump in the Soviet economy in the late 1970s slowed down the tempo of Soviet assistance. Cuba's involvement in Africa, while important politically for the Cuban leadership, had been costly, forcing mobili-zation at home and significant expenditures abroad to maintain 40,000 Cuban troops in Africa. The institutionalization of a Soviet-style centrally planned economy had burdened Cuba with a vast administrative bureaucracy that stifled the innovation, productivity, and efficiency necessary for sustained economic growth.*

In an attempt to increase economic efficiency and in line with Soviet objectives, the Cuban Communist party, which now num-bered some 482,000 members, was expanded and strengthened. The aim was for greater party conformity to the needs of a socialist soci-ety, with principal emphasis on a higher level of ideological training and the acquisition of specialized knowledge by party members.

Throughout the 1960s the party had remained weak and unable to play a key role in the political process. Established in 1961 through the merger of Castro's 26th of July Movement with the Partido

---

*See Lawrence H. Theriot, *Cuba Faces the Economic Realities of the 1980's* (Washing-ton: U.S. Department of Commerce, U.S. Government Printing Office, 1982).

Socialista Popular (PSP) and the Directorio Revolucionario, the new structure was called Organizaciones Revolucionarias Integradas (Integrated Revolutionary Organizations, or ORI), a preparatory step toward the creation of the United Party of the Socialist Revolution (PURS), transformed in 1965 into the Communist Party of Cuba (PCC), the island's ruling and only party.

During the early period the party remained small, disorganized, relegated to a secondary position vis-à-vis the military. It lacked a clear and defined role. Internal leadership and coordination remained poor, and meetings were scarce and of questionable value. Evidently Castro saw little need for a well-developed party structure that would have reduced or at least rivaled his *personalista* style of leadership. Conflict between old-guard Communists and Fidelistas also created tension and prevented the development of a strong organization. Competition from the military and the bureaucracy took the best talents away from the party. These cadres saw better opportunities for advancement in those other sectors than in a party riddled with factionalism and not warmly supported by the *líder máximo*.

The decade of the 1970s was one of expansion and consolidation for the party. During the first half, membership expanded from some 55,000 in 1969 to 202,807 at the time of the First Party Congress in 1975. During the second half, the rapid rate of expansion slowed somewhat. By the time of the Second Party Congress in 1980 there were fewer than 400,000 members and candidates. As the Third Party Congress was approaching in 1995, Fidel Castro disclosed that full members and candidates numbered 482,000. Recently, greater emphasis has been placed on candidates active in production, teaching, and services. Since many of the earlier party members had been promoted rapidly within the ranks and had become party bureaucrats, the need was for cadres working in industry and agriculture and, therefore, hopefully being more aware of production problems and in closer contact with the realities of the economy.

Also an attempt was made to bring more women into the party. From the time of the party's organization, women had been underrepresented in its ranks and leadership organs. Even when more women were entering the labor force, few were attaining leadership status. Since 1975, attempts have been made to correct this situation.

The First Party Congress in 1975 was a watershed in legitimizing the position of the party as the guiding and controlling force in society. It reassured the Soviet Union of Cuba's loyalty and friendship, extolling the Soviets' continuous military and economic aid to the Cuban revolution, and rehabilitated old-guard communists, some of whom had been mistrusted and persecuted by the Castroites. Three old-guard Communists, Carlos Rafael Rodríguez, Blas Roca, and Arnaldo Milián were elected to the Political Bureau.* The Congress also expanded the party's Central Committee from 91 to 112, increased the Political Bureau from eight to thirteen, and maintained the Secretariat at eleven members with Fidel and Raúl as first and second secretaries.

In his report to the Congress, Castro attempted to reconcile the adoption of Soviet-style institutions in the island with a renewed emphasis on nationalism and on the historical roots of the Cuban revolution. He emphasized that Cuban socialism was the culmination of a struggle against Spanish colonialism and U.S. neo-colonial involvement in Cuban affairs. With total disregard for Martí's ideas, Castro linked the Cuban independence leader with Lenin in order to justify Cuba's move into the Communist camp. The Congress adopted a Five Year Plan calling for closer economic integration with the Soviet Union and an economic system modeled on other socialist states. The approval of the party's platform stressing "Marxist-Leninist principles and the leading role of the party" was further evidence of the impact of Soviet-style orthodoxy in the island.

Of paramount importance was the adoption of Cuba's first Socialist Constitution, which was approved by a 97.7 percent majority in a popular referendum in early 1976. Modeled upon other Communist constitutions, the Cuban document recognized the party as "the highest leading force in state and society" and defined the function of mass organizations such as the Committees for the Defense of the Revolution and the Federation of Cuban Women. It divided the island into fourteen new provinces instead of the six old ones.** It recognized freedom of speech, religion, the press, and association so

---

*These included in addition to Fidel and Raúl Castro, Juan Almeida, Guillermo García, Ramiro Valdés, Armando Hart, Osvaldo Dorticós, Sergio del Valle, Pedro Miret, and José Ramón Machado. During the Second Party Congress in 1980 the Political Bureau was expanded to sixteen members. The new members were Osmani Cienfuegos, Julio Camacho, and Jorge Risquet. Milián died in 1983 as did Dorticós, who committed suicide.

**The new provinces are Camagüey, Ciego de Avila, Cienfuegos, Ciudad de La Habana, Granma, Guantánamo, Habana, Holguín, Las Tunas, Matanzas, Pinar del Río, Sancti Spiritus, Santiago de Cuba, and Villa Clara.

long as these did not conflict with the objectives of socialism; enumerated the rights and duties of Cuban citizens; and created a host of new governing institutions, particularly the Organos del Poder Popular, or People's Power Apparatus.

These institutions consist of three sets of "elected" assemblies at the municipal, provincial, and national levels. At the base of the structure were 10,725 members elected in 1976 to some 169 municipal assemblies. These in turn selected 1,084 delegates to the provincial assemblies and 481 delegates to the National Assembly. The National Assembly selected a thirty-one-member Council of State consisting of Fidel Castro as president of the Council, Raúl Castro as first vice-president, five other vice-presidents, a secretary, and twenty-three other members. The Cuban state is formally represented by a president, Fidel Castro, who is designated Head of State. In addition, the president appoints and presides over a Council of Ministers that is approved by the National Assembly and has primary responsibility for administering the country. The National Assembly is also empowered to legislate, regulate production, and appoint Supreme Court judges.

Real power, however, resides with the smaller Council and ultimately with the Political Bureau of the party. The National Assembly has been largely a rubber-stamp body that meets for only a few days a year to discuss mostly social legislation and to approve laws and proposals submitted and previously agreed to by the Council. In turn, the fact that the Council is dominated by members of the party's Political Bureau, and also that most of the National Assembly is composed of party members, assures that at all levels the party's position will be dominant. Every important issue or legislation is reviewed by the Political Bureau, which in some instances either acts independently of any other governmental agency and makes important decisions on its own or vetoes proposed legislation. The party, therefore, enjoys a veto power in decision making somewhere between the drafting of laws and their adoption by the National Assembly.*

Perhaps the most important effect of the People's Power Apparatus has been the increase in communication and responsiveness at the local level. Whereas prior to this time Cubans had little input

---

*See William M. Leogrande, "The Communist Party of Cuba Since the First Congress," *Journal of Latin American Studies* (November 1980), pp. 399–419.

into the decision-making process, these organizations provide an avenue for channeling a limited amount of criticism. The vast network of municipal assemblies at the local level, furthermore, offers easier access to state officials and a mechanism for resolving local problems.*

The party has devoted great efforts to ensuring its control over the managerial and state bureaucracies. Not only are party officials involved in the management and supervision of industries and agriculture enterprises, as well as at all levels of government, but the party has also developed an internal machinery to oversee and control all aspects of society. Within the party, eighteen departments are important links with other organizations. Eight departments deal with economic issues; five with internal party matters; two with foreign affairs; and three act as liaisons with other organizations. A department of religious affairs was created to monitor and supervise religious activities in the island. The fact that five departments are devoted to internal party affairs indicates the importance attached by the leadership to the building of a strong party machinery. The party has also created a National Control and Revision Committee to supervise the work of party members within the party and in other organizations, thus signaling a further tightening of party control and influence.

The second PCC Congress convened in December 1980 and solidified the main tenets of the 1975 Congress report while presenting new dictums for the 1980s. At the international level, the Congress reaffirmed Cuba's strong ties with the Soviet Union, defended such internationalist principles as support for revolutionary movements abroad (with special reference to Nicaragua and Grenada). Within this context, the FAR's external as well as internal roles of assistance to national liberation struggles and national defense buildups were exalted. Regarding U.S.-Cuban relations, the party anticipated an escalation of tensions between the two countries as a result of Ronald Reagan's election. In the economic sphere, the Congress emphasized the need for more state planning and warned of a possible decline in production and exports due to the world economic situation. The 1980 Congress strengthened the PCC structure and func-

---

*See William M. Leogrande, "The Theory and Practice of Socialist Democracy in Cuba: Mechanisms of Elite Accountability," *Studies in Comparative Communism* (Spring 1979), pp. 39–62.

tion in the political sphere. Following traditional Marxist-Leninist principles, the PCC was envisioned as the vanguard of the people.

The degree of penetration of society by the political system has been exceptionally high and effective. Most citizens are involved in "voluntary" organizations and are mobilized constantly for active participation in the political process. They are swept up in successive campaigns to fulfill any conceivable aspects of human endeavor in the form of "tasks." These "tasks" or "goals" are emphasized primarily in the fields of industrial production, ideology, and education. Of maximum importance is the understanding of Marxism-Leninism, which requires not only taking formal courses in educational institutions but also attendance at party meetings.

The Communist euphemism that the state will "wither away" is nowhere to be found in Cuba. On the contrary, the state is monolithic and its managerial capabilities depend on the party and a new class of technocrats. A tightly knit leadership led by the Castro brothers envisages far into the future its role in initiating, coordinating, and controlling policies and functions in Cuban society. They claim not only to exercise legitimate power but also to interpret the wishes and will of the people.

A highly intolerant and hierarchical party structure has developed. It has been molded through the successful attempts of the leadership to monopolize political functions such as recruitment, socialization, and articulation, as well as to inculcate uniformity of beliefs and conformity of behavior within the party and throughout society.

Castro has never shown any concern over the use of coercion and deceit. He justifies these techniques as necessary and correct under Marxist-Leninist doctrine to protect the revolution against foreign and domestic enemies and to expand its influence abroad. He is a master in the manipulation of public opinion and in the propagation of partial truths, repeated incessantly in his speeches and in the controlled media until accepted as reality. He believes that the preservation of his revolution requires massive doses of coercion and the use, for a long time, of techniques of centralized administration and repression to crush any resistance.

Of the several institutions in the Cuban panorama, the military continues to be the most powerful, most influential, and best organized. The stability of the regime and the continuity of the revolutionary process seem guaranteed primarily by the power and loyalty of Cuba's armed forces. Headed by Raúl Castro, the Cuban military has been transformed into a highly professional institution completely loyal to the Castro brothers.

When on December 31, 1958, General Batista fled Cuba, most organizations that had supported his regime crumbled. Among these, the military was particularly affected because of its slow and weary campaign against the guerrillas and because of an internal process of demoralization and decomposition that had been taking place for several years. As soon as Castro was entrenched in power, he proceeded to eliminate the national armed forces and to replace them with the so-called Rebel Army, made up of guerrillas who had fought in the Sierra Maestra mountains.

During the first few years of the Revolution this Rebel Army constituted, together with a hastily organized militia, the only armed forces in the island. As the regime grew stronger and as ties with the Soviet Union began to develop, a reorganization of its cadres was initiated, which led to the development of a professional military establishment. Also, the Ministry of the Revolutionary Armed Forces was created, and Raúl Castro was named to head it. Castro's aim was a totally loyal military organization. As he saw it, it would have been impossible to consolidate the revolution unless the military was actively included in the great political process that was under way. The example of Guatemala in 1954, where the armed forces became the vehicle through which Colonel Castillo Armas overthrew the leftist Jacobo Arbenz regime, loomed large in the minds of the Cuban leadership.

The very nature of the Rebel Army, composed of different ideological tendencies, complicated the problem of creating a disciplined armed force. The inherent problems were further complicated by the ideological shifts implemented by Castro himself in the early days. The way out was the establishment of complete loyalty to Fidel as the paramount ideological requirement for the military. The more moderate factions within the armed forces who opposed Communist participation in the government or who rejected the rapid pace of reform had to be purged or eliminated. In the first three years of the revolution a widespread purifying operation took place that affected not only old adversaries but any "comrade" of the revolution suspected of being lukewarm, opposing the government, or harboring anti-Communist sentiments.

The purges were followed by intense indoctrination of the army cadres. The presence of representatives of party political organs was evidence of an ideological conditioning that very much resembled circumstances in other Communist countries. According to government statements, the majority of the officers today belong to the Communist party or to the Union of Young Communists. Dozens of high military officers are members of the Central Committee.

All this occurred not without resistance in the armed forces. Over the course of years, the shifts, dismissals, and changes created a lack of confidence and misgivings among many members of the military. But these misgivings have over time been compensated by a new role. Not only did the military receive new and sophisticated weaponry but it also assumed a predominant role in the management of the economy and an external role in promoting Castro's policy primarily in Africa. Its responsibilities as well as its prestige and importance have thus been augmented.

Relations between the Cuban Communist party and the armed forces appear quite good. The numerous safeguards that have been established against party infringement upon the authority of military officers prevent any possible independent activity by the party in the armed forces. The presence of numerous military men in the party's Central Committee and the political and economic functions which Castro assigns many officers also reflect obvious confidence of Castro himself in the military, and have led to a degree of participation without parallel for other institutions of the country.

The Cuban armed forces faced another problem in its early stages of development. This was the lack of technically skilled personnel to man and handle the increasing quantity of sophisticated equipment being shipped by the Soviet Union and Eastern European countries to Cuba. In many instances it was necessary not only to train technically capable officers but even to instruct in the most basic techniques the vast number of recruits who, attracted by the revolutionary enthusiasm of the early days, responded to the call of the armed forces.

Faced with these problems, the Cuban government had to set up officers' schools in all branches and send a number of students to Eastern European countries. As the years have gone by, a new military technical elite has come into being within the armed forces. Castro's old companions still enjoy his confidence, and most of them continue to occupy high positions in the military establishment. Yet as subordinate cadres become technically qualified, pressure will be exerted on Castro's old comrades to move out and give way to this new military group.

With the growth and strengthening of the party's role in society, the use of military techniques to boost productivity and the employment of troops as a labor force were partially curtailed. The organizational advantages that the military enjoyed in the early years were rivaled by the party, which increased its role in managing the economy. Soviet pressures for a clearer differentiation of civilian and military roles in Cuba, the need to build a strong military apparatus for defense, and the external mission assigned to the military in places like Angola, Ethiopia, and Nicaragua gravitated against an extensive and continuous involvement of the armed forces in administration and production, a trend that was again reversed in the 1990s.

Cuba's activist foreign policy, geopolitical situation, and ties with the Soviet Union placed the country in a position of constant mobilization and tension. What existed in the way of a foreign threat, whatever its degree of danger, meant greater responsibility for the military and was used to justify demands of the armed forces, apart from propagandistic rhetoric, for fresh and continuous commitments. Cuba's armed forces developed a dual defense function: one, to watch the foreign front, and two, to watch the internal front. This dual-defense dimension, although it is in the nature of a universal principle for all armed forces, acquired a certain singularity in Cuba. The Cuban military, therefore, combined training for guerrilla warfare to face possible internal subversion with training on how to handle modern weapons systems to deal primarily with a major defensive action. In addition it received extensive combat training through its involvement in Africa.

The Cuban armed forces were organized into the three classical branches: land, sea, and air. It is estimated that a total of 225,000 men were on active duty. In addition there were 190,000 trained reservists who were subject to annual refresher training. The land army had the largest number of men, totaling an estimated 200,000. It was well supplied with modern and sophisticated Eastern European armored equipment and artillery. The air force had an estimated two hundred combat aircraft including Soviet MIG23 interceptors, and later MIG 29s, fighter bombers, and helicopters. The much smaller navy had some submarines, several patrol boats, and missile launchers.

The army units were deployed in three geographical sectors. Each sector has elements of all weapons needed to make up an independent force. In general, the entire concept of deployment was oriented to defense against landings, to mobility, and to mutual support among the forces. Many coastal sectors were protected by heavy artillery and numerous fortifications. In addition, large-scale anti-aircraft defenses covered the entire territory. Army reserves, exceeding 100,000 men, could be mobilized quickly. The regime in 1964 instituted compulsory military service for the armed forces. The decree issued by the government stated that all Cubans, age sixteen and over, have a three-year commitment to serve in regular military units, or will receive military instruction in the training centers for short periods of time.

A National Militia was created parallel with the development of the armed forces. The Militia was developed for the purpose of mobilizing the population, creating an organization in support of the armed forces, and using this manpower for the military's developmental needs. The organized Militia was given thorough military training. Yet in the 1970s its role and importance were downplayed as a professional military developed. In 1980, Fidel reestablished a territorial militia estimated at a strength of 500,000 men and women to "defend the revolution from the aggressive machinations of U.S. imperialism."

In the 1970s the Cuban armed forces became without a doubt the strongest military establishment in the western hemisphere next to the U.S. armed forces. Cuba, with a GNP of $13.3 billion, spent over $1 billion on defense. A great deal of the training and preparation was under the direction of Soviet experts. The USSR sent numerous technicians and advisers to the island and maintained a strong military presence including a ground-force brigade of 2,600 men, a military advisory group of more than 2,000, and an intelligence-gathering facility. It is also estimated that there were about 8,000 Soviet and Eastern European civilian advisers in the island. The cost of Soviet arms delivered to Castro since 1960, all sent free of charge to the Cuban government, exceeded $3.2 billion. In the early 1980s the Soviets escalated weapons deliveries to Cuba and reequipped the Cuban military in an unprecedented fashion.*

---

*Only prior to the 1962 missile crisis did the Soviets deliver a larger quantity of equipment to Cuba, some 250,000 metric tons. During 1981 alone, Soviet merchant ships delivered some 66,000 tons of military equipment, as compared with the previous ten-year annual average of 15,000 tons.

This military buildup was motivated by various factors. First, U.S.-Cuban tensions increased after the Reagan Administration took office, and Castro was apprehensive about U.S. policies toward Cuba. Second, more equipment was needed to arm the territorial militia being organized to support the military. Third, there was a need for larger weapon stockpiles in the island because of Cuba's military aid to Nicaragua, Grenada, and other insurgent groups in the area. Some of the older weapons found their way to Cuban-supported guerrillas in Central America, particularly in Nicaragua, El Salvador, and Guatemala. Finally, by providing Cuba with this vast new arsenal the Soviets were reaffirming their commitment to protect the Cuban Revolution and reward their Caribbean ally for past and future services to the cause of international communism.

The Cuban armed forces, according to their technical profile, constituted the most solid institution in the national political spectrum. The army's attitude, its deployment, and its weapons were primarily oriented to the defense of the island and to the implementation of revolutionary policies. It was not only well equipped but it also was superbly organized and trained, and a great number of recruits and reservists saw combat in Africa. The vast and modern air force provided Cuba with a capability for intervention in the Caribbean and Central America. The future of the revolution and the continuity of the leadership were based on the loyalty and power of the military establishment.

Threats to Cuba from abroad did not seem to represent a serious risk for the Castro regime so long as such threats did not find sufficient dynamic support inside the island. Internal opposition to Castro was disorganized and disillusioned. The military strength of the regime and its coercive organs were able to infiltrate and thwart any attempt at rebellion. The massive refugee exodus from Mariel to the United States in 1980 and others earlier worked as an escape valve for discontented elements, eliminating possible opposition to the regime. Repeated failures of various incursions into the Cuban territory from surrounding areas confirmed the strength and power of the Cuban military and the weakness of its opposition.

Both the party and the military were enlisted in a fight against *burocratismo* (bureaucratism). To be a bureaucrat, it was felt, was to be an enemy of the revolution. Castro and his followers took every opportunity to blame the bureaucracy for the various failures suffered by the Cuban economy. As the economic crisis deepened in the late 1970s, Castro's impatience with the party and the bureaucracy grew. In December 1979, he asked the National Assembly to transfer to the Council of Ministers its authority to consider and write tougher crime laws. This was followed by a massive political shake-up that included the firing of various ministers and state-agency administrators. Instead of replacing those dismissed, the top leadership acquired new powers and responsibilities. The end result was a greater concentration of power in the hands of the Castro brothers and their trusted allies.

Guidelines adopted at the Second Party Congress in 1980 called for greater efficiency and productivity of labor and outlined cutbacks in imports, signaling a further shortage of consumer goods and tougher times ahead. Fidel also vowed to wage a battle against corruption and abuse of position by employees of state agencies. He explained that the government was struggling to come to terms with the *mercado libre campesino,* a free market established to stimulate agricultural productivity by allowing farmers to sell surplus products; the free market, however, was manipulated by middlemen whom Castro referred to as "bandits."[*]

The effect of such attacks was to reduce rather than increase the efficiency of those responsible for implementing the goals of the revolution. For one thing, the attacks almost completely destroyed the initiative of lower-echelon functionaries. Also, the demands made by the party for more sacrifices and more dedication greatly taxed the resources of higher government functionaries, resulting, among other things, in increased absenteeism.

Within the bureaucracy itself, marked class distinctions developed. The intermediate and high-level cadres, furnished either by the army, the party, or the state administration, exercised a sort of paternalistic-authoritarian leadership at all levels. It seems that a new class was emerging in Cuba, a new elite that enjoyed living conditions that contrasted with those of the average population. Better housing, clothing, and transportation, and even more food were some of the privileges reserved for this group. They had, therefore, a vested interest in the preservation of the regime as well as in the consolidation of their own power and position.

Aiding the military and the party were the Committees for the Defense of the Revolution (CDR). This massive apparatus, with

---

Havana Domestic Radio, May 1, 1982.

more than three million members out of a total population of some ten million, was assigned the task of mobilizing and controlling the population.

Initiated in 1960, the CDR continue to be an organ of neighborhood vigilance. During the Bay of Pigs invasion in 1961 they were a key factor in keeping the population under control and rounding up real and suspected counterrevolutionaries within hours after the outbreak of fighting. Over the years, however, they have become much more than committees of revolutionary vigilance. They have become a mass organization to aid other state organs. Just as the CDR help the Ministry of Interior in its fight against counterrevolutionaries, so it helps the Ministry of Education in school enrollment and attendance, the Ministry of Public Health in its special campaigns, and the National Bank in savings campaigns. The CDR also has a vital role in local government, serving as links between the municipal administrations and the neighborhoods. Well-functioning committees keep an eye on the quality of services at local stores and bring shortcoming to the attention of the manager or his superiors.

In early 1968 the CDR played a major part in the execution of the "revolutionary offensive" leading to the expropriation of close to 55,000 Cuban bars, nightclubs, and other small private businesses. The very day the government decreed the confiscation of almost all remaining private businesses in the island, the neighborhood CDR throughout the country assigned volunteers to guard the local stores and officially took them over in the name of the revolutionary government. They appointed "People's Administrators" and opened the stores for business, thus completing the confiscation process in a single day.

In order to raise the ideological level of members, the CDR placed much emphasis on study seminars at the neighborhood level. The Cuban government estimates that more than 1.3 million people a month take part in these seminars. Recent themes of study include Cuban history, the struggle against American imperialism, and the need for more sacrifices to increase productivity. Still, the effectiveness of the seminars is questionable. Participants have pointed out that the quality of the instructors is rather low and that people are usually bored with the repetitious and monotonous lectures.

The new man and the new society envisioned by Castro and his regime were to be significantly different from the past and required a change in the values and attitudes of many Cubans. The belief that events are determined by nature had to be transformed, and the orientation toward the present modified. Devotion to the cause of communism and love of the fatherland must prevail. The church's faltering influence had to be eliminated completely; so must be the aversion of Cubans to manual labor and the notion that a woman's place is in the home. The new man would consciously labor for the welfare of society, each working for all and all for one. "That is what is meant by revolution," explained Fidel, "that everyone shall benefit from the work of everyone else." Racial prejudices will be eliminated. Honesty and truthfulness would guide everyone's life. The young would be taught to respect and admire party leaders, especially Fidel, and to obey party discipline. Consciousness of social duty and intolerance of any violation of social interest would predominate.

The new socialist morality would preserve those virtues demonstrated by Castro's rebel army while fighting in the mountains against Batista; a spirit of sacrifice, abnegation, courage, discipline. After emphasizing that communism is a question of developing human awareness, as well as material wealth, Fidel described the type of man his regime proposed to create: "We will bring up human beings devoid of selfishness, devoid of defects of the past, human beings with a collective sense of effort, a collective sense of strength." Castro explained his great dream—that "of advancing toward a Communist society in which every human being with a superior awareness and a full spirit of solidarity is capable of contributing according to his ability and receiving according to his needs."

The new society would be abundant in material wealth, but man would be less concerned with obtaining material goods for himself, preferring to work to produce for the whole society. "From an early age," explained Fidel, "children must be discouraged from every egotistical feeling in the enjoyment of material things, such as the sense of individual property, and be encouraged toward the greatest common effort and the spirit of cooperation." Although society would enjoy material wealth, money would be abolished. "There will arrive the day," said Castro, "when money will have no value. Money is a vile intermediary between man and the products man creates."

Other material incentives would similarly be eliminated. Recalling Che Guevara's preachment of the superiority of moral over material incentives, an editorial in *Granma*, the official newspaper of Cuba's Communist party, lashed out at "economism," which it described as "the tendency to consider that men produced more and better as they received more and better," and stressed that the new Communist ideology will be developed only through a gigantic effort to organize the productive, social, educational, and cultural activity of the Cuban people. "Men produce more and better," concluded *Granma*, "as they improve the organization of work, as technical training is improved, technological and scientific resources are more extensively employed, and Communist awareness becomes greater."

In foreign affairs the Cuban masses had to be irreconcilably opposed to the enemies of the fatherland, especially the United States. Cubans should demonstrate solidarity with the peoples of developing countries, of the socialist camp, and particularly of Latin America, as well as friendship and brotherhood toward the people of the Soviet Union. As James Reston pointed out after a trip to Cuba as early as 1967, "A remarkable new generation of Cubans, more literate and disciplined than any other, is being indoctrinated systematically with the idea that the United States is the embodiment of everything that is narrow, selfish, and evil in the world today." A new anti–United States vision based on intense internal struggle and commitment, it is not to be mistaken for more moderate Latin American versions, as in Peru or Mexico.

All efforts were directed toward committing the younger generation to these principles, for if the drive to create the new socialist man failed, the revolution would fail, too. Without the proper attitudes, the millennium could not be reached. Faithful to Lenin's ideas that the school should "educate and prepare members of a Communist society," the Castro regime seemed convinced that, under the direction of the party, education could be used as an indispensable tool in developing the new society and the socialist man. Politburo member Armando Hart described the objective of socialist education as "the ideological, scientific, and technical formation of whole generations capable of actively constructing socialism and communism." "The task of teaching and the ideological struggle are intimately related," he explained. "It is necessary to educate man against the individualistic ideology and to instill in him the work methods derived from the Marxist-Leninist concept." "Education," Castro emphasized, "is society's basic instrument to develop worthy individuals able to live within communism." Particularly from intellectuals and writers, the revolutionary leadership demanded commitment to the revolutionary goals; *homo poeta* (the intellectual) must support the dominant role of *homo faber* (man the maker).

The "new man," however, is nowhere to be found. Despite significant efforts, the regime has been unable to root out old habits and values. Even forty-two years of revolution have not destroyed all that was "bad" in Cuba's cultural legacy. Youthful apathy, pessimism, and cynicism characterize contemporary Cuban society.

The pervasiveness of tradition cannot be easily overcome. The memory of past ideas and values weighs heavily on the minds of the Cubans, and historical experiences are not easily eradicated. Despite the government's attempts to rewrite and reinterpret Cuban history, the past is still too close for total forgetfulness. Yet the regime uses its own historical interpretations as weapons in the political struggle. These new interpretations have become the established dogmas to be inculcated in old and young alike. Fidel and the party link their present policies with broad aspirations and sentiments of the people while using whatever national or cultural symbols they consider appropriate to obtain their desired goal.

This attack on the past has not meant a total rejection of Cuba's cultural tradition. On the contrary, the regime emphasizes certain aspects of the past, such as African cultural contributions, as well as Cuban sacrifices at the time of the wars of independence. The cult of Martí flourishes, though Martí's writings have been carefully screened to select those that reflect his anti-Americanism and his admiration for some socialist ideas.

Nationalism and anti-Americanism guide the revolution's efforts at cultural changes. It seems as if the regime is attempting to find a new identity by taking what it considers "good" from Cuba's past and by preserving some aspects of Cuba's political tradition, such as nationalism, while emphasizing "bad" aspects more strongly, such as the role of the United States. Castro and the Cuban leadership present the revolution as the embodiment of the ideas of the independence movement and the frustrated 1933 revolutionary process. A history of Cuba written as a text especially for the members of the Cuban armed forces concluded by pointing out that the failure of the 1933 revolution proved that true progress for Cuba could be achieved only in opposition to the United States. This search for a nationalistic identity is definitely influencing present cultural directions and certainly will shape the thinking of the new socialist man.

There is no doubt that the emerging Cuban intelligentsia will differ significantly from that of pre-Castro times. The latter was cosmopolitan and had been exposed to both Western and Eastern ideas.

Its origins were chiefly middle- or upper-class. Today a part of the new intelligentsia has worker and, in some instances, rural backgrounds. Its view of other cultures, particularly that of the United States, has been deliberately distorted to conform to the objectives of the Cuban Communist party by reason of the unavailability of diverse reading materials and the educational policies of the regime.

Far beyond the sphere of formal education, the whole of society had to be geared toward producing the proper conditions for the development of the new man. A massive social apparatus was thus devised to mold the minds of the growing generation. It included the press and the mass-communication media, as well as social, cultural, and workers' organizations. The party, the Union of Young Communists (UJC), and the army all provide political instruction. As early as June 1964 an article in the theoretical journal *Cuba Socialista* indicated the regime's awareness of the important role movies, radio, television, and the press play in the "cultural and ideological formation of the masses" and reiterated that the efforts of all the revolutionary leaders, beginning with Fidel Castro, were directed at making radio and television "informational and educational vehicles through which the masses could be both *informed* and *formed*."

Recognizing early that one of the most stubborn obstacles to the ideological conversion of the Cuban people was the cultural and political legacy documented in the works of Cuban writers, the Castro government launched a purge of all literature incompatible with the Communist view. Not only were old textbooks eliminated but many were rewritten to justify the Castro revolution and its movement into the Communist camp. The government also embarked on a massive effort to disseminate the writings of foreign and particularly communist and socialist authors.

Schools at all levels formed the core of the social apparatus. But before schools could be effective, the old "bourgeois" intelligentsia had to be either eliminated or won over, the schools had to be transformed, and a whole new generation of teachers had to be indoctrinated.

To eliminate the old intelligentsia was relatively easy. Some members of this group left the country voluntarily during the first years of the revolution. Others were expelled, purged, or pensioned off from their bureaucratic and academic positions. Still others, who accepted the regime, were at first incorporated only to be later replaced by more trustworthy younger cadres.

Why Castro allowed the old intelligentsia to leave Cuba requires some explanation. Underlying the regime's thinking was the assumption that a generation reared under the capitalist system could not be trusted or converted to Marxism-Leninism. Every disloyal intellectual who left therefore could be substituted by a loyal follower. In addition, a policy of allowing Cubans to leave the island diminished opposition and released internal pressures. Undoubtedly a group of disloyal writers, professors, intellectuals, and *pensadores* could influence public opinion and become a source of potential trouble.

Before his death in Bolivia in 1967, Che Guevara described how the educational system worked in Cuba. The process of educating the young, he explained, was twofold: on the one hand, society acted upon the individual by means of direct and indirect education while, on the other hand, the individual underwent a conscious phase of self-education. Direct education was the job performed by educational institutions, the party information organs, and the mass media. Indirect education consisted mainly of the pressure exerted by the educated masses and the social apparatus on the uneducated individual. "The individual receiving the impact of the social power," wrote Guevara, "realizes his inadequacy and tries to adjust to a situation. He is educating himself."

Fidel Castro after the Moncada Attack, July 1953.

Ernesto "Che" Guevara (1959).

Raúl Castro (1959).

Castro's rebel army in the Sierra Maestra, 1958.

Fidel Castro (right) and Manuel Urrutia (center), the first revolutionary president, in the days following Batista's overthrow.

Manuel Urrutia, Armando Hart (former minister of education and organization secretary of Cuba's Communist party), and José Miró-Cardona (first revolutionary prime minister who resigned in February 1959 to allow Castro to become prime minister).

Anastas Mikoyan (right), Soviet deputy prime minister, visiting a Cuban factory in February 1960.

In pre-Castro Cuba, sugar was the main source of foreign currency earnings. After more than forty years, sugar is still "king," and today Cuba is still dependent on sugar exports. Since the revolution, Russian equipment and spare parts have been brought in to run the sugar mills. *Courtesy of the Organization of American States.*

Tourism has always been a major source of Cuban foreign currency earnings. The pre-revolutionary Hotel Nacional was refurbished to accommodate a new wave of tourists, primarily from Canada, Europe, and Latin America. *Courtesy of the Organization of American States.*

Havana was a thriving metropolis in the 1950s. Construction of high-rises, a booming economy, and a vibrant night life characterized the city. *Courtesy of the Organization of American States.*

Fidel and younger brother Raúl reviewing a military parade. In the past few years, the military has become the dominant institution in Cuban society. Military officers direct the economy and manage agricultural and industrial enterprises. Despite recent reductions, the Cuban military remains a powerful fighting force. *Courtesy of the* Miami Herald.

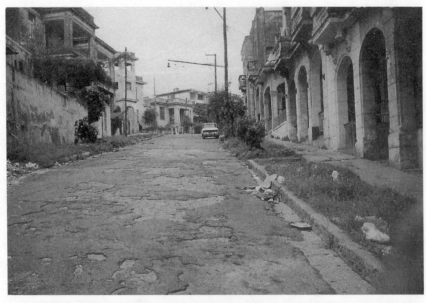

A residential street in Havana, 1999. The capital has deteriorated significantly during the Castro era. *Author's collection.*

Beautiful Varadero Beach in Matanzas Province, 1999. Cuba's tourist industry is one of the few areas of the economy that is booming. Europeans and Canadians flock to the special tourist hotels, which are off-limits to Cuban citizens. *Author's collection.*

The lush vegetation and rolling hills of Viñales Valley in Pinar del Río Province, 1999. *Author's collection.*

Pre-Revolution American cars are still a common sight in Cuba. Cubans have become very skilled at doing makeshift repairs to keep these vintage autos on the road. *Author's collection.*

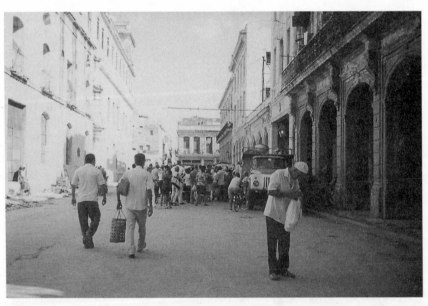

Cubans queuing up for food, 1999. After the collapse of the Soviet Union, the standard of living and the availability of goods in Cuba dramatically declined. *Author's collection.*

14

THE REVOLUTION
CONTINUES: THE
EIGHTIES AND NINETIES

IN the early 1980s, the Cuban revolution reached a critical stage in its development. Persistent structural and managerial problems in the economy, low prices for Cuba's export products, and inability to break away from economic dependence on the Soviet bloc forced a reexamination of basic goals. Since production in most key sectors had fallen short of expected targets, emphasis was placed on increased planning with more modest goals. The regime adopted Soviet economic methods, decreased emphasis on moral incentives, and attempted to create more efficient economic organizations. The Cubans suffered more austerity, with greater rationing of food and consumer goods, and, therefore, harder times. Life became increasingly difficult, with long lines to obtain the most basic goods, with a collapsing public transportation system, and with rapidly deteriorating education and health systems. In desperation, Cubans preferred to risk dying in the straits of Florida fleeing the island in flimsy rafts rather than continue to live in Castro's Cuba.

The establishment of a Soviet-type centrally planned economy burdened Cuba with a vast and cumbersome bureaucracy that stifled innovation, productivity, and efficiency. The island continued its heavy reliance on sugar for development of the domestic economy and for foreign trade, with little attempt made to achieve agricultural diversification or industrialization. Dependence on sugar ensured that erratic swings in hard currency continued. At the same time, Cuba relied on the Soviets for massive infusions of aid to meet minimal investment and consumption needs and depended almost entirely on Soviet oil exports for energy requirements.

Meanwhile, Cuba's per capita debt grew into the largest in Latin America, four times that of Brazil and three times that of Mexico. The approximately $10 billion debt was more than two hundred times that of 1959. Cuba's loans were short-term, floating-rate types and had to be refinanced constantly at interest rates that rose sharply after the debt was incurred. Cuba's interest payments increased at a staggering rate, while Western commercial banks were reluctant to provide new hard-currency loans.

Popular expectations of rapid economic improvement were replaced by pessimism. There was decreasing enthusiasm among Cuba's labor force and increasing signs of weariness with constant revolutionary exhortations. Underemployment was rampant, and labor productivity was at a low point. Absenteeism from the job place became common. Cubans stole from state enterprises and fed an already growing black market for food and goods. Graft and corruption became widespread as Cubans rejected socialist morality and laws and struggled to survive on a daily basis.

Yet this is only one side of the picture. It is in the nature of totalitarian regimes that the key question related not to economics per se but rather to the effects of economic factors upon the levers of political and social control. In an effort to increase productivity and forestall any further decline in revolutionary momentum, the regime increased the militarization and regimentation of society and institutionalized its rule by expanding the role and influence of the party throughout society. This progressive institutionalization contributed to the further stabilization of the system, while reducing its vulnerability to threats of external subversion and internal revolt. From an institutional standpoint, the regime appeared equipped to withstand the difficult years ahead. Fidel Castro was still dominant. He remained "the revolution," "the maximum leader." The evidence seemed to indicate that significant segments of the Cuban people continued to be attracted by his personalized style of government. Some regarded him as a protection against the state structures, an uncontrollable and unpredictable leader ready to change or challenge policies of which he was the author. His lengthy speeches before huge throngs served both as a pedagogical device and as an instantaneous plebiscite. Despite some friction within the military after the U.S. invasion of Grenada embarrassed the Cubans, to all appearances, he maintained absolute control of his government, with no other public figure in a position to challenge his undisputed authority. Speeches by ranking government and party officials were replete with laudatory remarks about the commander in chief. Mass organizations, such as the Committees for the Defense of the Revolution and the Federation of Cuban Women, continued to display slogans extolling Castro's personality, calling for unswerving loyalty to the maximum leader and insisting on supporting Fidel "until victory."

Even with the significant institutionalization of the power structure, Castro's hold on the reins was unchallenged. Yet the very fact that he surrounded himself progressively with the more hard-line elements in the party and the military was certainly indicative of Castro's predilections. Starting in December 1979, the ranks of the "technocrats" in the regime, led by Vice-President Carlos Rafael Rodriguez and Minister of Trade Marcelo Fernandez, were decimated by purges that victimized Fernandez and twenty-two other ministers, presidents of state committees, and other high officials, removing them from the Council of Ministers and, in nine cases, from the new Central Committee that was installed in December 1980.

The political elite's values, policy goals, and organizational interests were driven to reinforce Castro's political inclinations and policy preferences. The hard foreign policy objectives of this group were (1) maintaining Cuba's independence from, and opposition to, the United States; (2) actively supporting violence and terrorism in Latin America; (3) promoting national liberation and socialism in the Third World; (4) acquiring influence and supportive allies among the Third World states; and (5) securing maximum military, economic, and political commitments from the Soviet Union. The Castro brothers and their respective followers were also in full control of the pivotal Executive Committee of the Council of Ministers, which was assigned enlarged powers under the governmental reorganization in the early 1980s. The old guard of civilian guerrilla veterans, the *fidelistas* and *raúlistas*, along with the Cuban armed forces, occupied the top posts of the party and the government to an extent unparalleled since the 1960s. The profile of the regime indicated that it would be no more amenable to moderation or conciliatory policies toward the United States than it was two decades ago.

In foreign affairs, the Cuban revolution achieved significant successes. In the late 1970s, Castro emerged as the leader of the nonaligned movement. There he espoused four important themes for the future that became the cornerstone of Cuba's policy toward the developing world: support for violent revolution, anticolonialism and anti-Americanism, an end to white supremacy in Africa, and a reduction of dependency on the Western economies. These policies coincided with Soviet objectives and produced a convergence of Soviet and Cuban actions in the developing world. Castro's willingness to commit his Soviet-equipped, well-trained armed forces in the African continent gained for Cuba much respect and admiration but also created some fear among African leaders.

The Cuban leadership saw its support for revolution as an integral and critical part of Cuba's foreign policy. Helping leftist insurgents throughout the world is a revolutionary commitment that ensures these allies will come to Cuba's aid in times of need. But more important, worldwide revolution directed against the United States and its supporters weakens the United States, the principal enemy of the Cuban Revolution, diverts its attention and resources, and may ultimately restrain its policies and actions against the island. This, in turn, will ensure the survival of the Cuban Revolution and its present leadership, the most important objective of Cuba's foreign policy.

Armed struggle has remained fundamental to Castro's mystique as well as to the image that he has projected onto the larger world stage where he is determined to play. Other revolutionary leaders may shed, in time, doctrinaire excesses in favor of the pragmatic pursuit of comfortable rule. Yet there is truly nothing in Castro's personal makeup to suggest that he could forsake the global floodlights and renounce his internationalist commitments.

Perhaps the Sandinista victory in Nicaragua and the establishment, albeit temporarily, of a Marxist regime in Grenada were Cuba's most important revolutionary achievements in the western hemisphere. Although the overthrow of the Somoza regime in Nicaragua was as much the result of internal opposition as of external aid, Cuba claimed a joint effort with Venezuela and Panama in bringing down the Somoza dynasty. Cuba pointed out, furthermore, the vindication of the Cuban line, which had been emphasizing for years the need for violence and particularly guerrilla warfare to attain power in Latin America.

The Sandinista victory gave new life to revolutionary violence and terrorism in Central America, much of it supported by Cuba. Yet Cuba's support for insurgent groups in the area, particularly in El Salvador and Guatemala, was channeled increasingly through Nicaragua. Using Nicaragua or other third countries facilitated the flow of weapons, propaganda, and aid, while making the task of detection and resistance that much harder. Cuba also denied supporting revolutionary groups, thus weakening U.S. credibility and influence, while at the same time facilitating relations with more conservative governments in Latin America. Castro's willingness to come to the aid of the Argentine military regime during the Falklands War was a further indication of Cuba's pragmatic and opportunistic foreign policy. In Argentina, Castro sided with a military dictatorship that had important commercial relations with the Soviet Union and that was fighting Great Britain, a close U.S. ally.

Throughout these maneuvers in Cuba's foreign policy, Castro remained closely tied to the Soviet Union. While there were frictions between Castro and the Kremlin, the latter's influence and presence in the island were far more extensive than ever before. At the same time, solidarity with the Soviet Union remained a vital element of Cuba's foreign policy. Cuba's policies and actions in the international arena operated in the larger framework of Soviet objectives. Castro continued to pursue his own policies only as long as they did not clash with those of the Soviets. To an American journalist who visited Cuba in 1984 and questioned Fidel's loyalty to the Soviets, Castro replied, "I am not Sadat," meaning he would not leave the Soviet camp as Egyptian leader Anwar Sadat had.

Uncomfortable as he felt in the embrace of the Russian bear, Fidel's options were limited. Although relations with China improved from the nadir in 1967, the Chinese seemed unable or unwilling to take Cuba on as an expensive client. Castro's support of Moscow's policies were decried by Beijing as "revisionist," and his denunciations of Mao in the late 1960s were still remembered with bitterness and anger by the Chinese.

Increased commercial ties with Canada, Western Europe, and Japan beckoned as a healthy development from Cuba's standpoint. Yet the ability of these countries to absorb the island's sugar exports was limited, and Havana had scant cash reserves with which to purchase European and Japanese goods. Cuba's heavy economic commitment to the Soviet Union and eastern European countries was an additional deterrent to a broadening of its scope of trading partners, while U.S. pressures on Western allies tended to limit their willingness to trade with Cuba.

To be sure, all of this could have enhanced the desire of the Castro regime to reduce its reliance on the Soviet Union and to reach some accommodation with the United States. Rapprochement with the United States could have led to a loosening of the embargo and the travel ban and even access to an important and proximate market, if the United States were willing to buy Cuban sugar. It could have bolstered Cuba's immediate security position and provide Castro with leverage in his dealings with the Soviet Union. U.S. recognition would have meant an important psychological victory for Castro. In Latin America, it would have been interpreted as a defeat for "Yankee imperialism" and as an acceptance of the Castro regime as a permanent, albeit irritating, phenomenon in the Caribbean.

It is a measure of the strange and pervasive economic determinism in the American outlook that we tend to assign priority to economic analysis in trying to understand the motivations of revolutionary Marxist regimes like the one in Havana. The history of the past decades offers clear proof that economic considerations have never dominated Castro's policies. On the contrary, many of the initiatives and actions that the Cuban leadership has undertaken abroad, such as intervention in Angola, Ethiopia, Grenada, and Nicaragua, as well as constant mass mobilizations at home, have been costly, disruptive, and detrimental to orderly economic development. If the economic welfare of the Cuban people had been the leitmotif of Castro's policies, we would be confronting a totally different Cuba today.

Cuban moves toward accommodation with the United States would have posed some major problems for the Kremlin. The Soviets were not averse to some amelioration in Cuban-U.S. tensions, especially if this resulted in reducing Cuba's heavy demands for Soviet aid. The Kremlin was fearful, however, that ties with the West could foster desires for increasing independence by other Soviet bloc members and lead to progressive internal liberalization, as the results of the West German efforts to establish diplomatic and trade relations with Eastern Europe showed. Although Cuba was not so critical to the Soviet Union as Eastern Europe, a resumption of Cuba's relations with the United States and significant weakening in Soviet-Cuban ties was seen as leading to the eventual subverting of the revolution and the renunciation of membership in the "socialist camp." Moscow viewed Cuba's possible defection as a blow to its prestige and as damaging to the Soviet power posture vis-à-vis the United States.

Rapprochement with the United States would have also been fraught with danger and uncertainties for the Cuban leadership. It would have required a loosening of Cuba's military ties with the Soviet Union, the abandonment of visible support for violent revolutions in Latin America, and the withdrawal of Cuban troops from Africa and other parts of the world. These were conditions Castro was not willing to accept. He perceived them as attempts by the United States to isolate Cuba and strengthen anti-Castro forces within the island, thus posing a threat to the stability of his regime. Moreover, the economic embargo engendered in Cuba a sort of siege mentality, which facilitated the mobilization of the population and justified the constant demands of the government for more work and sacrifices, while at the same time providing a ready-made excuse for economic failures. The close ties of the Cuban economy to the Soviet Union prevented a rapid reorientation toward the United States, even if this were politically feasible. Castro, therefore, was not able or willing to offer meaningful concessions that would be indispensable for U.S.-Cuban rapprochement. Statements of intention or meaningless tactical concessions are no substitutes for substantive policy changes. In the past, Castro has periodically extended ostensible olive branches to the United States, only to retract them. Even in those years, the complex diplomatic avenues between Washington and Havana have never been completely barricaded. Negotiations have proceeded and ad hoc agreements have been struck; for example, with respect to the treatment of skyjackers or the Mariel refugees. The question, therefore, is not whether Castro is willing to negotiate. The question, rather is whether he stands ready to render the kinds of meaningful concessions that he has barred in the past—concessions concerning Castro's support for revolutionary and terrorist groups and Cuba's respect for human rights and development of a pluralistic society.

It is unlikely that a profoundly anti-American, megalomaniac, and cunning leader such as Fidel will be happy as simply another friendly authoritarian/paternalistic caudillo relegated to an insignificant tropical island. Castro's political style and ideology and his apprehensions about U.S. motivations make him more prone to maintain a hard line. His awareness of Cuba's vulnerability is reinforced by the hostile activities of Cuban refugees in the United States. Commitment to violent revolution and solidarity with anti-American regimes such as Iraq, North Korea, Iran, and Libya are cornerstones of his foreign policy. The preservation of a radical position is felt to be necessary for the defense of the revolution and to encourage the anti-U.S. struggle. He cannot modify, let alone abandon, these cornerstones without risking his power and obscuring his personal place in history—a consideration that may be becoming more important in Castro's mind.

Meaningful Cuban overtures to the United States seem unlikely, all the more so because of the prospect of a continuing erosion of the U.S. embargo and the travel ban. Castro prefers to make the U.S. boycott an important issue in his anti-U.S. campaign in Latin America. Although of little economic significance for the revolution, Latin American moves toward reestablishing economic and diplomatic relations with Cuba are viewed by Havana as a major political defeat for the United States in Latin America, which could result both in some isolation of the United States in the region and in pressures for it to recognize the Castro government.

This is not to say that Cuban-Soviet relations were without serious irritants. Moscow's claim to leadership of the "socialist bloc" and its interference in Cuba's internal affairs clashed with the forces of Cuban nationalism. Given Castro's personality and past policies, his suspicion, if not dislike, of the Soviets, and his desire to play a leading role in world affairs, he remained an unstable and unpredictable Soviet ally. Yet, in the 1980s, Castro had no choice but to follow the Soviet lead, while attempting to emerge from his isolation in Latin America and improve Cuba's faltering economy.

In the late 1980s and early 1990s, Castro faced some of the old problems that plagued the Cuban Revolution in the past, as well as new and critical challenges. Internally, there was growing evidence of disillusionment with the party's and Castro's exhortations. Absenteeism and youth apathy were increasing. Castro seemed to be losing the battle to create a new generation devoted to the party and to the revolution. Despite thirty years of revolution, the "new man" was yet to be created. The loss of this generation represents, perhaps, the greatest challenge for the future stability of the regime.

Economically, the revolution was extremely weak. Persistent

structural problems in the economy, low prices for Cuba's export products, and the inability to obtain greater quantities of aid from the Soviet Union forced yet another reexamination of basic goals. The deepening economic crisis, aggravated by events in Eastern Europe, produced a new frenzy of planning activity and greater regimentation, in the hope of stimulating productivity. While rejecting *perestroika* (restructuring) and *glasnost* (political opening), Castro returned to the failed paths of the past, insisting that the Cubans should work harder, sacrifice more, and expect less in the years ahead. Among the populace, pessimism and cynicism replaced revolutionary fervor.

Externally, Castro remained a willing ally of the Soviet Union. While frictions developed after Gorbachev's assumption of power, the Soviet Union's influence on the conduct of Cuba's foreign policy remained strong, and Cuba's solidarity with the Soviets was one of the main cornerstones of Cuba's foreign policy. Without abandoning his commitment to anti-Americanism and internationalism, Castro became more selective in supporting revolutionary groups in Latin America and elsewhere. He expanded ties with the new Latin American democracies and tried to project a statesmanlike image in the area. He also negotiated, on his own terms, a solution to the Angolan conflict and the withdrawal of Cuban troops from the continent of Africa.

Mild overtures from Castro toward the United States encouraged those in this country who believed it was time for a rapprochement with Cuba. In 1989, Castro tried and executed three high-ranking officers of the Interior Ministry and General Arnaldo Ochoa, former commander of Cuban troops in Africa, accusing them of drug trafficking. The execution seemed more connected with the elimination of a potential rival than with drugs. Denying his or his brother's involvement with drugs, a denial few believed, Castro called on the United States for cooperation in fighting the drug trade. As he had in the past, Castro was willing to negotiate and to cooperate with the United States on specific issues.

Castro was not ready then, or since, to make major concessions. It is interesting to note that Fidel's overtures to the United States are usually followed with the now standard qualifier: "Since certain things are sacred—independence, the country's sovereignty, its revolutionary principle—its political and social systems cannot be renounced. Whoever destroys them will have to fight us." In a bitter and vitriolic anti-American speech on July 26, 1989, the thirty-sixth anniversary of the Moncada attack, Castro reemphasized his commitment to socialism and rejected any possibilities of change.

Yet successive U.S. administrations have hoped for an accommodation with the Cuban Revolution. Castro has periodically (especially before U.S. elections) extended ostensible olive branches to the United States, only to retract them. The expectation remained, however, that somehow a negotiated settlement could be found in the 1980s to contain Castro's internationalism and the accelerating currents of instability and conflict in Central America, and to relieve the difficult choices that the United States confronted in responding to these developments. Optimistic appraisals of the possibility of a deal with Castro were also encouraged by the spectacle of Cuba's deepening economic problems.

Before the revolution, most of Cuba's foreign trade was with Western nations, almost 70 percent with the United States. Since Castro's takeover, Cuba's trade was reoriented primarily toward Socialist countries. Almost 80 percent of Cuba's trade was with non-Western nations. To many American businesses, the possibility of reopening this market to American products seems natural, given the pre-revolutionary tradition, the geographical proximity of the island, and the needs of the Cuban economy for American know-how and technology. The notion of trade with Cuba is also surrounded by a certain mysticism that misestimates the true potential of the Cuban market, enhanced by the vision of selling to a state-controlled economy with its massive purchasing power.

There is little question about Cuba's chronic need for U.S. technology, products, and services. Yet need alone does not determine the size or viability of a market. Cuba's large foreign debt, owed to both Western and Socialist countries; the abysmal performance of its economy; and the low prices for its major exports make the "bountiful market" perception a perilous mirage.

Given Cuba's dismal economic picture, Castro's ability to use its scant foreign exchange to buy U.S. and Western products will remain very limited for the foreseeable future. The island's economy has fallen from a position of regional economic leadership to a level below the median Caribbean per capita income. In the process, Cuba has amassed a massive foreign debt, and the servicing of this debt has created an added burden to the economy. Yet this debt does not take into consideration the more than $19 billion the USSR had granted Cuba between 1961 and 1988, including commodity subsidies and absorption of balance-of-trade deficits. Cuba's indebtedness to the Soviet Union and the high level of assistance it received from Moscow until 1992 vouched for its dependency, for its subordination to decision-making mechanisms other than its own, and for its inability to divert significant resources to purchase Western goods.

Obviously, Cuba's dependence on foreign powers has greatly increased, relative to the pre-revolutionary era. That exacerbation of dependency must be judged in terms of Cuba's loss of economic flexibility and alternatives as a result of the political ideological commitment to the revolution. This commitment exacted a high economic price not only through heightened international dependency, but also through a massive concentration on sugar that weakened Cuba's possibilities to diversity its exports, as well as its choice of trading partners.

If a resumption of U.S.-Cuban economic relations were to take place, the United States must be prepared to barter its products for Cuban sugar. Cuba's chronic shortage of hard currency means bartering or loans are the only mechanisms available to the Castro regime to acquire U.S. goods. But Cuba's gain of any share of the U.S. sugar market must come at the expense of other sugar producers in the Caribbean, as well as sugar producers in the United States itself. This arrangement would deal a considerable blow to the American sugar industry, but it would be particularly devastating to the economies of a score of friendly nations structurally dependent on sugar exports to the United States. Such nations as the Dominican Republic, Costa Rica, Guatemala, and El Salvador would face additional hardships, stifled growth, and enlarged debt burdens that could threaten their political stability, and thus, U.S. regional security interests.

It is also important to point out that domestic protectionism in the United States has already resulted in reduced sugar quotas for most regional producers. A specific danger is that Cuba could subsidize sugar exports and sell below marginal cost. To some Caribbean sugar states, this would represent an economic dislocation of the first magnitude. The same argument holds, in varying degrees, for other potential Cuban exports such as biotechnology, nickel, tobacco, citrus, and rum.

Cuba's products are neither economically nor strategically important to the United States. From the U.S. point of view, therefore, the reestablishment of commercial ties with Cuba would be at best problematic. It would create severe market distortions for the already precarious regional economy of the Caribbean and Central America, since the United States would have to shift some of these countries' sugar quota to Cuba. It would provide the U.S. market with products that are of little value and in abundant supply. And while some U.S. firms could benefit from a resumed trade relationship, it would not help in any significant way the overall U.S. economy. Cuba does not have the potential to become an important client like China, Russia, or even Vietnam.

Under the protective umbrella of the Soviet Union, Castro continued to play a great power role in Africa, Latin America, and the Middle East into the 1990s, supporting violent revolution in three continents and leading the non-aligned movement—a role totally out of proportion to Cuba's size and resources—and at the expense of the Cuban people. The Cuban leadership saw its support for revolution as an integral and critical part of Cuba's foreign policy. The Soviets provided Cuba the protection that allowed Castro's adventurism in the world. While not providing the principal motivation for Castro's policies, the protection and aid of the Soviet Union enhanced Cuba's policies and actions. Yet it is important to emphasize that the Soviets were neither able nor willing to prevent Cuba's involvement with revolutionary groups. In the 1960s, Castro engaged in revolutionary exploits throughout the world, many times to the chagrin and dismay of the Soviets. To understand Cuba's world role requires a unique analytical lens.

American analysts generally neglect the personal factor as a key to the behavior of a revolutionary society dominated by the charisma and philosophy of a single personality. Notwithstanding the prominent attention that has been given to Castro the leader, there is still inadequate appreciation of Castro the man, and of the integral roles that violent revolution and "internationalism" exert upon his personal makeup.

By the 1990s, Cuba's international relations had developed into seven main themes: (1) the survival of the Castro revolution; (2) the internationalization of Castro's personal prestige and charisma and the resulting power and influence this conveys; (3) the maintenance, until the collapse of communism, of a close alliance with the Soviet Union and its interests throughout the world; (4) the preservation of an anti-American posture in an attempt to weaken American power and influence worldwide; (5) the acquisition of influence and supportive allies among Third World states; (6) the development of a "new international economic order"; and (7) the continuous support of "movements of national liberation" in Asia, Africa, the Middle East, and Latin America.

The Cuban government helped a broad range of "progressive forces," terrorist groups, and religious fanatics opposing the United States. Since the 1970s, however, the regime has been increasingly willing, in spite of its Marxist rhetoric, to establish ties with conservative Latin American states. Clearly, ideology is not the sole factor shaping Cuba's external behavior. Cuban interest in developing such relations has been motivated by a desire to foster Cuban and, in the past, Soviet objectives, and to undermine U.S. interests in the area.

Another interesting characteristic of Cuba's foreign policy is the attempt to achieve goals with low risks. Failures abroad would hurt Castro's prestige and weaken his leverage. Successes, however, feed the leader's ego and bring with them tangible rewards; worldwide influence, leverage vis-à-vis other countries, and internal support, which compensates for the continuous economic failures and hardships endured by the Cuban people. Successes abroad justify sacrifices at home.

Despite the expansive role of Cuba and the successes of certain daring Cuban initiatives (especially in Africa), Cuban foreign policy has had its share of failures and has shown signs of possible decay. The U.S. invasion of Grenada is a case of forced Cuban reversal. The eventual electoral defeat of the Sandinistas in Nicaragua, as well as the peace accord in El Salvador, shows the limits of Cuba's internationalism and influence.

The image of a non-aligned Cuba was repeatedly tarnished by Castro's close partnership with the Soviets. His failure to condemn the Soviet invasion of Afghanistan cost him dearly. It was difficult for Castro, the "champion" of non-intervention and a constant critic of past U.S. interventions, to justify the brutal Soviet intervention in Afghanistan. It was also difficult for honest and responsible leaders of the Third World to accept this dual standard. Castro's failed attempt to rally Latin American leaders to repudiate their foreign debt contrasted sharply with Cuba's commitment to pay its own debt to the Soviets. It is difficult to reconcile preaching morality at home and practicing cynicism abroad.

In 1988 Angola, South Africa, and Cuba signed an agreement

mediated by the United States calling for the removal of Cuban troops from Angola and establishing the independence of Namibia. With this agreement, Castro achieved his original goal of consolidating a Marxist regime in power in Angola, as well as securing the independence of Namibia. On July 26, 1988, he proclaimed that Cuba was "willing to participate in a just and dignified solution that includes the security of Angola and the independence of Namibia." He also achieved world status—he shared the negotiating table with bigger powers. The U.S. had negotiated with a leader of a small, insignificant Caribbean island and considered his wishes and demands. Castro's prestige and leverage increased. Furthermore, Castro left Angola only gradually over several years, thus minimizing the impact of returning his troops to Cuba and helping to guarantee the survivability of the Popular Movement for the Liberation of Angola, the Angolan Marxist regime.

Cuba emerged as the real victor. Castro achieved at the bargaining table what he was unable to achieve on the battlefield. The agreement allowed him to extricate his troops from a difficult, indeed a no-win, situation. In over ten years of fighting, he had been unable to emerge victorious in the Angolan conflict, and Cubans suffered thousands of losses. Opposition had been growing to a winless war, and there was less enthusiasm within the military to remain indefinitely in Angola. In addition, returning troops increased the AIDS epidemic on the island.

Cuban policies and actions in the world were usually conducted with Soviet support or acquiescence and, in the case of Angola, with direct Soviet military involvement. Yet it should be emphasized that commitment to revolutionary violence has been a Cuban policy since the beginning of the revolution. Fidel sees this commitment as his most significant contribution to modern revolutionary theory and as the policy that will provide for him a place in history.

Despite *perestroika* and *glasnost* in the Soviet Union and differences with Gorbachev, Castro remained a close Soviet ally until the end of communism. Since the late 1960s, the relations between Havana and Moscow had taken the form of a progressively closer alliance. The incorporation of Cuba into the Soviet camp was evident not only in economic terms (Cuba was a member of the COMECON and was heavily dependent on Soviet economic and military aid and trade) but was clearly manifested in its model of government and its international behavior. The nature of this alliance was more complex than the theories that describe Cuba as a simple satellite or the Soviets as the center of an empire with a series of allies in its periphery. Undoubtedly, Cuba was subservient in most cases to Soviet interests, but Havana had considerable leverage with Moscow as well as some freedom to act and react in external affairs (especially in the Caribbean and Central and Latin America). What best defined the relationship is a commonality of interests and a mutuality of gains.

In spite of this intimacy, the Soviet-Cuban connection had encountered differences, temporarily souring the partnership. The early years of the 1980s were marked by minor but revealing tensions. The Soviets quarreled with Castro over his somewhat independent ideological maneuvering and his failure to put order into Cuba's faltering economy. Castro attempted to underscore his limited independence in international policies vis-à-vis the Kremlin but mitigated possible negative repercussions by praising the Soviets' vital economic lifeline to his regime.

Tensions between Cuba and the Soviet Union also can be traced to the Grenada invasion. The successful U.S. invasion represented a setback for Cuban influence in the region. Wishfully expecting a stronger Soviet reaction, the Cubans were disappointed by the Kremlin's lack of support. Consequently, several regional leftist organizations, such as the Worker's Party of Jamaica, criticized Cuba for not providing military assistance to that radical violent communist faction that took control of Grenada after the assassination of Prime Minister Maurice Bishop, the Coard group. Castro, in turn, blamed his military commanders in Grenada for having failed to resist the U.S. intervention, demoting several officers whose performance was deemed unacceptable.

Castro also showed impatience with the Soviet level of support for Nicaragua and with the Kremlin's unwillingness to challenge the United States in defense of the Sandinista revolution. Castro's failure to attend the COMECON meeting in 1984, and the absence of a high-level Soviet delegation at the anniversary celebration of the Cuban Revolution that same year were additional signs of strains in the relations.

By early 1985, Havana and Moscow were beginning to reconcile differences. Raúl Castro and a top-level Cuban delegation attended Chernenko's funeral in Moscow. In 1986 and 1987, Fidel attended the anniversary celebrations of the Bolshevik Revolution in Moscow, and insisted that there was no friction with the Soviets, and claimed that relations were better than ever. He proclaimed the 1987 celebration his best visit to the USSR.

Gorbachev's visit to Cuba in early 1989 produced mixed results. While Castro balked at Gorbachev's insistence on the need for *perestroika* and *glasnost* on the island, they agreed on other more fundamental issues dealing with international relations. Cuba and the Soviet Union supported the renunciation of the utility of force in international relations, the reduction of regional conflicts, and the continuous global emphasis on the problems of humanity. Cuba would seek greater economic aid from Western countries, including, if possible, the United States, so as to alleviate the Soviet burden of supporting the Cuban economy. As long as the Soviets were not directly involved nor their image tarnished, Cuba would continue to support movements of national liberation. Armed struggle in certain countries remained, from Cuba's standpoint, the only possible road to further power.

As on previous occasions, the areas of agreement in Soviet-Cuban relations seemed greater than those of disagreement. Despite Castro's rejection of economic reforms and his clinging to old Marxist-Leninist ideas, he recognized and supported the value of Gorbachev's "new thinking" in international affairs as a strategy to weaken the Western alliance and undermine U.S. interests, particularly in Latin America.

As the decade of the 1990s began, despite advancing age and mounting internal problems, Castro remained a troublesome adversary of the United States. Little did he expect that communism would collapse in the Soviet Union and that his critical ally would fragment into smaller republics following market economic policies and a more democratic path.

15

YEARS OF CRISIS

Few anticipated the rapid and dramatic collapse of the Soviet Union and its empire in Eastern Europe in the early 1990s. Even fewer anticipated the end of communism in the Soviet Union. Western nations rejoiced at the spectacle of an independent and free Eastern Europe, the breakdown of the Soviet Union into sixteen republics, and the development of a market-oriented and more open society in Russia. For Cuba, it was a devastating blow. Cuba lost not only the protection of the Soviet political umbrella but also the economic support that had been the lifeline of the Castro regime. Soviet aid and subsidies suddenly vanished. Access to Eastern European and Soviet products at subsidized prices disappeared. The Eastern Europeans and the new republics demanded cash payments for their goods. The weakness and dependence of Cuba's economy became painfully evident.

The years that followed saw a deepening economic crisis in Cuba, a theme that plays in constant repetition. Severe shortages of Russian and Eastern European petroleum, fertilizers, spare parts, raw materials, and foodstuffs crippled the economy. Sugar harvest production declined to the lowest levels since the revolution. Nearly three-quarters of factories on the island stopped or reduced production for lack of spare parts and raw materials. Transportation and communications suffered drastic cuts. Cuba's imports and exports fell by 70 to 75 percent. Unemployment and underemployment increased drastically. The low standard of living of the Cuban people sank to new levels of misery and suffering. Hope for the future was replaced with even deeper pessimism and despair. A terrible sense of alienation from the state gripped Cuban society.

The government's initial economic-policy response to the crisis was further rationing of limited supplies of consumer goods (belt tightening), to allow Cuban citizens to briefly hold dollars; to purchase goods in special stores previously reserved for tourists, diplomats, and government functionaries; and to increase efforts to attract foreign investments, especially in non-traditional export industries, mainly tourism and mining. Some profound reforms were contemplated, but not implemented, by the government's central planning agency. These included cost accounting by enterprises, establishment of investment funds by state firms, balanced budgets and price liberalization, and the private ownership of property by Cubans.

This first response was virtually a non-policy. The government sought economic survival by husbanding its meager resources. Rations were reduced, labor brigades were organized, security and repression increased, and rhetoric was used to boost morale and maintain social unity. At the same time, the military was given a greater role in controlling the economy. Officers in the armed forces were entrusted with running agricultural and industrial enterprises and producing goods for themselves as well as for the population. It was the hope of the Castro brothers that the militarization of the economy would bring order and discipline and reverse the deteriorating economic situation. At the same time, involvement in the economy provided a new mission to a military, demoralized by the arrest and execution of several of its leaders, and by the lack of mission since its involvement in Africa.

In mid-1990s, the government permitted the establishment of farmers' markets where agricultural products were sold by growers directly to the public. Similar peasant markets had flourished for about four years in the mid-1980s until Castro shut them down claiming that Cubans were becoming "little capitalists" and that the goals of the revolution were being undermined. The regime now hoped that a return to these free agricultural markets would help alleviate the critical food shortage and weaken the expanding black market.

The economic reforms not related to foreign direct investment have been extremely limited and designed to alleviate the most immediate problem: Cuba's lack of hard currency. In 1992 Cuba expanded the list of consumer goods that exiles could send to relatives on the island, including many foodstuffs (e.g., beans, rice, and coffee) that were previously prohibited. Cuban officials also announced in 1995 an increase in the number of visas that they would process for travel from the United States to Cuba. Cuban-Americans that travel to the island usually bring money and non-perishable goods to relatives on the island. The objective of these policies were to capture officially some of the dollars that now circulate in the black market and to encourage more exiles to visit the island or send monetary remittances to their relatives.

Cuban officials realized that these reforms create sharp economic inequalities among the Cuban population, mainly benefiting those who work in the dollar-earning sectors, principally tourism and related services, and/or those who have generous relatives abroad. The need for foreign exchange, however, is critical, and officials were willing to accept the negative side effects. These reforms led to some improvement in Cuba's economic situation. Yet these measures remained readily reversible by the regime on short notice.

The most significant response to the crisis was the reforms in Cuba's foreign-investment laws and the country's active posture in seeking joint ventures with foreign companies. One may speculate that Cuba would like to be as successful as China in attracting foreign investment, but it has yet to emulate the structural economic reforms that China has adopted. Cuban technocrats, as well as critics of the Castro government, have noted that there are significant differences between the two countries, which work to Cuba's disadvantage.

In 1982, Cuba enacted its joint-venture law that permitted foreign direct investment (FDI) in Cuba. Not much FDI activity took place until 1992, when Cuban officials began liberally interpreting the 1982 law and encouraged foreign investment by offering fiscal incentives such as the exemption of joint ventures from tariff duties on imported materials and from all taxes but social security. Actual terms are negotiated on a case-by-case basis, with the fiscal incentives often limited to the initial years of the project. Foreign firms have also been allowed to conduct business in hard currency, introduce their own management techniques, dismiss workers at their own discretion, set wages, and repatriate profits freely. In July 1992, new legislation permitted the limited transfer of state property to foreigners, the creation of autonomous (but regulated) enterprises, and the export and import of goods without prior government approval.

The exact number of joint ventures that have resulted from Cuba's efforts is difficult to determine, as various officials and Cuban publications from time to time report different figures. Most of the joint ventures have been in tourism, and most of the foreign partners have been from Spain. Of the non-tourist investments, the Cuban government reported mostly Spanish, Canadian, French, and Mexican companies as joint-venture partners in mining, rum production, and oil exploration. Most of the Mexican investments were part of a debt-for-equity swap in which the Cuban government reduced its debt to Mexico by providing various Cuban enterprises to Mexican businessmen. For all of Cuba's efforts, the number of joint ventures is quite small for an economy of its potential size, and many of the publicized investments have not actually been consummated.

Cuba's desire to emulate the Chinese model will most likely be unfulfilled, as Cuba is unlikely to achieve the success that China has attained in its FDI efforts. China began to attract foreign investors in the late 1970s and established a series of complementary economic reforms that supported their development strategy. Authorities created special economic zones in the early 1980s that combined material, fiscal, and labor incentives in strategic geographic locations. Individuals, not just firms, were afforded greater freedom in economic decision making. The Chinese focused their FDI efforts on manufacturing, with particular emphasis on activities that would introduce new technology into the country. China permitted foreign firms to pay higher wages than those found in the rest of the country, rewarding and stimulating labor productivity increases. Workers resettled in those special areas and often remitted part of their earnings to family members back home, or sent home consumer goods purchased within those zones. The economic zones served as small islands of quasi-capitalism within the larger communist state. China was also able to attract significant amounts of investments from Hong Kong and Taiwan, which has contributed greatly to the development of China's Guandong province.

In contrast, Cuba has promoted investments in tourism as its highest priority and only recently has begun to promote investments in other sectors. Cuba has not yet attempted to link FDI with technology transfer. Nor has it permitted greater individual freedom in economic matters. While the Cuban government is allowing some workers to operate independently, these activities are highly regulated, with increased taxation and licensing costs. Unlike China, Cuba has not legalized private agriculture or manufacturing. No foreign trade that is independent of the state is permitted, either.

The Cuban constitution still outlaws foreign ownership of most properties and forbids any private Cubans from participating in joint ventures with foreigners. Moreover, it is still illegal for foreign companies to hire Cuban workers directly. Foreign employers must pay the wages owed to their employees directly to the Cuban government in hard currency. The Cuban government then pays out to the Cuban workers in Cuban pesos, which are worth a fraction of the hard currency, pocketing the difference. Furthermore, while the new foreign-investment law provides protection against government expropriation, all arbitration must take place in the corrupt and arbitrary government offices, where little protection is given to investors.

Foreign investors must also confront political uncertainties that do not exist in many countries. They must contend with the possibility of the regime's reversing its present open-door policy, the legal problems posed by the U.S. embargo, the legal questions surrounding previously confiscated properties, and potential sanctions against foreign investors that cooperated with the Castro government in the event that an anti-Castro government eventually comes to power.

Cuba's economic future is also clouded by a relatively large convertible currency debt. Cuba's external debt amounts to about $10 billion, and Castro has failed to make either principal or interest payments on this debt since 1986, when he unilaterally declared a debt moratorium. The non-performing status of this debt represents a nearly insurmountable obstacle to obtaining a large renewed flow of international credit.

There is a degree of contradiction among the stated economic goals of Cuban officials. Some indications suggest that Cuba is attempting to implement a slow transition from a command economy to what some in the Cuban leadership call a mixed economy, composed of state, private, and cooperative enterprises (public/ private partnerships). Yet Castro and hard-line supporters are resisting the adoption of market reforms, or what they derisively refer to as capitalism.

Such resistance creates a major dilemma for Cuba's economic

transition. Opposition to market reforms will limit the extent to which the private sector emerges and functions effectively and thereby slows, if not prevents, attaining a measurable degree of economic recovery. While Castro and hard-liners recognize the need for economic recovery, they also see the likely erosion of political power and control that accompanies the restructuring of the economy along free-market rules. Adoption of market reforms may well represent a solution to the economic crisis, but a full-blown reform process carries with it the risk of loss of control over society, as well as the economy, and threatens to alienate some of the regime's key constituencies.

In foreign relations, Castro scrambled to create new relationships and obtain foreign aid for his troubled economy. A number of Latin American countries normalized diplomatic and trade relations with Cuba. Venezuela under president Hugo Chavez developed close relations with Cuba and provided the Castro regime with subsidized petroleum on long-term credits. Calls for Cuba's readmission into the Inter-American system are often heard, and democratic countries like Colombia, Brazil, and Chile are willing to trade with, and invest in, Cuba. The English-speaking Caribbean countries have welcomed representatives from Cuba to their meetings, and an attempt is being made to integrate Cuba with the Caribbean Community (CARICOM). Cuba was welcomed into the newly formed Association of Caribbean States (ACS), despite U.S. protests. Mexico has reaffirmed its long-standing relationship with the Castro government. Yet relations are not as close since the departure of Ernesto Zedillo Administration and the assumption to power of Vicente Fox. Fox has expressed mild opposition to U.S. policy toward Cuba and offered himself as a possible mediator, while insisting that Cuba needs to improve its human rights record.

The immediate economic impact of improved foreign relations between Cuba and other Latin American nations, with the exception of Venezuela, is not likely to result in a noticeable change in Cuba. Approximately one-third of Cuba's meager foreign trade occurs with Latin America, and this trade occurs on a strictly commercial basis (i.e., payment in hard currency is required). Cuba, moreover, incurs a trade deficit with these countries, especially with respect to its trade with Mexico. The political effects may be more important than the economic effects, however.

The general trend among new democratic governments throughout Latin America is to pressure the United States, albeit mildly, to change its policy toward Cuba. The belief persists among some Latin American statesmen that, through negotiations and economic inducements, Castro may change his policies and provide for a peaceful political transition in the island. Optimistic appraisals of the possibility of a "deal" with Castro were also encouraged to a large extent by the spectacle of Cuba's anemic economy. This view holds that, if the crisis deepens, Castro will have no choice but to liberalize both the economy and the political system. Thus far, however, there has been little evidence to support this view.

One of the government's responses to the deepening crisis was to tacitly permit Cubans to take to rafts to flee the island. In 1994, thousands of Cubans set sail in flimsy rafts. Many perished in the Florida straits. Others reached American shores. Most were captured by the U.S. Coast Guard at sea and sent to the U.S. naval base in Guantánamo in eastern Cuba. After prolonged negotiations, most of the refugees in Guantánamo were allowed to enter the United States. The United States government agreed to provide 20,000 yearly visas to Cubans seeking to immigrate to the United States, and Havana promised to prevent illegal migration.

The Clinton Administration reversed the country's long-standing policy of allowing refugees from Cuba to enter the United States. Unless they reach American soil, rafters are now intercepted at sea and only if they can show a clear case of political persecution in Cuba, are allowed into the United States, otherwise they are returned to the island. While the massive exodus stopped almost completely, the potential for a new migration crisis still looms on the horizon.

The Castro government has also shown no signs of making meaningful concessions in the political and human rights arena. Indeed, in late 1995, the Castro regime began to slow down the lukewarm pace of economic reforms and to insist that Cuba will remain a Communist state. There has been no indication that the government truly intends to open up its political system or to promote a negotiated solution with the United States or with Cuba's budding opposition to the deepening crisis. History reveals times when strong, and even autocratic, political leaders have mellowed with age and softened their positions, but there is no evidence that this is the case with Castro. On the contrary, as Castro has aged, he has become more intransigent and difficult. In meetings with Latin leaders and in speeches from Havana, he reaffirmed his opposition to the United States and his unwillingness to relinquish power even after forty years at the helm of this troubled island. "There is an idea," Castro declared, "that socialism is declining and the time is right to exact from Cuba the price of more than thirty-five years of revolution. No price will be exacted here."

Until 1996, however, the Clinton Administration seemed willing to depart from the policies of previous administrations toward Cuba in two areas. The administration was willing to relax the travel ban to Cuba for Cuban-Americans and Americans and was ready to increase telecommunications and other media contacts with the island. Secretary of State Warren Christopher issued statements regarding "U.S.-calibrated responses" to Castro's actions, an indication of U.S. willingness to consider moving in a direction of gradually normalizing relations with Cuba. There was the hope among U.S. policy makers that this policy of engagement would lead to economic changes in the island, the building of a civil society, and, finally, the undermining of Castro's personal power. The speed of the U.S. response would be conditioned by the internal changes in Cuba, the actions of the new U.S. Congress, the pressures from the Cuban-American community, and the other priorities of the Clinton Administration.

The lifting of the travel ban could have provided the Castro regime with much-needed foreign exchange. While U.S. tourism will not in itself resolve Cuba's economic situation, it could provide the regime with a sufficient influx of dollars to allow its economy to muddle through for quite a number of years. It could also result in a decrease of Cuban visas to Cuban-Americans to visit the island. This group is feared by Cuba's leadership for its potential in subverting the values of the revolution. No such concern exists regarding U.S. tourists.

The lifting of the travel ban could also lead to serious pressure from U.S. business groups to increase other types of trade with Cuba and relax the ban on U.S. investments in the island. The long-term strength of Cuba's tourist industry needs significant numbers of visitors from the United States, a prerequisite for major development of that industry. U.S. businesses in the hotel and travel industry would clearly want to participate in the growth of the market. U.S. airlines and U.S.-based cruise companies would also want to capture a major share of that developing tourist market. A significant relaxation of the travel ban would represent one of the first steps in ending the U.S. embargo on Cuba.

Castro encouraged this U.S. policy of engagement. He mobilized significant resources to force the United States to unilaterally and without concessions lift the embargo and the travel ban. He invited U.S. religious, political, business, and academic leaders to the island. He reached out to moderate Cuban-Americans to begin a dialogue and to weaken Cuban-American opposition to a Cuba-U.S. rapprochement. He even visited New York in 1995, dressed not in his usual military uniform but in a business suit, enticing American entrepreneurs with a vision of major bonanza, if Cuba opened up to them.

Castro's calculated moves were designed to gain time and to force the United States into concessions regarding the embargo and the travel ban. He hoped that U.S. and world opinion would force the Clinton Administration to soften its policies and that U.S. attempts at subverting his revolution could be handled by Cuba's efficient security apparatus. His short-term tactics did not contemplate the dismantling of communism in Cuba or the weakening of his personal power over the Cuban people. Castro's minor concessions and tactics failed.

In early 1996, Cuban-U.S. relations took a turn for the worse. The slowing down of the pace of reforms in Cuba was an indication of Castro's unwillingness to move Cuba toward a market-oriented economy. The government's brutal repression of dissident groups in the island, and the arrest of more than one hundred of their members in February also emphasized Castro's opposition to a political opening. Then on February 24, two small, unarmed civilian aircraft flown by Brothers to the Rescue, the Cuban-American humanitarian group based in Miami, were destroyed by Cuban MIGs over international waters, killing the four occupants of the planes. Although Brothers to the Rescue had dropped anti-Castro leaflets in Havana on earlier occasions, their primary mission was to spot Cuban rafters fleeing the island and advise the U.S. Coast Guard so they could be rescued.

The United States reacted swiftly. The Clinton Administration supported the passage of, and signed into law, the Helms-Burton Act, which punished foreign companies and nationals that invested in properties confiscated by the Castro government, prohibiting the principals in those companies from traveling to the United States and allowing U.S. citizens to sue foreign companies in U.S. courts to obtain compensation (this last section has never been implemented). The law was aimed at discouraging foreign investments in Cuba and setting a standard of morality and fairness regarding properties illegally confiscated by the Castro government. Although the law generated significant criticisms, particularly in Canada, Europe, and Latin America, the United States administration and Congress refused to budge, claiming that it was important to punish the Castro government for its actions. Later, a Federal Court awarded $186 million to the families of the Cuban-Americans killed by the Cuban air force. The administration also restricted travel to Cuba and tightened the embargo.

By its actions prior to the downing of the planes, the Castro government served notice that the internal period of limited liberalization had come to an end. Castro had once again showed that political considerations were more important than economic ones. He risked upsetting the mild thaw in U.S.-Cuban relations, trade deals with the European Union, and condemnation by the world community in order to maintain internal control and external security. Fearful that a broader economic opening would lead to a political opening, he rejected both.

Commitment to a command and communist economy, violent revolution, internationalism, anti-Americanism, and personal rule remain the cornerstones of Castro's polices. He has been unwilling to modify, let alone abandon, these cornerstones for fear of risking his power and obscuring his personal place in history, a consideration that is perhaps now uppermost in Castro's outlook. He and his brother Raúl, head of the Cuban military, seem to have neither the wish nor the will to modify this totalitarian course, and on the basis of their stated beliefs and recent actions, change seems quite unlikely.

16

PREPARING FOR SUCCESSION

As a new millennium began Castro faced some of the same old problems that had plagued the Cuban Revolution in the past, as well as new and critical challenges. Internally there was growing evidence of disillusionment with the party's as well as with Castro's exhortations. Popular discontent, migration efforts by increasing numbers of Cubans, and defections of government, cultural, and athletic officials grew. Youth apathy and absenteeism increased. Pessimism and cynicism replaced revolutionary fervor. Castro seems to have lost the battle to create a new generation of Cubans devoted to the party and the revolution. Despite more than forty years of education and indoctrination, the "new man" is nowhere to be found. The loss of this generation represents, perhaps, the greatest challenge for the future stability of the regime.

Economically, the revolution reached a critical juncture. The collapse of the Soviet Union and the communist governments of Eastern Europe, persistent structural problems within the economy, low prices for Cuba's export products, and Cuba's inability to obtain greater levels of foreign aid forced the government to reexamine basic economic goals. The deepening economic crisis produced a frenzy of planning activity and greater militarization in the hope of stimulating productivity and of muddling through a difficult period.

The Cuban government failed to demonstrate any significant resolve to embark on a path of real market reforms and instead revived old strategies that have failed to generate real economic growth and new ones that are creating profound contradictions in society. Castro called for Cubans to work harder, sacrifice more, and expect less in the years ahead. At the same time he continued strategies based on tourism, remittances from abroad, and foreign investments to help him survive the difficult times.

While critically important, remittances and tourism accentuated the differences in society between those with and those without dollars and deepened racial tensions, since most dollars are received by Cuba's white population. For the foreseeable future, the economic difficulties will continue and Cubans can expect more austerity, greater food and consumer-goods rationing, and, therefore, much harder times.

In foreign affairs, Castro moved closer to the Chinese, which provided limited aid and investments together with telecommunications technology, spare parts, and small weapons. Castro also renewed close relations with radical Middle Eastern countries and leaders, and with Venezuela's Chavez.

At the Fifth Party Congress in 1997, he reaffirmed his opposition to the United States and his unwillingness to relinquish power, even after thirty-eight years at the helm of this troubled island. In February 1999, he introduced the most severe legislation Cuba has ever experienced, condemning dissidents, journalists, and others who deviate from the party line to twenty to thirty years of prison.

This crackdown on Cuba's budding civil society has clear implications. Castro and the Cuban elite are concerned with the growth of independent organizations in the island and their future potential. But more important, it is an attempt to impose greater orthodoxy on the population and to guarantee a smooth succession to younger brother Raúl once Fidel disappears. In the past several years, and on repeated occasions, Fidel has alluded to his mortality and to the need for the revolution to continue and survive after his departure from this world.

The Fifth Party Congress in 1997 was significant not for what it did but for what it did not do. Once more, as he has done for the past four decades, Castro showed that in Cuba politics dictates economic decisions. Despite mounting economic problems, the party did not introduce any major reforms that would propel Cuba into the world market. Fearing that economic openings would lead to political openings, Castro emphasized: "We will do what is necessary, without renouncing our principles. We do not like capitalism, and we will not abandon our Socialist system."

Castro also reiterated his long-standing anti-American posture, accusing the United States of waging economic war against his government and calling for "military preparedness against imperialist hostility."

The final party document and Castro's long speech to the Congress showed a determination to stay the course. Aware of his advancing age, Castro tried to ensure that his revolutionary legacy of anti-Americanism, heightened nationalism and Marxism-Leninism would endure beyond his death. He showed determination and confidence that despite the collapse of communism in Eastern Europe and Cuba's difficulties, his hard line would be vindicated. Immediately following the Party Congress, Castro held a meeting in Havana of Communist groups and leaders from all over the world to reassert the supremacy of communist ideology and to plan for a "comeback when capitalism fails." "Neoliberalism and globalization create consumer societies like the U.S. throughout the world," he explained, "and this is not a model for anyone."

The Party Congress was also significant in other ways. It reasserted Raúl Castro's position as the undisputed heir to Fidel's dynasty. Both in the party's private meetings and in public, Fidel praised his brother and summoned the faithful to support him to ensure the continuity of the revolution.

Raúl's position as vice-president, head of the military, and second secretary of the party makes him the obvious replacement of Fidel, and it seems that the older brother wanted to make it absolutely clear to the party cadres and the population at large that the younger brother, as his anointed heir, should be supported and obeyed and that his leadership would be best for the future of Cuba.

To reinforce his power, Raúl promoted an old guard Communist, Raúl Valdés Vivó, as the new party ideologue in charge of education. Valdés Vivó was a former leader of the old pro-Soviet Partido Socialista Popular (PSP), Cuba's Communist party before the Castro revolution, and Raúl Castro's political "godfather." It was Valdés Vivó who brought Raúl into the Juventud Socialista, the youth branch of the PSP in the late 1940s, and introduced him to communist ideology.

In a speech closing the Party Congress, Raúl Castro also announced that the party would reduce from 225 to 150 the members of the Central Committee and from twenty-six to twenty-four the members of the Political Bureau. Several of the new members were from the military, clearly showing the growing trend toward the militarization of society.

Of the three institutional pillars of most Communist regimes, the party, the military, and the security apparatus, in Cuba the party seems the least important. First, there is Castro's dislike for institutions. His style of leadership is personal, Stalinist, and *caudillista,* and he views institutions as instruments to carry "his" policies rather than as policy-making bodies. He has never been a strong vocal advocate of the party.

Second, the Communist Party (the old PSP) played a small role in the revolutionary victory and was victimized by Castro in the early years of the revolution. Castro, unlike European communist leaders, did not rise to power through the party ranks or owe his successes to the party machinery. Even as the new Communist Party of Cuba was organized in 1965, it was a Castro creation, an attempt to legitimize an already existing Communist regime.

Third, since 1965 the relevance of the party has been limited. While major decisions in Cuba are discussed and made at the Party Politburo, it is Castro, and to a lesser extent his brother, who dominates this small body. Party Congresses have always been held at irregular intervals and then only to discuss and ratify pre-approved policies.

Finally, the military, which preceded the party in its organization and development, is now not only independent from the party but superior to it. Neither military personnel policy nor military doctrine and internal control is handled by the party. Increasingly, military figures have taken key positions not only in the Politburo but in other key party positions. The militarization of the party is consistent with the militarization of society and the economy.

The Cuban military is unquestionably the most important institution in contemporary Cuba. It has achieved significant professionalism, legitimacy, and respect. First, the FAR (Fuerzas Armadas Revolucionarias) are the heir to the Ejercito Rebelde or Rebel Army that fought a guerrilla campaign against the Batista dictatorship in the late 1950s. They emerged in 1959 as a nationalist force and only later became an internationalist military supportive of Soviet policies throughout the world. Yet even in this latter capacity, Castro attempted to maintain a semblance of independence from Moscow as evidenced, for example, when he established conditions for the Cuban military withdrawal from Angola and when Cuban officers shared with Moscow and Washington military the negotiating table that led to a peace accord in Africa.

Second, there seems to have developed among the Cuban population a significant degree of respect for the military. It is seen as the defender of the nation and of Cuba's national sovereignty. It has refrained from involvement in repression and abuses, thus escaping the stigma of the old Batista military. Finally, military sacrifices on foreign soil, particularly in Africa, are admired by various sectors of the population. This admiration, however, has begun to wane with the passage of time and with the questioning of the direct benefits it produced for Cuba.

The military today is a professional, highly technical, disciplined, and loyal force. Aside from the old "historico"-type military leaders, there is a new breed of well-trained and educated generals that have been promoted after 1959. Most of these officers belong to the inner circle of Raúl Castro. They have been nurtured and promoted by Raúl and seem fiercely loyal to their military boss. There is a camaraderie that seems to have developed around Raúl with various circles of friends, some closer, others one layer away. It seems clear to these officers that closeness to Raúl not only provides an avenue for upward mobility in the ranks but also for protection from intrigue from other officers.

The largest group is made up of generals and colonels who were not members of the Rebel Army because they were too young in the 1950s. They came from urban lower-middle-class or working-class families.* Their average age is mid-fifties. The bulk of these officers are from provinces other than Havana with most from Cuba's eastern provinces. The majority had no previous connections to existing political parties and movements; their affiliations and loyalties are associated with developments after 1959. There is a significant growth of blacks and mulattoes among the generals and colonels recently promoted.**

---

* They include Alvaro López Miera, José Legró, Orlando Almaguel, Silvano Colás, Rolando Alfonso Borges, Leonardo Ramón Andollo, Eladio J. Fernández Cívico, Arnaldo Tamayo, Orlando Carlos, Roberto Milian, and Alejandro Ronda.

** Examples include Harry Villegas, Silvano Colás, Jose Legró, Humberto Omar Francis, and Arnaldo Tamayo.

The average general has had several combat experiences on foreign soil together with numerous graduate and post-graduate courses in the best Soviet (Voroshilov, Frunze, and others) and Cuban academies (Curso Basico, Superior de Guerra, Máximo Gómez), as well as field experience in Vietnam, Angola, and the Middle East.

There is a growth of highly professional technocrats associated with technological development; business, financial, and industrial administration; engineering; and logistics within the ranks of the general staff and moving from there to key civilian positions.*

The areas that are currently under the jurisdiction of the military include the tourist enterprise *Gaviota, Military Industries, State Reserves, Banca Metropolitana, Tecnotec,* and others. In addition, key positions in fisheries, sugar, merchant marine and ports, transport, telecommunications, and civil aeronautics are in the hands of highly qualified technocrats emerging from the FAR. Most of these technocrats come from rearguard services/logistics of the army, air force, and navy, and especially from the air force and navy because of their expertise in the fields of complex technology, computer systems, international standards, and other specialized requirements.

This military leadership seems loyal to Fidel and his brother. They apparently share and evidently follow the leader's views and commands. Either because of fear for their own safety, concern about a future without Castro, or shared ideology and power, they have generally remained loyal.

The possibility of factionalism in the military is also diminished by the constant rotation of officers, which prevents the creation of personal loyalties within the services, and by tight supervision and control, both through electronic surveillance and through the party and counter-intelligence units within the military. Fear and distrust characterize the higher echelons of the military. Trusting no one, it is difficult for a disgruntled military leader to share his unhappiness with others or to plan actions against Fidel. Even if able to obtain the support of a few colleagues, it is impossible for unhappy officers to secure the support of a large number of military personnel whose loyalties and beliefs are unknown. Successful rebellion within the armed forces is, therefore, unlikely.

Only in a situation of massive disturbances and popular upheaval

---

* Such as Leonardo Andollo, Jose Legró, Orlando Almaguel, Silvano Colás, and Eladio Fernández Cívico.

in which the security apparatus is unable to establish order will the military be called in to repress the population. Under this scenario, it is likely that factionalism, desertions, and unrest would occur within the military, hastening the collapse of the Castro regime. Until now, the Castro brothers have refrained from using the military to deal with popular discontent, perhaps aware of the potential dangers involved.

Unlike those of Eastern Europe, Cuba's security apparatus is monolithic and highly centralized. Castro learned well the lesson of Rumania, where forces from the Ministry of the Interior and the military fought each other. He eliminated possible rivals within his military and security forces and placed the Ministry of the Interior under the control of the military, headed by an officer he and Raúl trusted.

Among the Cuban people, there is a strong belief about the efficacy of the security services and an overwhelming fear of their repressive capabilities. Castro has dealt harshly with real and potential enemies; he has infiltrated and destroyed opposition groups, has imprisoned and intimidated dissidents and anyone suspected of anti-Castro activities, and has prevented the development of any civilian group that threatens his authority. Recently, opponents of the regime have been given the choice of long imprisonment or exile.

Developing a civil society in a country jealously dominated by a political elite and a leader who has resisted change for four decades is not easy. Cuba has a vigilant security apparatus and a leader who sees the development of a civil society as a major challenge to his absolute control of power on the island. Whether the limited gains made by a civil society independent of the Castro brothers in the past few years is the result of the collapse of the Cuban economy, the growing unhappiness with the Castro regime, the influence of outside forces, or a deliberate relaxation of the system of control is difficult to tell. Perhaps it is a combination of all of these. Yet civil society in Cuba remains weak, not very effective, and watched carefully and constantly by the Castro regime.

In the past decade the Catholic Church has regained limited influence. The pope's visit in 1998 and his message *"no tengas miedo"* (do not fear) emboldened some and provided hope to others that the Castro regime would tolerate a broader opening for the church as well as for other groups. The honeymoon was short-lived. Although Castro declared Christmas an official holiday, he did not allow a significant increase of priests in the island, refused the church access to the government-controlled media, and continued the prohibition of religious education.

Under these circumstances the church remains a weak adversary for the regime. The need to preserve its limited gains in a very difficult environment and to concentrate on religious rather than political matters weakens the church as a major force for change now or during a transition.

Other religious denominations have fared no better. Protestant groups have proliferated throughout the island, but they still remain splintered and devoted primarily to evangelical preachings. Probably the Afro-Cuban religious groups, the largest religious communities, command significant popular allegiance. Yet their message and structure, organized into small independent groups, do not represent a potential threat to the regime.

Non-religious non-governmental organizations (NGOs) have proliferated in the past few years. Most of these are government controlled or are infiltrated by the security apparatus. They were created or encouraged by the Cuban Communist party. These GONGOS (governmental NGOs), as they are referred to in Cuba, were created for two main purposes. First, to obtain assistance from legitimate NGOs in Western Europe, Canada, and even the United States, and second, to project an image that the regime was allowing an opening to the world and that Cuban society was becoming more tolerant of dissent and opposition. Castro succeeded on both counts. Many in the United States and throughout the world incorrectly saw this as an indication of a more mellow, less repressive regime in the island and increased support to these groups.

Human rights activists and organizations and independent journalists recently have received the brunt of government repression. Since the creation of Concilio Cubano in 1995, an umbrella organization of about one hundred small groups, activists have been harassed, jailed, or exiled. This ambitious attempt to consolidate all of these groups and present a united front against the regime represented a major challenge to Castro. He reacted violently, crushed the Concilio, and arrested its major leaders. To date, no other such organization has emerged.

This is not to say that there is no opposition in Cuba. Opposition manifests itself in low productivity in the workplace, disobedience of Communist laws, alienation from the party and from the constant demands of the leadership, graft and corruption, and an increasing desire to leave the island. Independent groups of journalists and professionals, as well as religious organizations, have emerged under very difficult circumstances. Many of their leaders have shown enormous courage in defying the regime. Yet, time and again, the security apparatus has infiltrated these groups and eventually discredited or destroyed them.

Fearing the system's repression and the dreaded possibility of long prison terms, Cubans seem resigned to await the end of the Castro era and the beginning of better times. Disillusionment and alienation characterize Cuban society. Resistance and open defiance carry too high a price, a price Cubans are unwilling to pay.

17

BEYOND CASTRO

THE views toward Castro's Cuba of many in the U.S. policy establishment have been influenced by a variety of erroneous assumptions. First and foremost, there is the strong belief that economic considerations could influence Castro's policy decisions and that an economically deteriorating situation would force the Cuban leader to move Cuba toward a market economy and eventually toward political reforms. This has not happened. Castro has introduced limited economic reforms in an attempt to muddle through a difficult situation. Yet the reforms are not structurally profound, nor are they propelling Cuba to the marketplace. In Cuba, economic decisions are influenced by political and ideological considerations.

The second assumption, among many in the United States, is that the embargo is the cause of Cuba's economic ills. This notion has been propagated continuously by the Castro regime in an attempt to force the United States to unilaterally lift U.S. sanctions. In reality the cause of Cuba's economic problems is not the embargo but a failed economic system. Like the Soviet and Eastern European Marxist economies, Cuba's system is antiquated, inefficient, and corrupt. It does not encourage productivity or individual initiative. If Cuba were to export and produce more, it could buy any products it needs from other countries. For Cuba the United States is the closest but not the cheapest market. What the Castro regime would like is

American tourists and credits to help scrape by without making major economic changes.

The third assumption is that leaders from other countries are very much like American leaders, except that they speak a different language. We assume that these leaders share our values and perceptions and that, therefore, they will behave as we do. We believe that we can negotiate with them most, if not all, of our mutual problems, that we can find common ground and work out differences. Nothing could be further from the truth. There are leaders, particularly in the developing world, who don't share Western values. They see the world very differently than we do. Perhaps the result of their educational, religious, or cultural background, perhaps the result of their own experiences, they think and act very differently. Iraq's Hussein, Libya's Qaddafi, and Cuba's Castro belong to this group. What characterizes these leaders is a self-righteous assurance that they know what's best for their countries and an unwillingness to compromise their views even to the extent of sacrificing their people in the pursuit of their ideas. They are anti-Western and particularly anti-American. They have a commitment to remain in power, since they believe that no other individual can carry out the anointed task of transforming and leading their countries. Compromise is seen as a short-term, sometimes forced, tactical move to achieve long-term strategic objectives. Negotiations with these leaders are usually of little value, and agreements of short duration.

America's long-held belief that, through negotiations and incentives, we can influence Castro's behavior has been weakened by Castro's unwillingness to provide major concessions to the United States or to other Western leaders. Castro prefers to sacrifice the economic well-being of his people rather than cave in to demands for a different Cuba, politically and economically. Neither economic incentives nor punishment have worked with Castro in the past. They are not likely to work in the future.

Which brings us to the obvious conclusion that not all differences and problems in international affairs can be solved through negotiations, or can be solved at all. This reality vitiates an assumption that has permeated American foreign policy for decades. There are international disputes that are not negotiable and can be resolved only through the use of force or through prolonged patience until the leadership disappears or situations change. While some differences naturally can be solved through negotiations, others are irreconcilable.

Yet the belief that Cuba's economic crisis will lead to major political changes continues to permeate American thinking about Cuba. We seem to cling to an outdated economic determinism in trying to understand events in other societies and the motivations of their leaders. Despite growing economic difficulties, Castro has not budged, and the Cubans have not rebelled and forced out the present leadership.

Optimistic appraisals of a rapid end to the Castro regime have been encouraged by the collapse of communism in Eastern Europe and the Soviet Union. For many observers, Cuba seemed the next domino to fall. Unlike Eastern Europe, however, Cuba is not dominated by a corrupt and weakening Communist party led by second- or third-generation leaders who lack real political legitimacy. Cuba is dominated by a strong military and by the original leader who made the revolution. Despite diminishing popularity, Castro retains a degree of legitimacy. Not unlike Tito in Yugoslavia, Franco in Spain, and Mao in China, Castro is the leader who overthrew the old order and established the new. He conquered power by force and will relinquish it only by force or in death. Once changes occurred in the Kremlin and the Soviet leadership refused to intervene in Europe as it had in the past, nationalistic forces surfaced to take political control and transformed their societies away from the communist system.

The possibility of regime continuity seems stronger for Cuba than it was for other communist states. Although their end came suddenly and swiftly, it took decades of decay to weaken critically the Eastern European regimes, and Soviet disengagement and acceptance were required to hasten their collapse. In Poland, where the trade union Solidarity was born in 1980 as the first non-government trade union in Communist history, a military-led government took control and remained in power for a decade. In China, the Communist regime obtained a new lease on life following Mao's death in 1976, initially through Deng's reforms and then ultimately through increased repression, particularly against student protesters. In Syria and North Korea children of the former leaders took and retained power.

In Latin America, many non-Communist authoritarian regimes held out for decades despite external pressures and internal weakness—among them, Trujillo's regime in the Dominican Republic, Somoza's dynasty in Nicaragua, Pinochet's dictatorship in Chile, and the Institutional Revolutionary Party (PRI) in Mexico. The last case is particularly instructive. Despite profound financial and economic crises and the erosion of popular support for the official party, the PRI-based regimes remained sufficiently strong to stay in power for seventy years until recently, while radically altering Mexico's economic course.

The Castro regime is bound to draw lessons from the negative experiences of Eastern Europe and the electoral defeat of the Sandinistas in Nicaragua and to incorporate the lessons offered by the Chinese and Mexican experiences, particularly the Chinese. In recent years the higher echelon of Cuba's military visited China and Chinese officials reciprocated with numerous visits to Cuba. While these experiences are interesting and instructive, it is doubtful that Castro needs any foreign examples to influence his predilections on how to govern or to reinforce his dislike for democracy and the electoral process. He has done pretty well in maintaining his totalitarian control since 1959.

For the regime, the problem of succession is crucial. No totalitarian regime has been able to devise a smooth system of transition, and Castro's disappearance could touch off an internal power struggle. Most likely, however, this power struggle would take place within the revolutionary ranks rather than outside them. Despite Castro's overwhelming presence, it seems doubtful that the revolution would collapse were he to die or become incapacitated. The stability of the regime is based primarily on the strength of the armed forces, undoubtedly the most vital of the three "legs" on which the revolution stands. The other two, the party and the security apparatus, serve, under increased military supervision, to control, mobilize, socialize, and indoctrinate the population. The organization and strength of the bureaucracy that has grown up around these institutions seem to assure the continuity of the revolution. Thus, while Castro is unquestionably the motor that maintains the revolutionary momentum, with a replacement, the machinery might slow down but would still continue to work.

A revolt against Castro's rule in the absence of large-scale outside intervention seems highly unlikely, especially as long as the Cuban armed forces remain loyal to him and to their immediate commander in chief, Castro's brother, Raúl. The continued loyalty of the armed forces appears highly likely. Not only do they represent a Castro creation but they have also developed a large measure of professionalism, are thoroughly integrated into the political system, and enjoy an important and trusted role in the general management and control of society. While Fidel's harsh criticism and punishment of some of his officers stationed in Grenada, the prolonged Cuban presence in Angola, and the execution of General Ochoa and others caused some stress with the military, they have not led to increased instability within the Cuban government.

Yet the Castro era may be coming to an end, if for no other reason than biological realities. Fidel Castro is now seventy-five years old and seems to be deteriorating physically. During a speech in mid-2001 he collapsed. His brief fainting spell, shown on Cuban TV, produced significant anxiety within the island and increased speculation about succession.

Depiction of Cuba's immediate future without Fidel Castro is problematic because the conditions at the time and the cause of his demise are impossible to know. Will the succession be orderly, or will it be violent and accompanied by mass protests and civil disorder? The key question, however, about post-Castro Cuba is not who its new rulers will be or what they would like to accomplish. The key question is whether the institutionalization of the revolution, as we understand it now, will survive the transition from the totalitarian, paternalistic rule of Fidel Castro. And equally important, what can any emerging leadership hope to accomplish within the existing sociopolitical and economic context?

Other questions still remain to be answered: What options in foreign affairs are open to Cuba's leaders after Castro? How can they rectify Cuba's troubled domestic economy? What are the chances that the new rulers will be unable to exercise any major options at all? Will they fear upsetting the multilevel balance of interests upon which a new government will certainly depend?

The role of the United States may become critical. Can the U.S. government act quickly and decisively enough to take advantage of any opportunities that might arise? Will the leadership be constrained by domestic political considerations? Will increased U.S. involvement generate stronger nationalism? Will a violent transition, accompanied by mass migration, force the United States to exercise military options?

A possible, but not likely, scenario at this time could develop in which Castro may want to end his rule fighting the United States. An aging, sick leader facing a decaying and collapsing revolution and increased civil war and violence that threatens his power could decide to provoke Washington. A Cuban military attack on the Guantanamo Naval Base or on south Florida would force the United States to react militarily, leading to massive destruction in the island and, perhaps, a U.S. military occupation. This unlikely, and for many people unthinkable, *Götterdämmerung* scenario should be considered, given Castro's anti-Americanism, failing revolution, and historical mind-set. His earlier actions, such as his call upon the Soviets to launch a nuclear strike against the United States during the missile crisis in 1962, his continuous massive buildup of reinforced underground tunnels throughout the island, his development of a massive biotechnology industry—allegedly only for peaceful purposes—and his numerous appeals to "Socialism or death" should give us serious concerns. In a speech, Castro called for the Cuban island to sink into the ocean before surrendering to U.S. imperialism.

At this time the succession line in Cuba seems clear. If Fidel were to die or become incapacitated, Raúl Castro would succeed as ruler of Cuba. Most likely Raúl would allow for a collective leadership with himself remaining in command of the military and the party and for a civilian as President of Cuba. The three most likely civilians are Ricardo Alarcón, President of the Popular Assembly, Carlos Lage, Vice-President in charge of the economy or Marcos Portal, Minister of industries and Raúl's sister's son-in-law. Yet the certainty that the younger brother will outlive the older could be a dangerous assumption. Raúl is also in frail health and he may die or become incapacitated before his older brother.

But assuming that Raúl survives Fidel and takes power, he would face significant challenges. A bankrupt economy, popular unhappiness, the need to maintain order and discipline in the population at large, as well as to increase productivity within the labor force, are some of the more pressing problems. Raúl would continue to be critically dependent on the military. Lacking the charisma and legitimacy of his brother, he would also need the support of key party leaders and technocrats within the government bureaucracy. He thus would likely create a framework for collective leadership controlled by the military. It is probable that, after a period of consolidation and harsh repressive rule, this collective leadership would initiate limited economic reform.

Perhaps the critical challenge for a Raúl Castro regime would be to balance the need to improve the economy and satisfy the needs of the population with maintaining continuous political control. Too rapid economic reforms may lead to a loosening of political control, a fact feared by Raúl, the military, and other allies bent on remaining in power. Some overtures to the United States also seem possible after a period of time, especially if no major opposition develops within the island. While maintaining an anti-U.S. posture, a consolidated Raúl regime may welcome American tourists and limited U.S. trade and investments.

Under this slow and most likely succession scenario, limited political and economic changes would take place. While a significant number of U.S. citizens would visit Cuba if the U.S. travel ban were to be lifted, investment would be on a small scale. If the U.S. embargo were modified or lifted, trade would develop as U.S. companies attempt to penetrate the Cuban market and stake a claim, as some Canadian and European companies have done.

Given Cuba's need for all types of products and consumer goods, the potential for trade is significant. Yet demand alone is not sufficient. Cuba must have the ability to pay for foreign goods and services. These resources will come initially from tourist dollars spent on the island. Eventually, Cuba must sell its products, primarily sugar, tobacco, agriculture, seafood, and nickel in the U.S. market. Trade will flourish only with massive U.S. tourism in Cuba and large-scale U.S. purchases of Cuban products.

Investments would be limited, however, given the lack of an extensive internal market, the uncertainties surrounding the long-term risk to foreign investment, an uncertain political situation, and the opportunities provided by other markets in Latin America and elsewhere. Modest initial investments would be directed primarily to exploiting Cuba's tourist, mining, and natural-resource industries.

Unless major reforms were to take place, it is unlikely that the U.S. government or corporations will be willing to commit significant investment funds in Cuba. The U.S. government could provide limited financial aid but would not grant Cuba other benefits such as Caribbean Basin Initiative (CBI) or North American Free Trade Agreement (NAFTA) membership. Foreign investments would be limited in scope as U.S. firms wait for Cuban measures that would assure investors that the reforms taking place are irreversible and that they represent a major step toward a comprehensive transformation of the economy.

Under a faster and much less likely scenario, a government without either Fidel or Raúl might open up the economy and encourage private, domestic, and foreign investments, as well as provide political change and respect for human rights. Laws would be introduced protecting foreign investments; negotiations might begin either to compensate or return to their original U.S. and Cuban owners companies and properties confiscated by the Castro regime in the 1960s; Cuban exiles would be welcomed to visit, invest in, and trade with Cuba. The U.S. government would lift the travel ban and end the embargo and would initiate foreign-aid programs to help the island's economic development. The United States might also lead a major international effort to encourage multilateral organizations, such as the World Bank and the Inter-American Development Bank, to provide quick financing for investment programs needed to begin the process of rebuilding Cuba's economy. The U.S. government itself could be a provider of credit to the Cuban government for the purchase of U.S. products. The United States, after a formal understanding is reached regarding repayment of Cuba's debt to Western creditors (approximately U.S. $10 billion), might allow Cuba to participate in the financing programs of the Export-Import Bank and the Commodity Credit Corporation. The U.S. might also provide investment insurance to U.S. investors through the Overseas Private Investment Corporation (OPIC). The United States could move to integrate Cuba into the CBI and grant other trade benefits, such as Most Favored Nation status. Cuba would likely also move up on the priority list for countries to be incorporated into the North American Free Trade Agreement.

Under this scenario the Cuban economy would improve rapidly. U.S. tourism and investments could jump-start the economy and release Cuban entrepreneurial creativity and talent, long suppressed by the Castro government. Cuba would export to the United States not only its traditional products—sugar, rum, tobacco, nickel—but also other exports such as vegetables, citrus, fish and seafood, and biotechnology.

Under either a fast or slow transition scenario, however, any post-Castro government will face significant challenges and problems. There will be the awesome task of economic reconstruction. Cuba's extreme dependence on Soviet bloc trade and the adaptation of its economy to an unnatural and immense subsidy inflow for nearly four decades created an artificial economy, which disappeared. Cuba does not have a viable economy of its own. As nearly every category of imports keeps decreasing, a vicious circle of poverty descends without mercy.

Cuba has a weak internal market. Consumption is limited by a strict and severe rationing system. Whatever transactions take place outside are in the illegal black market, which operates with dollars and merchandise stolen from state enterprises or received from abroad. The Cuban peso has depreciated considerably, and its purchasing power has decreased. Huge and persistent government deficits and the absence of virtually any stabilizing fiscal and monetary policies have accelerated the downward spiraling of the economy.

Production of sugar, Cuba's mainstay export, has dropped to levels comparable to those of the Great Depression era, and prices of other Cuban commodities continue their downward trend in international markets. While other countries have diversified their exports, Cuba has clung to sugar. With low prices, a decline in consumption worldwide, an increase in competitive producers, and widespread use of artificial sweeteners, sugar is a losing commodity with dire future prospects.

In addition to these vexing economic realities, there will be also a maze of legal problems posed by the issue of the legality of foreign investments and the validity of property rights acquired during the Castro era. Obviously, Cuban nationals, Cuban-Americans, and foreigners whose properties were confiscated during the early years of the revolution will want to reclaim them or will ask for fair compensation as soon as this becomes feasible. The United States and other countries whose citizens' assets were seized without compensation stand ready to support their nationals' claims. Cubans living abroad await the opportunity to exercise their legal claims before Cuban courts. The Eastern European and Nicaraguan examples are good indications of the complexities, delays, and uncertainties accompanying the reclamation process.

Cuba's severely damaged infrastructure is also in need of major rebuilding. The outdated electric grid cannot supply the meager needs of consumers and industry; transportation services are totally insufficient; communication facilities are obsolete; and sanitary and medical facilities have deteriorated so badly that contagious diseases of epidemic proportions constitute a real menace to the population.

In addition, environmental concerns such as pollution of bays and rivers are in need of immediate attention.

Economic and legal problems are not, however, the only challenges facing Cuba's future. One of the critical problems that a post-Castro Cuba will have to deal with is the continuous power of the military. In the past, Cuba had a strong tradition of militarism. During recent years the military, as an institution, has acquired unprecedented power. Under any conceivable scenario, the military will continue to be a key, decisive player. Not unlike Nicaragua, Cuba may develop a limited democratic system with Cubans able to elect civilian leaders but with the military exercising real power and remaining the final arbiter of the political process.

Any immediate significant reduction of the military may be difficult, if not impossible. A powerful and proud institution, the armed forces would see any attempt to undermine its authority as an unacceptable intrusion into its affairs and as a threat to its existence. Its control of key economic sectors under the Castro regime will make it more difficult in the future to dislodge it from these activities and to limit its role to a strictly military one. Reducing the size of the armed forces will be problematic as the economy may not be able to absorb the unemployed members of the military or the government may not be able to retrain them fast enough to occupy civilian positions.

The role of the military will also be determined in part by social conflicts that may emerge in a post-Castro period. For the first half century of the Cuban republic, political violence was an important factor in society. A belief developed in the legitimacy of violence to effect political changes. This violence will probably reemerge with a vengeance in the future. The Castro communist rule has engendered profound hatred and resentments. Political vendettas will be rampant; differences over how to restructure society will be profound; factionalism in society and in the political process will be common. It will be difficult to create mass political parties as numerous leaders and groups vie for power and develop ideas on how to organize society, what to do about the economy, what type of regime should be established, and how to unravel the legacy of decades of communist dictatorship.

A free and restless labor movement will complicate matters for any future government. During the Castro era the labor movement has remained docile and under continuous government control. Only one unified, Castro-controlled labor movement has been allowed. In a democratic Cuba, labor will not be a passive instrument of any government. Rival labor organizations will develop programs for labor vindication and demand better salaries and welfare for their members. A militant, vociferous, and difficult-to-manage labor movement will surely characterize post-Castro Cuba.

Similarly, the apparent harmonious race relations of the Castro era may collapse in a free society. There has been a gradual African-ization of the Cuban population over the past several decades. In part because of greater intermarriage and miscegenation, in part because of the out migration of a million mostly white Cubans, there is a greater proportion of blacks and mulattoes in Cuba. This has led to some fear and resentment among whites in the island. On the other hand, blacks feel that they have been left out of the political process, as whites still dominate the higher echelons of the Castro power structure. The dollarization of the economy has accentuated these differences with blacks receiving fewer dollars from abroad. The potential exists for significant racial tension, as these feelings and frustrations are aired in a democratic and free environment.

One of the most difficult problems that a post-Castro leadership will have to face is that of acceptance of, and obedience to, the law. Every day Cubans violate communist laws: they steal from state enterprises; they participate in the black market; they engage in all types of illegal activities, including widespread graft and corruption. They do this to survive. Eradication of those necessary vices from the past will not be easy in the future, especially since many of these pre-date the Castro era. Graft and corruption, as well as disobedience of laws, have been endemic in Cuba since colonial times. *"Obedezco pero no cumplo,"* "I will implement the laws but not obey them," is one of the most lasting and pervasive Spanish legacies to Cuba and the Latin American world.

The unwillingness of the Cubans to obey laws will be matched by their unwillingness to sacrifice and endure the difficult years that will follow the end of communism. A whole generation has grown up under the constant exhortations and pressures of the communist leadership to work hard and sacrifice more for society. The young are alienated from the political process and are eager for a better life. Many want to migrate to the United States. If the present rate of requests for visas at the U.S. consular office in Havana is any indication, more than two million Cubans want to move permanently to the United States. Under a U.S.-Cuban normalization of relations, Cubans will be free to visit the United States. Many will come as tourists and stay as illegal immigrants. Others will be claimed as legal immigrants by their relatives who are already naturalized citizens of the United States. A significant out migration from Cuba is certain, posing an added major problem for U.S. immigration authorities in particular and for U.S. policy in general at a time of increasing anti-immigration feelings and legislation in the United States.

While many Cubans will want to leave Cuba, few Cuban-Americans would abandon their life in the United States and return to the island, especially if Cuba experiences a slow and painful transition period. Although those exiles who are allowed to return will be welcomed initially as business partners and investors, they will be resented, especially as they become involved in domestic politics. Adjusting the views and values of the exile population to those of the island will be a difficult and lengthy process.

The future of Cuba is therefore clouded with problems and uncertainties. More than four decades of communism will surely leave profound scars on Cuban society. As in Eastern Europe and Nicaragua, reconstruction may be slow, painful, and not totally successful. Unlike these countries, Cuba has at least three unique advantages: proximity to, and a long tradition of close relations with, the United States; a major tourist attractiveness; and a large and wealthy exile population. These three factors could converge to transform Cuba's economy, but only if the future Cuban leadership creates the necessary conditions: an open, legally fair economy and an open, tolerant, and responsible political system. Unfortunately, life in Cuba is likely to remain difficult and improve slowly.

CHRONOLOGY 1492–2001

Colonial Period

1492	Christopher Columbus discovered and explored Cuba.
1508	Sebastián de Ocampo circumnavigated and explored the island.
1511	Diego Velázquez conquered the native peoples and established various settlements.
1519	Havana was relocated from its original site on the Gulf of Batabano to its present location on the north coast.
1523	Blacks were brought from Africa to work the mines and fields.
1538	Havana became the seat of government.
1538	Santiago de Cuba was formally selected as the capital of the island.
1555	French private Jacques de Sores captured and burnt part of Havana.
1595	Cattle raisers installed sugar mills on their lands and began sugar production.
1607	Havana was formally established as the capital of Cuba.
1628	Dutch pirate Piet Heyn captured the Spanish fleet off the north coast of Cuba.
1662	English navy captured and ransacked Santiago de Cuba.
1715	Political administration was centralized following the Bourbons' assumption of power in Spain. Bourbon reforms began to be introduced into Cuba.
1717	Veguero rebellion against Spanish tobacco monopoly.
1728	University of Havana founded.
1762	English forces captured and occupied Havana.
1763	Havana restored to Spain.
1764	The intendency system was introduced to improve efficiency.
1773	Real Colegio Seminario de San Carlos was founded.

1789	Cuba was divided into two ecclesiastical jurisdictions, one in Santiago and the other in Havana.
1790	First newspaper established.
1792	Sociedad Económica de Amigos del País was founded.
1808	Napoleon overthrew and captured the Spanish King, Ferdinand VII.
1809	Joaquín Infante organized the first independence conspiracy.
1812	José Aponte organized a conspiracy of slaves and free blacks.
1814	Ferdinand restored to the Spanish throne.
1817	England and Spain signed a treaty proclaiming the end of legal slave trade effective 1820.
1818	Spanish royal decree opened Cuban ports to free international trade.
1823	Rayos y Soles de Bolívar conspiracy was organized. The United States issued the Monroe Doctrine.
1828–30	Aguila Negra conspiracy was organized.
1830s	Spain imposed harsher authoritarian controls.
1837	Cuba's first railroad commenced operation linking Havana with Bejucal and Guines.
1844	La Escalera, a slave conspiracy, was suppressed.
1845	Spain ended the slave trade.
1850	The Ostend Manifesto calling for the purchase of Cuba was issued.
1848–51	Conspiracies, expeditions, and death of Narciso López.
1865	Spain created the Junta de Información.
1867	Spain disbanded the Junta de Información.
1868	Grito de Yara began the Ten Years' War.
1869	Guáimaro Constitution was drafted.
1873	Rebel boat Virginius was captured and fifty-two passengers, mostly Americans and Englishmen, were shot by Spanish authorities.
1878	Peace of Zanjón ended the Ten Years' War. Protest of Baraguá-General Antonio Maceo rejected the Peace and called for the abolition of slavery.
1879–80	La Guerra Chiquita took place.
1886	Spain abolished slavery.
1892	José Martí formed the Partido Revolucionario Cubano.
1895	Grito de Baire began the War of Independence. Martí killed on the battlefield. Jimaguayú Constitution drafted.
1896	Antonio Maceo killed on the battlefield in Havana.

1898   The U.S. battleship *Maine* blown up in Havana harbor.
Spanish-American War began.
United States occupied Cuba.

1899   In the Treaty of Paris, Spain relinquished Cuba.

1899–1902 The United States occupied Cuba militarily.
Tomas Estrada Palma was elected president under the new 1901 constitution.

1901   Cuban Constitution was drafted, incorporating the Platt Amendment, which gave the United States the right to intervene.

Republican Period

1902   The Republic was proclaimed and U.S. intervention ended.

1903   U.S.-Cuban Treaty signed whereby the United States obtained Guantanamo base.

1905   President Estrada Palma obtained a second term by defeating liberal candidate Jose Miguel Gomez.

1906   Guerrita de Agosto, a Liberal Party uprising, hastened U.S. intervention.

1906–09 Second U.S. intervention.

1908   Liberal candidate Jose Miguel Gomez won election to a four-year term.

1912   Short-lived racial uprising led by the Agrupación Independiente de Color.

1912   Conservative Mario G. Menocal was elected to a four-year term.

1917   Cuba declared war on Germany.

1917   Short-lived uprising in Oriente and Camagüey led by the Liberal Party.

1920   Collapse of the sugar boom.

1920   Liberal Alfredo Zayas won election to a four-year term.

1923   U.S. representative Enoch Crowder sent to Cuba to "reform" political process.

1924   Gerardo Machado elected to his first four-year presidential term.

1924   Short-lived revolt by the Association of Veterans and Patriots.

1925   Gerardo Machado assumed the presidency.
Cuban Communist party was founded.

1927   The anti-Machado Directorio Estudiantil Universitario was founded.

1929   Machado was "reelected" to a new six-year term.

1930   The U.S. Hawlley-Smoot Tariff Act reduced the Cuban share of the U.S. market.

1930   Mass student and popular demonstrations against the Machado regime occurred.

The clandestine ABC organization was established.

1931   Carlos Mendieta and former president Mario G. Menocal organized a short-lived uprising in Pinar del Río.

Carlos Hevia and Sergio Carbó's expedition from the U.S. was crushed by the Machado army.

1933   U.S. became involved in mediating between Machado and various groups seeking to overthrow his government.

Machado was ousted and Carlos Manuel de Céspedes became provisional president.

Revolt of the Sergeants led by Fulgencio Batista hastened the fall of Céspedes.

Dr. Ramón Grau San Martín became president of a revolutionary government.

1934   Batista overthrew Grau's regime and appointed Mendieta as provisional president.

Platt Amendment was abrogated. Partido Revolucionario Cubano (Auténtico) organized.

1935   A general strike forced the resignation of President Mendieta, who was replaced by Jose A. Barnet.

1936   Miguel Mariano Gómez "elected" president.

1936–?   Federico Laredo Brú became president.

1939   Grau San Martín elected president of the Constitutional Assembly.

1939   The Confederacion Nacional Obrera, created in 1925, is reorganized into the Confederacion de Trabajadores de Cuba (CTC).

1940   Constitution was drafted. Batista elected president for a four-year term.

1942   Cuba declared war on the Axis powers.

1944   Communists changed their party name to Partido Socialista Popular.

Dr. Ramón Grau San Martín elected president.

1947   Eduardo Chibás formed the Partido del Pueblo Cubano (Ortodoxo).

Cayo Confite expedition against Dominican dictator Rafael L. Trujillo was thwarted by the Cuban government.

1948   Fidel Castro participated in the "Bogotazo" in Colombia.

Carlos Prío Socarrás elected president.

1951   Eduardo Chibás committed suicide.

1952   Batista seized power through a military coup.

1953   Resistance organized and led primarily by Auténticos and university students.

Castro launched the ill-fated Moncada attack.

1954   Batista "reelected" president for a four-year term.

1955   Attempt at political compromise organized by Sociedad de Amigos de la República failed.

1956   Montecristi conspiracy within the military squashed by Batista.
Auténticos attacked unsuccessfully the Goicuría army barracks.
Castro's Granma expedition landed in Oriente province.

1957   Members of the Directorio and the Auténticos attacked unsuccessfully the Presidential Palace.
Directorio leader José Antonio Echeverría killed by police.
Strike paralyzed almost all the western provinces of the island.
Castro consolidated his guerrilla operations in the Sierra Maestra.

1958   Castro-organized general strike collapsed.
Castro expanded guerrilla operations into Las Villas province.
Military offensive against the guerrillas failed.
U.S. gradually withdrew support for the Batista regime.
Rigged election produced the victory of Batista's candidate, Andrés Rivero Agüero.
Increased demoralization and corruption led to the gradual collapse of Cuba's armed forces.
Batista and his close associates escaped to the Dominican Republic.

Revolutionary Period

1959   Fidel Castro assumed command and began consolidation of power.
Castro visited Caracas, the United States, Canada, and Buenos Aires.
First Agrarian Reform Law promulgated.
Castro became prime minister and replaced Manuel Urrutia with his hand-picked candidate, Osvaldo Dorticós.
Major Camilo Cienfuegos died in a plane crash.
Major Huber Matos sentenced to twenty years in jail.

1960   Cuba and the Soviet Union signed a commercial treaty and reestablished diplomatic relations.
Major foreign businesses were confiscated by the government.
Transportation, banking, communications, and the media and educational systems were taken over by the government.
Central Planning Board (JUCEPLAN) created to plan and direct the economy.
The Committees for the Defense of the Revolution (CDR) were organized.
Castro issued the Declaration of Havana, claiming Cuba's right to export revolution and calling for Soviet support.
The Soviet government purchased Cuban sugar the United States had refused to buy.
Soviet bloc armaments began arriving in Cuba.

1961 The United States broke off diplomatic relations with Cuba.

Fidel Castro proclaimed the socialist character of the Cuban Revolution.

U.S.-sponsored Bay of Pigs invasion was defeated.

The United States declared an embargo on trade with Cuba.

The Cuban government proceeded to socialize the economy.

Castro declared himself to be a Marxist-Leninist.

1962 Cuba was expelled from the Organization of American States. Castro issued the Second Declaration of Havana, calling for continued revolution at home and abroad.

Castro formed the Integrated Revolutionary Organizations (ORI), an amalgamation of revolutionary groups and the Communists.

The Cuban government introduced rationing of most items, including food.

The Cuban missile crisis brought the United States and the Soviet Union to the brink of nuclear conflict.

1963 Castro visited the Soviet Union for the first time. Second Agrarian Reform Law was issued.

Support for revolutionary and terrorist groups, particularly in Venezuela, increased.

Cuba refused to sign the Nuclear Test Ban Treaty.

1964 Castro visited the Soviet Union, signed a long-term trade agreement providing for Cuban sugar deliveries for 1965–1970 of twenty-four million tons at a fixed price of U.S. $.06 per pound.

Marcos A. Rodríguez tried and executed.

Partido Socialista Popular leaders purged.

Castro announced that Cuba would produce ten million tons of sugar in 1970, signaling a return to dependence on one agricultural crop and the abandonment of plans for major industrialization.

Conference of Latin American Communist Parties held in Havana subscribed to the Soviet line.

1965 Cuba participated in the Consultative Meeting of Communist Parties held in Moscow.

Ernesto "Che" Guevara initiated a series of trips to Asia and Africa to promote anti-U.S. violence.

Three-year Soviet-Cuban trade agreement signed.

Fidel Castro assumed greater personal control over the economy.

Cuban Communist Party (PCC) created.

Cuba allowed for the exodus of tens of thousands of Cubans.

Castro rejected the Communist doctrine on "the leading role" of Communist parties in the revolutionary struggle and criticized bitterly Latin American Communist parties for not supporting guerrilla warfare.

1966 Cuba and China criticized each other, straining relations. Tricontinental Conference held in Havana, and the Organization for the Solidarity of the Peoples of Asia, Africa, and Latin America (OSPAAL) was founded to support anti-American revolutionary and terrorist groups.

Castro and delegates from most Latin American leftist groups formed the Latin American Solidarity Organization (LASO). The economic situation continued to deteriorate, and Castro proclaimed the supremacy of moral over material incentives.

1967   Castro admitted to Cuban-Soviet disagreement over Cuban support for guerrilla activities in Latin America.

First Latin American Solidarity Organization (LASO) conference held in Havana.

Flights resumed to take U.S. citizens out of Cuba after one-year suspension.

Che Guevara killed in Bolivia.

Castro sent weapons and provided training to the PLO and the National Front for the Liberation of South Yemen.

Cuba refused to sign the Nuclear Non-Proliferation Treaty.

Cuba published a book by French Marxist Regis Debray, *Revolution in the Revolution*, promoting guerrilla warfare in Latin America.

1968   The microfaction, nine pro-Soviet members of the Central Committee including Aníbal Escalante, were tried as "traitors to the revolution" and received jail terms.

All remaining private businesses except small agricultural plots were confiscated.

The University of Havana was placed under strict military discipline and control following student demonstrations.

Castro made a major address justifying the Soviet invasion of Czechoslovakia.

Castro supported and trained Colombian guerrillas.

1969   Castro committed Cuba to a long-range agricultural-development plan, thereby postponing the country's move to industrialization.

The United States and Cuba signed an agreement to return passengers aboard airliners hijacked to Cuba.

Cuba became the first nation to establish formal relations with the Vietcong (National Liberation Front).

Cuba participated in the Moscow-based World Conference of Communist Parties.

Soviet defense minister Marshall Andrei Grechko visited Cuba.

Soviet naval squadron visited the island for the first time.

1970   Castro announced the capture of leaders of exile group Alpha 66, which had landed in Cuba in April.

A "Mini Manual for Revolutionaries" was published in the official LASO publication *Tricontinenatal,* written by Brazilian urban terrorist Carlos Marighella. The manual gives precise instruction in terror tactics, kidnappings, etc.

Cuba's attempt to produce ten million tons of sugar failed, and the Labor Ministry reported that productivity among sugar workers was so low that the cost of the 1970 harvest was three times higher than its value on the world market.

Economic problems compelled Castro to replace several civilian ministers with military officers.

The possibility of a Soviet naval base in Cienfuegos led to a diplomatic exchange between the United States and the Soviets and a final statement by the latter that they were not building "military bases in Cuba . . . [nor] doing anything that would contradict the understanding reached between the governments of the U.S.S.R. and the U.S. in 1962."

Cuba faced economic crisis with declines in production in almost all sectors, and the Labor Ministry attributed the problems to "widespread passive resistance" by all workers.

Castro called for closer ties with the Soviet Union and acknowledged that forms of struggle other than Castroism were possible in Latin America.

A joint Inter-Governmental Soviet-Cuban Commission for Economic, Scientific, and Technological Cooperation was established, and Carlos Rafael Rodríguez was appointed chairman.

1971   Castro urged Cubans to work harder to increase low levels of productivity of Cuban economy.

Soviet Premier Alexei Kosygin visited Cuba.

Castro visited Salvador Allende in Chile.

Cuba and the Soviet Union signed a long-term economic and trade agreement.

1972   The Cuban government withdrew 600 million pesos from circulation (out of 3 billion total) to combat inflation.

Castro toured Africa, Eastern Europe, and the Soviet Union on official visits.

Cuba was formally admitted as the ninth member of COMECON, the Soviet bloc's economic alliance.

Castro signed a new long-term Soviet-Cuban economic agreement, whereby Cuba's large debt to the Soviets was deferred to 1986, after which time it would be repaid over the next twenty-five years at no interest.

Castro announced a major reorganization of administration strengthening the structural capacity of the government to manage major economic activities.

1973   The United States and Cuba signed an agreement on hijacking. Castro supported a pan–Latin American regional grouping that would exclude the U.S.

An experiment in local government, Poder Popular (People's Power), was begun in Matanzas province.

At a meeting of the Confederation of Cuban Labor (CTC), Castro announced the abandonment of moral incentives and the establishment of Soviet-type norms for the labor force in an attempt to increase productivity.

At the Conference of Non-Aligned Countries in Algiers, Castro praised the Soviets and attacked the theory of two imperialisms espoused by other non-aligned leaders.

1974   Soviet party leader Leonid Brezhnev visited Cuba on official mission.

Cuban-Argentine trade agreement of $1.2 billion signed—the largest between Cuba and any Latin American nation.

Cuba provided military support and personnel to Syria during the Yom Kippur War.

President Ford indicated U.S. support of the Organization of American States' move to improve relations between member nations and Cuba.

Castro created the America Department (DA) under the Communist Party. The DA became responsible for planning and coordinating Cuba's secret guerrilla and terrorist camps, networks for the covert movement of personnel and weapons from Cuba, and a propaganda apparatus.

Cuban Foreign Minister Raúl Roa García at United Nations declared there would be no normalized moves with the United States until the latter had lifted its economic blockade.

Cuba stepped up its training and support of Communist groups in Mozambique, Guinea-Bissau, and Angola.

1975   Cuban voter referendum on new constitution provided for National Assembly with five-year terms for those elected (by Cubans sixteen and older). Also involved, a thirty-one-member State Council with a president, a first vice-president, and five second vice-presidents.

The United States eased restrictions on exports to Cuba by foreign subsidiaries of American companies; direct trade remained embargoed.

The United States reported Cuban soldiers and advisers in Angola to support the Marxist group MPLA.

Castro presided over first Cuban Communist Party Congress, which approved Cuba's new Socialist constitution and five-year economic plan.

1976   Cuba announced it would not withdraw troops from Angola supporting the MPLA. U.S. secretary of state Henry Kissinger warned Cuba about its intervention in Angola.

Canadian prime minister Pierre Trudeau visited Cuba.

Cuba informed Sweden of its intention to withdraw half its troops from Angola by December 1976.

Castro accused the United States of sabotage in the crash of a Cuban passenger jet near Barbados.

Cuba's new socialist constitution was promulgated.

1977   COMECON announced decision to build a nuclear-power station in Cuba.

Week of Cuban solidarity with Nicaragua held in Havana.

Castro visited Africa and the Soviet Union and agreed with Brezhnev to continue support for national liberation movements.

Castro and Jamaican prime minister Michael Manley exchanged official visits to each other's countries.

President Jimmy Carter eased travel restrictions on U.S. citizens to Cuba, and "interest" sections of consular officials were set up in Washington and Havana.

Cuban military advisers and combat troops entered Ethiopia. All Cuban officials were expelled from Somalia as a reaction to Cuban presence in Ethiopia.

Castro reasserted Cuba's determination to help black African liberation movements, reaffirmed support for Puerto Rican independence, and claimed that Cuba's presence in Africa was non-negotiable with the United States. *Granma* article complained about Chinese attacks on the Cuban Revolution and Cuba's internationalist commitments in Africa.

1978   Cuba hosted the World Youth Festival.

Cuban radio hailed the ratification of the Panama Canal treaties.

Cuban troop strength in Ethiopia reported by the United States at 3,500 to 5,000.

Abu Iyad, a close aide to Yasser Arafat stated that hundred of Palestinians had been sent to Cuba's terrorist camps.

The United States accused Cuba of supporting invading rebels in Zaire.

Tomás Borge, leader of Frente Sandinista de Liberación Nacional (FSLN), arrived in Cuba and met with party leaders.

Castro attacked the foreign policies of the United States and China.

One hundred fifty Cuban-American political prisoners allowed to leave Cuba.

Central Planning Board President Humberto Pérez explained that Cuba had not reached a rate of economic growth allowing it to emerge from underdevelopment.

Castro developed closer ties with and sent military advisers to Iraq.

1979   Cuba supported Vietnam and condemned China's "military aggression."

The Soviet Union commenced a buildup and modernization of the Cuban military by providing the Castro government with its first submarine and two torpedo boats.

Cuba announced the release of several hundred political prisoners.

Cuba's America Department helped unify Sandinista factions fighting Somoza.

Castro provided personnel and weapons to anti-Somoza groups in Nicaragua.

National Assembly of People's Power met in Havana.

Castro called for higher discipline and working standards. He criticized public services, especially transportation.

Cuba and Jamaica signed economic, scientific, and technical cooperation agreements and continued to maintain close relations.

Cuban military, technical, and economic advisers arrived in Nicaragua following the overthrow of Somoza's government. Close relations and collaboration developed between the two countries.

Cuba's Movement for Peace and Sovereignty of Peoples (MPSP) appealed for solidarity with the people of El Salvador in their struggles.

Cuba's America Department operated a weapons pipeline to the Farabundo Martí National Front (FMLN), a terrorist group attempting to gain power in El Salvador.

The United States charged that a Soviet combat brigade was stationed in Cuba; Castro denied it.

The Sixth Nonaligned Summit Meeting was held in Havana. Grenada admitted that it received arms from Cuba but only for defensive purposes. The two countries signed a two-year technical and economic cooperation agreement.

1980   Castro shuffled Cuban cabinet, assumed personal control over Ministries of Defense, Interior, Public Health, and Culture.

Ten thousand Cuban refugees entered the Peruvian Embassy in Havana seeking asylum and starting a mass exodus of Cubans to Peru and the United States.

Cuba and Nicaragua signed an economic, scientific, and technical agreement and established a joint intergovernmental commission to set the standards of relations in those fields.

Angolan President José Eduardo Dos Santos visited Cuba and signed an agreement establishing bilateral exchanges between Cuba and Angola.

Cuban MIGs attacked and sunk the Bahamian patrol boat *Flamingo*. The Cuban government apologized, saying "it sincerely regretted the incident."

The M-19 guerrilla group that held diplomats hostage in the Dominican Republic's embassy in Colombia for sixty-one days arrived in Cuba with eleven hostages. Hostages were released while the guerrillas remained in the island.

Daniel Ortega, member of the Nicaraguan governing junta, and Grenadian prime minister Maurice Bishop addressed the May Day rally in Havana. Cuba and the USSR signed an agreement for the building of a nuclear research center in Cuba.

Fidel Castro and a large delegation attended the first-anniversary celebrations of the Sandinista victory in Nicaragua.

Cuba and the USSR signed a bilateral economic-cooperation agreement for 1981–1985. Trade would increase by 50 percent and would average over U.S. $8 billion per year.

Raúl Castro announced the creation of territorial militias.

President Carter accused Cuba of aiding the supply of arms and insurgents to leftist groups trying to overthrow the government of El Salvador.

The Cuban Institute for Friendship with the Peoples (ICAP) organized a drive of solidarity with Puerto Rico to help Puerto Rican people gain their full sovereignty and independence.

During Mexican president José López Portillo's visit to Cuba, the two countries signed a joint communiqué that included a call for ending the economic blockade against the Cuban people and the cessation of violations of Cuban air space. The Mexican president condemned the cold war and the arms buildup, noting that nothing could be achieved without détente.

Addressing the Second Cuban Communist Party Congress, Fidel Castro admitted failing to reach the goal of 6 percent economic growth set by the First Congress during 1976–1980.

1981   Eleven new "alternate" members of the Politburo were named. Five of them, Humberto Pérez, Vilma Espín, Roberto Viega, José Ramírez Cruz, and Armando Acosta would represent "mass organizations" in order to facilitate grassroots relations. The other six members were all army leaders.

The government organized militias of territorial troops on a regional basis (Milicias de Tropas Territoriales—MTT). Many militiamen were veterans of Angola and Ethiopia. Militias would fight sabotage from exile groups.

Foreign Minister Isidoro Malmierca flew to Guyana on official visit.

Malmierca affirmed Guyana's territorial integrity in dispute with Venezuela.

Nominee for U.S. secretary of state Alexander Haig rejected notion of improved relations with Cuba during confirmation hearings.

U.S. FBI arrested seven anti-Castro Cuban exiles in Florida Keys. Exiles were linked to Alpha 66.

U.S. State Department failed to convince Castro to accept the return of 2,000 undesirables from 1980 Mariel boatlift.

Trade agreements signed with Guyana included increased technical assistance.

Government reported slight increase in rate of infant mortality from 1.93 percent in 1979 to 1.96 percent in 1980.

The United States reported that $532 million had been spent on entry and resettlement of 125,000 Cuban and 12,400 Haitian refugees who emigrated to the United States in 1980.

The United States expelled First Secretary of Cuban Interest Section, Ricardo Escortín, for illegal business deals with U.S. businessmen and for alleged intelligence activities.

Group of Cubans seized Ecuadorian embassy in Havana, holding Ecuadorian envoys hostage, demanding political asylum.

Valdilev M. Vasev, Minister Counselor of the Soviet Embassy in Washington, D.C., denied that the Soviet Union had supplied arms to Salvadorean rebels but said Soviets were shipping arms to Cuba without restrictions on their shipment to third countries.

Cuban security forces entered Ecuadorean embassy and arrested would-be Cuban emigrants.

Castro gave speech to Soviet Communist Party Congress, stating that the United States threatened a blockade and denying that Cuba was instigating the Salvadorean rebellion.

Castro met with Leonid Brezhnev. The Soviet leader assured Castro of Soviets' continued support.

Colombia broke off diplomatic relations with Cuba over Cuban links to Colombian guerrilla insurgency.

Alpha 66 reported thirty sabotage missions accomplished in six months inside Cuba, including attack at Regla power plant.

Castro reaffirmed solidarity with Soviet Union in a speech marking the twentieth anniversary of Bay of Pigs.

Fidel Castro made overtures to Christian groups for revolutionary unity in country.

U.S. assistant secretary of state Croker linked solution of Southwest African problem with withdrawal of Cuban troops from Angola.

ANAP President José Ramírez launched campaign to aid small, private farmers, especially those belonging to independent cooperatives, in new agricultural policy.

Costa Rica broke off diplomatic relations with Cuba over human rights issues.

Soviet four-ship naval squadron left Cuba after monthlong visit and maneuvers in the Caribbean.

U.S. Department of State reported Cuban transfer of Soviet-made T-55 tanks to Nicaraguan Sandinista government.

Vice-President Raúl Castro was awarded the USSR Order of the October Revolution.

Aid pact with COMECON signed in Sophia. Plans made to improve sugar production by modernizing mills and transport system. Aid package worth about $1.2 billion over ten years.

Cuba's largest cement factory, christened Karl Marx Plant, completed after six years of construction.

Manuel Urrutia Lleo, first president of Revolutionary Cuba, who later became a Castro foe, died in New York City at age 79.

Castro voiced "profound suspicion" over the origin of crop blights and dengue fever that killed 113 Cubans and damaged harvests. He said the epidemics had possibly been introduced by the CIA.

Castro met with President López Portillo of Mexico on the Mexican island of Cozumel. Castro accepted that his presence at the Cancún North/South summit would jeopardize meetings in light of U.S. warnings to stay away.

National Census put Cuban population at 9,706,369; Havana at 1,924,000. More than 97 percent of registered voters in Cuba voted in municipal elections to elect 9,763 members.

Jamaica broke diplomatic relations with Cuba, citing lack of cooperation in the extradition of Jamaican criminals.

Félix Fidel Castro Díaz, Fidel Castro's only son, became director of Atomic Energy Commission.

Mexican government offered to act as "communicator" between Castro regime and U.S. government.

Fidel Castro was reelected President of the Council of State with his brother, Raúl Castro, as first vice-president. Other vice-presidents elected were Juan Almeida Bosque, Ramiro Valdés, Guillermo García, Carlos Rafael Rodríguez, and Blas Roca. Flavio Bravo replaced Roca as council chairman.

Humberto Pérez announced 1981 budget deficit of 785 million pesos, compared to 249 million pesos in 1980. He blamed falling commodity prices and dengue fever for shortfalls.

Government raised prices 10 to 30 percent on rationed goods and most catering services (restaurants, bars, etc.). Two ministers, including Minister of Interior Trade Serafín Rodríguez, were ousted after public outcry swelled over excessive increases in some areas.

Manuel Vila Sosa replaced Fernández as Internal Trade Minister.

1982   Trade deal signed with Libya after visit by delegation headed by State Committee for Economic Cooperation President Héctor Rodríguez Llampart.

Andrés Rodríguez Hernández, a stowaway aboard Miami jetliner, was first refugee to be deported to Cuba.

President Ronald Reagan named F. Clifton White to lead Radio Martí, a U.S. broadcasting initiative designed to counter anti-American broadcasts from Cuba.

President Reagan said that Secretary of State Alexander M. Haig met secretly with Cuban vice-president Carlos Rafael Rodríguez in Mexico in the fall of 1980. Haig discussed arms shipments from the Soviet Union to Cuba.

U.S. Justice Department lifted embargo on Cuban publications to U.S. subscribers in effect since mid-1981.

Foreign Minister Isidoro Malmierca visited Angola; Deputy Foreign Minister Oscar Oramas, General Abelardo Colomé, and Politburo member Jorge Risquet visited Ethiopia, Mozambique, Tanzania, and Zimbabwe.

Cuban government liberalized restrictions on foreign investment in Cuba in effort to revive tourist industry and gain foreign exchange.

Reagan Administration announced new restrictions on travel to Cuba, banning tourist and business travel after May 15. Only academic and family-unification exit visas would be granted.

Castro rejected Reagan Administration's appeal for breaking off relations with the Soviet Union in a speech to Association of Small Farmers (ANAP).

ANAP President José Ramírez said that small, private farmers and cooperatives produced 70 percent of country's tobacco, 67 percent of cocoa, 54 percent of coffee, 50 percent of vegetables, and 18 percent of sugarcane and owned 21 percent of beef and dairy cattle stock. Castro admitted that "free market" food policy of 1980 was a failure due to unscrupulous "middlemen."

Vice-President Carlos Rafael Rodríguez visited France. Cuban government cracked down on "capitalist activities" in free markets for food and clothing and made 200 arrests.

Vice-President Carlos Rafael Rodríguez addressed UN General Assembly and said Cuba had received "huge quantities of modern and sophisticated weapons" from the Soviet Union and allies.

Torrential rains and flooding caused extensive damage to Cuban property and agriculture.

Cuban government announced that 180,000 foreigners had visited Cuba in 1981, bringing in $80 million.

The United States expelled two Cuban envoys at Cuban mission to the UN after finding sophisticated telecommunications equipment in an Orlando, Florida, warehouse.

Former foreign minister Raúl Roa died.

Fidel Castro, in Bayamo, in address during Moncada celebrations commemorating the Cuban Revolution, blamed the "capitalist crisis" for Cuba's economic woes. He asked Cuban people to work harder and endure and said Cuban troops would not leave Angola until all South African troops were out of Namibia.

1983   Cuban officials met in Panama with economic ministers from several Western nations to renegotiate payments on $2.6 billion in foreign debt.

The United States reported that Cuba—with Soviet backing—has expanded its amphibious fleet. Cuba also completed building shelters for a fleet of about 225 Soviet-built MIG fighter bombers and plans to receive four more Foxtrot submarines from the Soviet Union.

Former Cuban agent turned federal informer revealed, at U.S. Senate hearings, that his work as a drug dealer for the Cuban government earned $7 million for the Castro regime. The federal informer also estimated that 3,000 Cuban agents entered the U.S. during the 1980 boatlift.

Cuba rejected charges that two diplomats in their UN delegation in New York City were guilty of spying. The U.S. government ordered the Cuban diplomats to leave the United States within forty-eight hours.

Cuban government charged that U.S. reconnaissance plane violated Cuban airspace in a "deliberate and cold provocation."

U.S. assistant secretary of state Thomas O. Enders met with the head of the Cuban Interest Section in Washington, Ramón Sánchez-Parodi, to request that Cuba take back thousands of Cubans (who came to the United States via the 1980 Mariel boatlift) because of their criminal conduct in Cuba.

U.S. Senate Foreign Relations Committee voted thirteen to four to authorize Radio Martí.

Cuban vice-president Carlos Rafael Rodríguez claimed that Cuba was willing to open "serious negotiations" on reestablishing normal relations with the United States, provided that the Reagan Administration take the first step.

Castro provided funds for the Macheteros, a Puerto Rican terrorist group that highjacked a Wells Fargo truck in Connecticut and stole $7.2 million.

Osvaldo Dorticós Torrado, former President of Cuba, committed suicide.

Cuba informed the United States that it was willing to discuss the return of some of the Cubans who came to the United States illegally in 1980, but only as part of overall negotiations on "normalizing of migration" between the two countries.

President Reagan emphasized that the Soviet Union had repeatedly violated the 1962 agreement that ended the missile crisis by continuing to ship "offensive weapons" into the American hemisphere.

Americas Watch, a human rights organization, claimed that at least 250 long-term political prisoners were confined in Cuban jails under "brutal conditions" and that up to 2,000 former prisoners were denied decent work.

The United States intervened in Grenada, overthrew the Coard communist regime, and expelled all Cuban advisors.

The United States tightened its economic embargo against Cuba by banning imports of semi-finished nickel products from the Soviet Union, which is a major buyer of Cuban nickel ore.

Cuba reached a tentative agreement with its creditors to reschedule $810 million in short- and medium-term commercial debt and nearly half of its $3.5 billion debt owed to Western governments and banks.

1984

President Reagan accused Cuban leaders of having betrayed the Cuban people and not telling them the truth about Cuban activities around the world. Reagan said there were as many as 10,000 political prisoners in Cuban jails. Reagan also charged that Cuba's economy failed to meet even elementary needs.

The United States Immigration and Justice Department officials decided that 100,000 of the Cubans who came to the United States in the 1980 Mariel boatlift were eligible for legal status and citizenship opportunities under the 1966 U.S. law on earlier Cuban migration.

Fidel Castro visited Western Europe for the first time.

Castro made an unscheduled stop in Spain en route home from Yuri Andropov's funeral in Moscow.

Angolan guerrillas reported that Cuban-led Angolan forces opened a major offensive against rebel strongholds along the southeast border.

South Africa labeled "unacceptable" Cuba's heavily conditioned offer to withdraw its 25,000 troops from Angola, dimming hopes for efforts to negotiate independence for Namibia.

Roberto Veiga Menéndez, an alternate member of the Cuban Communist Party politburo and secretary general of the Cuban Federation of Workers, said that the Cuban government had doubled the size of its militia forces to more than one million men and women.

Jorge Vals, a prominent Cuban poet and political dissident, was released after being imprisoned for more than twenty years.

Several dozen Mexicans received training in terrorism and guerrilla warfare in Sierra del Rosario, Pinar del Rio, in Western Cuba.

The Reverend Jesse Jackson arrived in Cuba for a two-day visit and in-airport meeting with Fidel Castro, said that the United States and Cuba "must give peace a chance." Castro said that he invited the Reverend Jackson as a "gesture of friendship to the people of the United States." The Reverend Jesse Jackson returned to the United States with twenty-six freed American and Cuban prisoners.

Cuban and U.S. officials started discussions in New York about immigration issues, including the possible return of 1,000 Cuban refugees from the 1980 Mariel boatlift.

Supreme Court reinstated Reagan Administration's curbs on tourist and business travel to Cuba.

Western commercial banks reportedly agreed to reschedule about $100 million of Cuba's debts for this year on easier terms than those of 1983.

Foreign Minister Wu Xuequian said that China and Cuba agreed to improve trade, cultural, and technological ties despite their differences on international matters.

Fidel Castro, in speech marking thirty-first anniversary of the Cuban Revolution, said he would welcome any steps to lessen bitter hostility between the United States and Cuba.

State Department sees no change in Cuban policy reflected in Fidel Castro's speech; rules out comprehensive talks for now, demanding Cuba first make fundamental foreign policy changes.

1985   Fidel Castro ordered austerity measures expected to sharply slow the country's economic growth and possibly cause more reliance on the Soviet Union. The measures were aimed at saving badly needed foreign exchange.

Twenty-three Cuban 1980 Mariel refugees were returned to Havana. These were the first of more than 2,700 unwanted Cubans who could be sent back by the United States as part of an agreement with Fidel Castro's government.

The Reagan Administration claimed that Fidel Castro's absence from Soviet leader Konstantin Chernenko's funeral was evidence of friction between Cuba and the Soviet Union over economic aid. The Reagan Administration also viewed the absence as one of Castro's periodic urges to show his independence from the Soviet Union.

Cuban leader Fidel Castro said Cuba's relationship with the Soviet Union had never been better and that his absence from the funeral of Konstantin Chernenko was not significant.

Cuba offered to withdraw one hundred of its military advisers from Nicaragua but vowed to return even more if the United States continued its "dirty war" against Nicaragua.

Ecuadorean President León Febres Cordero arrived in Cuba for an official visit and was welcomed by Fidel Castro. Talks centered on the Latin American debt problem and unrest in Central America.

Radio Martí, the U.S. Information Agency news service for Cuba, began broadcasts to Cuba.

Havana suspended all immigration proceedings between Cuba and the United States in response to the start of Radio Martí. Cuban-Americans will be prohibited from visiting Cuba.

Fidel Castro suggested the United States and other industrialized nations pay the Latin American $4,360 billion debt.

The Cuban government sought to improve relations with churches and synagogues and urged mutual cooperation.

Cuban Central Planning Board head Humberto Pérez González was replaced by Construction Minister José López Moreno in a continuing government shakeup that is expected to lead to a more prominent role for Fidel Castro's younger brother, Raúl.

Fidel Castro said Cuba was going nuclear. A four-unit nuclear plant was already being built, and two more are planned.

Fidel Castro urged Latin American nations to band together and simply refuse to pay their foreign debt.

Castro refinanced Cuba's $3.5 billion debt and promised to continue making payments on loans.

U.S. and Cuba officials agreed that relations between the two countries had reached one of the lowest points in years. A slight warming in the relationship halted abruptly when the United States inaugurated Radio Martí's broadcast service to Cuba, which was denounced by Fidel Castro as a U.S. attempt at subversion.

Cuba signed a pact rescheduling $90 million owed to foreign commercial banks.

President Reagan imposed immediate restrictions on entry of Cuban officials into the United States.

Soviet foreign minister Eduard A. Sheverdnadze arrived in Cuba for talks with Fidel Castro.

About 20,000 protesters denounced the United States, outside the U.S. Mission in Havana, after Cuba protested what it called spy flights by U.S. surveillance planes.

Four Cuban embassy employees in Madrid tried to kidnap former Cuban official Manuel Antonio Sánchez Pérez, who had asked for political asylum. The attempt was foiled by the intervention of thirty bystanders. Four employees, including the vice consul, were arrested.

Cuba reportedly planned to reduce its outlays for military and public security in 1986, after failing to meet production goals for leading exports in 1985.

President Reagan warned that the United States had a legal right to defend itself against five nations that he claimed were sponsoring terrorist "acts of war" against America: Iran, Libya, North Korea, Cuba, and Nicaragua.

1986   Fidel Castro opened the third congress of the Cuban Communist party with a harsh attack on bureaucracy and inefficiency and praised the economic growth of 7.8 percent per year during the previous five years.

Cuba's Communist party reshuffled its Politburo and promoted women to full membership for the first time.

Fidel Castro marked the twenty-fifth anniversary of Cuba's Bay of Pigs victory with an attack on President Reagan and pledged to fight laziness and corruption in Cuban society.

In an effort to reschedule its $3.5 billion foreign debt, Cuba began new talks with its Western creditors.

The United States and Cuba agreed to negotiate the revival of the 1984 immigration agreement that enabled the United States to deport several thousand Cubans who had histories of crime or mental illness who had arrived in the United States as part of the Mariel boatlift of 1980. Talks collapsed when the United States refused to recognize Cuba's right to broadcast over an AM frequency in the United States to match Voice of America's Radio Martí transmissions.

President Reagan ordered measures designed to tighten the U.S. economic embargo of Cuba and responded to Cuba's decision to suspend immigration agreement by making it more difficult for some Cubans to enter the United States.

Cuba allowed seventy political prisoners, many of whom had been in prison for more than twenty years, to leave the country and fly to Miami. The U.S. Immigration and Naturalization Service reports that most prisoners had been members of the Cuban armed forces under dictator Fulgencio Batista.

One hundred thousand Cubans rallied outside the former U.S. embassy in Havana protesting what the Cuban government said was the overflight of a U.S. espionage plane over Cuban territory. Millions of Cubans took part in military exercises aimed at preparing the population to defend the island against a surprise air attack.

The Third Party Congress was held.

1987   Fidel Castro halted two ventures into capitalism he instituted—farmers' markets and private home ownership—in the face of signs that some people were accumulating wealth through them.

Antagonism between Cuba and the United States was greater than at any time in the previous ten years.

Bitter conflict between the church and the state in Cuba eased considerably.

Rafael del Pino Diaz, deputy chief of staff of the Cuban Defense Ministry and former chief of the Cuban air force defected to the United States; he had knowledge of significant military and political information.

Cuba agreed to release 348 political prisoners following a request from the U.S. Catholic Church.

The Cuban government charged that U.S. diplomats in Havana have been spying and plotting to assassinate Fidel Castro.

The Cuban government, in a policy reversal, agreed to restore an immigration pact with the United States by which 2,600 Cubans whose criminal records make them ineligible for U.S. residence will be deported from the United States and up to 20,000 Cubans will be allowed to emigrate to the United States each year.

Outraged at the prospect of being deported, Cuban inmates took over federal detention centers in Oakdale, Louisiana, and Atlanta. After several days of negotiations, the uprising ended and hostages were released. A new process to decide whether the inmates should be sent to Cuba was established.

Cuba's economy shrunk 3.5 percent in 1987 after growing 7.2 percent per year between 1981 and 1985.

1988   Pat Robertson claimed that Soviet missiles were pointed at the United States from Cuba; both the White House and Fidel Castro denied it.

United Nations Human Rights Commission unanimously agreed to accept an unexpected invitation from Havana to investigate human rights in Cuba. Even though UN specialists encounter harsh penal systems in Cuban prisons, they found no evidence to support U.S. charges of torture and executions. The official United Nations investigation concluded that abuses have declined.

Cuban National Bank documents obtained by a human rights group indicated that the Soviet Union was reducing support for the Cuban economy.

U.S. officials said they expect between 12,000 and 15,000 Cubans to emigrate to the United States by the end of the year in the first major exodus from the island since 1980.

In an apparent effort to improve his international standing, Fidel Castro moved toward reconciliation with Cuban Christians and the country's small Jewish population.

In the first five months since the protest riots in two federal penitentiaries, the U.S. government released 1,153 Cuban detainees from jail. Fidel Castro indicated that Cuba will not emulate Mikhail Gorbachev's plan for political and economic reform in the Soviet Union.

Restrictions on importing and exporting books, films, phonograph records, and other informational material to and from Cuba were eliminated by a trade bill signed into law by President Reagan.

Radio Martí expanded its Family Bridge program, which enables listeners in the United States to convey messages to relatives in Cuba.

Mikhail Gorbachev cut short a visit to the United States and canceled a trip to Cuba to return to the Soviet Union after news of a devastating earthquake in Armenia.

1989   Fidel Castro played down his differences with the Soviet Union even as he reaffirmed his refusal to adopt Mikhail Gorbachev's program of economic liberalization to remedy critical economic problems.

Cuban National Bank data showed Soviet Union cut its trade with Cuba by 12 percent in 1988's first quarter; data, presented to Western government creditors in June, showed Cuba's output of goods and services fell 3.5 percent in 1987; trade figures gave clear indication of USSR's effort to trim its $5 billion-a-year subsidy of the Cuban economy.

Leaders of Cuba's two main human rights groups said there has been increased pressure and new tactics government of Fidel Castro was using against dissidents since United Nations team looked into abuses of human rights in mid-September.

Americas Watch, a human rights organization based in New York, issued a report saying Cuba has improved its prisons and permitted some dissident groups to form, but it continues to commit serious violations of human rights.

A Soviet official revealed that Soviet nuclear warheads were deployed in Cuba and could have been launched at American cities within hours during 1962 Cuban missile crisis.

The United Nations issued a report on the human rights situation in Cuba; suggested that while there had been big improvements in church-state relations and treatment of political prisoners, basic political liberties were still widely denied.

Soviet leader Mikhail Gorbachev began visit to Cuba with effusive welcome from Fidel Castro.

Soviet leader Mikhail Gorbachev, in Havana, called for end to all outside military aid to Latin America and signed friendship treaty condemning use of force as instrument of foreign policy.

General Arnaldo T. Ochoa Sanchez of Cuba was arrested on corruption charges; American officials said action suggests dissension at highest levels of Cuban military. Cuba's transportation minister, Diocles Torralba Gonzalez, a friend of Ochoa's, was earlier relieved of his duties; Ochoa was accused of being involved in illicit sales in Angola.

Cuban officials said senior Cuban military officers helped Medellin drug cartel of Colombia smuggle six tons of cocaine and marijuana into United States over past two and a half years.

General Arnaldo Ochoa Sanchez was shown on Cuban television making abject confession to drug trafficking and corruption and saying "I deserve to die."

Cuba's interior minister, General Jose Abrantes Fernandez, was replaced as top security officer following official charges that high military officers in Cuba were involved in drug trafficking; Abrantes was not singled out as a key defendant in government's case.

Cuba announced that firing squad executed four Cuban army officers convicted by court-martial of conspiring to ship tons of cocaine and marijuana to United States; they include General Arnaldo T. Ochoa Sanchez, a highly decorated war hero.

Fidel Castro portrayed Cuba as nation under siege by the United States at a speech in Camagüey, marking the thirty-sixth anniversary of start of Cuban Revolution.

Cuba's former interior minister, Jose Abrantes Fernandez, and three other former officials were charged with corruption.

Cuban Communist party banned circulation of Soviet Union journals *Moscow News* and *Sputnik,* holding they promote bourgeois democracy and American way of life.

Sudden changes in East Germany and the rest of Eastern Europe appeared to be deepening political isolation of Fidel Castro and creating more problems for ailing Cuban economy.

A Havana court sentenced three Cuban human rights advocates to prison after convicting them of giving false information to foreign jounalists.

Fidel Castro vowed that Cuba will not undergo the profound political and economic changes now sweeping the rest of the Soviet bloc.

1990   Cuba's Communist party announced plans for reforms in the country's political system but made it clear that it will not abandon the one-party Communist rule.

The press in the Soviet Union painted an unflattering portrait of Cuba as an impoverished police state still mimicking Brezhnev-era Communism.

In his first visit to Brazil in thirty years, Fidel Castro said that Cuba may turn more to Latin American markets to make up for the loss of trade with the Eastern European countries that disapprove of his policies.

Experts on Cuba believe that despite growing economic problems, Fidel Castro's popularity remained too high to allow the sort of political change overtaking Eastern Europe.

The Communist party newspaper claimed that Cuba has almost completely succeeded in jamming broadcasts to the island by Radio Martí.

The Cuban government refused to negotiate the departure of Cubans seeking refuge in foreign embassies in Havana straining relations between Cuba and its most important Western economic partners, Canada and Spain; asylum seekers surrendered in exchange for a promise that they will not be punished.

The government of Fidel Castro, anticipating the end of large-scale Soviet economic subsidies, prepared the nation for a type of wartime austerity and full-scale mobilization.

Cuba's Communist party moved to streamline its bloated bureaucracy, slashing national and provincial party posts by 50 percent.

In the first phase of a program that envisions thousands of urban dwellers working for twenty-one-day shifts in the countryside to increase food production, the Cuban government sent several hundred office workers to plant potatoes.

The Cuban government forged ahead with crash efforts to create world-class industries in tourism and biotechnology.

The Soviet Union's decision to cut aid to Cuba and work with the United states to solve regional conflicts left Cuba as one of the last standard bearers in the ideological war against what it perceives as U.S. imperialism.

The Castro regime announced a series of austerity measures—the "Special Period."

1991

In a move seen as a sign of Havana's growing isolation, Czechoslovakia decided it will no longer represent Cuba in Washington. Switzerland, which sponsors U.S. diplomats in Havana, offered to sponsor the Cuban Interests Section in Washington to ensure that both countries have diplomatic representation in each other's capital.

The deteriorating economic situation in Cuba prompted a large increase in the number of Cubans seeking to leave their country.

The Cuban government rejected an appeal by President Bush for political change and accused him of being obsessively anti-Cuban.

With increased religious tolerance, Bibles were put on sale in Cuba for the first time in three decades.

Fidel Castro received only token gestures of friendship for his beleaguered government during a meeting with fellow Latin American leaders in Guadalajara, Mexico.

Cuba announced the lifting of restrictions on travel abroad; people aged twenty or over will be allowed to leave and visit other countries, provided that the host nation gives them a visa.

Cuban inmates seized control of the medium-security section of a federal prison in Talladega, Alabama, to avoid deportation; after ten days, federal assault teams stormed the prison cellblock, freed several hostages, and took custody of 121 inmates.

In order to remove a major obstacle to increased U.S. economic aid to the Soviet Union, President Gorbachev declared he will remove Soviet troops from Cuba and end the $2 billion-a-year trade subsidy Moscow gives Havana.

For the first time in the thirty-two-year leadership of Fidel Castro, Cuba banned foreign delegations and journalists from the Congress of its ruling Communist party.

The Cuban Communist party unveiled an economic plan meant to boost hard-currency exports, tourism, and foreign investment.

The presidents of Mexico, Venezuela, and Colombia met with Fidel Castro in Cozumel, Mexico, urged him to quicken the pace of reform in his country, and offered him prospects of closer relations in return.

The Castro government unleashed a violent crackdown on political dissent.

The Fourth Party Congress was held.

1992   The Castro government stepped up efforts to crush internal opposition as growing numbers of citizens took desperate measures to flee a life of hardship.

Eduardo Diaz Betancourt, a Cuban exile convicted of sabotage and terrorism, was executed by a firing squad in Cuba.

In a rare exception to the economic blockade of Cuba, the Bush Administration granted permission to AT&T to expand telephone services between Cuba and the United States; Cuba rejected AT&T's proposal.

A growing number of U.S. companies, lured by the prospect of approaching change in Cuba as the island tries to ward off economic collapse, followed their foreign counterparts in showing interest in the island.

Cuban officials said that the thirty-year U.S. economic embargo against Cuba has cost the island more than $20 billion and was blocking Cuban efforts to renegotiate a $7 billion debt to U.S. allies.

Havana began a sophisticated campaign to court U.S. businessmen in the hope that their thirst for opportunities will bring them to lobby in Washington for a change in U.S. relations with Cuba.

Americas Watch, a human rights organization, claimed that anti-Castro Cuban-American leaders in Miami use violence and intimidation to quiet exiles who favor the softening of U.S. policies toward Cuba.

Russia and Cuba agreed to the withdrawal of a former Soviet infantry brigade that had been on the island since the Cuban missile crisis in 1962.

Cuba halted monthly gasoline rations for private vehicles admitting that the government lacks foreign currency to buy fuel.

Cuba and Russia signed trade accords for new ties based on mutual benefits; Cuba would trade sugar for Russian oil at world market prices.

The United Nations Assembly overwhelmingly approved a resolution calling for an end to the thirty-year U.S. trade embargo against Cuba.

1993   Cuban industry was reported to be all but paralyzed by shortages of oil, electricity, and spare parts.

Fidel Castro said he was willing to negotiate his departure from power in exchange for the lifting of the U.S. economic embargo against Cuba.

General Raúl Castro, Fidel's brother, said Cuba is reducing its armed forces as a result of not having received any weapons from the former Soviet Union since 1990.

Cuba offered to negotiate reparations for U.S. properties confiscated in the 1960s. Challenging the hegemony of the Cuban American National Foundation and other established groups, new voices calling for a more flexible attitude toward Fidel Castro's government emerged in Miami's Cuban-exile community.

The last remaining members of a Soviet military brigade that was sent to Cuba after the missile crisis of 1962 left the island.

Cuban officials said they would open their economy by permitting Cubans to hold dollars and foreigners to open joint-venture banks on the island.

In a meeting in Salvador, Brazil, leaders of Latin America, Spain, and Portugal called for an end to the U.S. trade embargo against Cuba.

Cuba took a step toward the establishment of a mixed economy authorizing limited individual private enterprises in a wide range of trades, crafts, and services.

The Clinton Administration, in secret talks with Fidel Castro, agreed to hand over to Havana some 1,500 Cuban inmates held in U.S. federal prisons, spreading waves of alarm among Cuban exiles in Miami; Cuba denied such an agreement.

As Cuba's economic and political crisis deepens, exiles in Miami reach out to their kin on the island as never before by sending aid, exchanging visits, and seeking their advice on how to ease Fidel Castro from power.

Of 900 Cuban athletes participating in the Central American and Caribbean Games in Puerto Rico, thirty-nine defected and twenty-seven formally applied for U.S. asylum.

1994   A granddaughter of Fidel Castro, sixteen-year-old Alina-Maria Salgado Fernandez, was allowed to leave Cuba and be reunited with her mother, Alina Fernandez Revuelta, who fled in December 1993.

Record number of Cuban refugees floated to Florida in 1993; the Coast Guard reported that the total amount, 3,656, was up 43 percent from the 1992 total.

A federal appeals court ruled that Cubans from the 1980 Mariel boatlift cannot be held indefinitely in federal prisons; Cuba sent off many prisoners and mental patients. U.S. authorities later revoked freedom of those who committed new crimes.

Cuba announced a series of measures aimed at encouraging more Cuban-Americans to visit and to attract foreign investment, hosted three-day conference in Havana that is first sizable meeting between Communist leadership and representatives of exile population in sixteen years.

Dozens of Cubans broke into Belgian ambassador's residence in Havana, demanding political asylum.

Brazil and Cuba agreed on a way for Cuba to start repaying part of nearly $40 million debt through export of Cuban medicine to Brazil.

Three Cuban gunboats trying to stop a freighter loaded with people trying to flee Cuba fired on the vessel for more than four hours sinking it; thirty people were killed.

Fidel Castro broke his thirty-five-year tradition of wearing military uniforms in public and wore civilian clothes at summit meeting in Cartagena, Colombia, of Latin American, Spanish, and Portuguese leaders; leaders, in an indirect slap at U.S. embargo of Cuba, called for elimination of "unilateral coercive economic and trade measures." Clinton Administration, responding to Fidel Castro's threat to unleash a flood of refugees on the United States, warned it would not permit a repeat of the 1980 Mariel boatlift, in which Cuba dropped emigration curbs and 120,000 Cubans fled to the United States.

Clinton Administration ended open-door policy toward Cuban refugees, who will be detained for an indefinite period after they arrive in United States, effective immediately.

The United States stopped refugees aboard rafts and boats off Florida coast and began detaining them at its Guantanamo Bay base, as President Clinton ended long-standing policy of welcoming fleeing Cubans.

President Clinton barred Americans from sending cash to Cuba and cut off flights to the island to intensify pressure on Castro regime and punish it for encouraging Cubans to set out in boats.

The United States moved to beef up patrol vessels in Florida straits as hundreds of Cubans set sail despite the Clinton Administration's efforts to stem exodus.

Clinton Administration, alarmed that its new policy failed to stem flow of Cuban refugees, considered expanding capacity of Guantanamo Bay naval base to handle them.

Secretary of State Warren Christopher said the administration would react positively if Fidel Castro took meaningful steps, such as allowing free elections; denies administration's policies are driven by domestic politics.

Once quiet U.S. naval base at Guantánamo Bay was crowded with thousands of Cuban and Haitian refugees, all uncomfortable and angry over failure to make it to the United States.

Cuba and the United States reached an agreement under which Cuba pledged to stop citizens from fleeing in small boats and the United States promised to accept at least 20,000 Cuban immigrants a year.

The flood of Cuban refugees ended as Cuban government implemented terms of agreement reached with the United States aimed at halting exodus.

Cuba took a step away from highly centralized Communist system that has defined its economy for more than three decades; it would for the first time allow all farmers to sell part of their produce on open market.

The Clinton Administration gave American telecommunications companies permission to establish direct telephone links with Cuba.

In an interview, Fidel Castro, who celebrated his thirty-sixth anniversary in power, admitted he has real reservations about the market-oriented reforms his government has undertaken to save the economy devastated by collapse of Soviet bloc but said he recognized that the world economy has changed.

Appointment of Jaime Cardinal Ortega y Alamino as Cuba's first Roman Catholic prelate in more than thirty years, and the passionate reaction of his flock, are seen as new signs of reinvigoration of the Catholic Church in Cuba.

1995   President Francois Mitterrand welcomed Fidel Castro to France for a three-day private stay that has hallmarks of a state visit.

Cuban officials and athletes at Pan American Games admit for the first time that nation's worsening economic crisis and political isolation severely erode sports programs.

The Clinton Administration ended thirty-five years of special treatment for Cuban refugees and started returning them to homeland after admitting final group of about 20,000 held at Guantanamo Bay Naval Station.

The Clinton Administration, which was signaling new cooperation with Cuba, opposed Republican bill to tighten thirty-three-year-old U.S. trade embargo.

The Cuban government, in an effort to make Cuba's sagging economy more efficient, abandoned one of most cherished concepts of Communist state—guarantee of full lifetime employment—and began layoffs.

Role and responsibilities of Cuban armed forces expanded rapidly while those of the Communist party sharply decline. The military, traditionally one of Fidel Castro's principal pillars of support, produced and distributed between a quarter and a third of country's food supply and set up highly profitable tourism, construction, and retailing companies of its own, and officers were put in charge of many state enterprises.

U.S. officials report Cuba has arrested fugitive financier Robert L. Vesco and approached the United States about extraditing him; Vesco fled the United States in 1973 to avoid prosecution for allegedly swindling mutual-fund investors out of $224 million.

Latin America increasingly ignored U.S. trade embargo on Cuba, choosing to develop full economic and diplomatic ties.

Cuba passed a new foreign-investment law, which allows foreign investors access to all economic sectors, except defense, health care, and education, and to fully own businesses in Cuba.

U.S. House voted 294 to 130 to tighten trade embargo against Cuba, despite Clinton Administration's veto threat.

President Clinton signed executive order to ease restrictions on travel to Cuba by Cuban-Americans, academics, artists, and clergymen.

Fidel Castro addressed UN General Assembly as part of the world body's fiftieth-anniversary celebration, revisited Harlem for the first time in thirty-five years.

The Cuban government permitted citizens to buy and sell foreign currencies on open market for the first time in more than thirty years in an attempt to challenge flourishing black market for American dollars and to soak up surplus pesos that have fueled inflation.

Fidel Castro visited China, whose leaders welcomed him warmly and pledged a small increase in economic aid.

The Cuban government restored the personal income tax in an effort to go after newly affluent Cubans who earn money in dollars and other foreign currencies.

1996   Canadian foreign minister Lloyd Axworthy briefly visited Cuba to sign human rights statement and foreign-investment declaration and met with Fidel Castro and aides.

The Clinton Administration's annual report on human rights in 193 countries concluded that despite U.S. efforts, human rights performance worsened last year in China, Nigeria, Cuba, and Myanmar.

The United States closed tent city on Guantanamo naval base, allowing remaining refugees to enter the United States.

The coalition of Cuban dissidents and human rights groups Concilio Cubano canceled plans to hold conference in Havana, citing crackdown by state security apparatus against organizers of event.

Two small unarmed aircraft belonging to Brothers to the Rescue, a Miami-based Cuban-exile group, were shot down by Cuban air force MIG jet fighters over international waters, killing four.

President Clinton denounced Cuba's downing of two private American planes as flagrant violation of international law, suspended air charter travel between countries, and pledged to reach an agreement with Congress on a pending bill to tighten economic sanctions.

President Clinton agreed to a package of sanctions, the Helms-Burton Act, to punish Fidel Castro by curbing foreign investment in Cuba.

The Communist Party of Cuba called for crackdown on dissent and on economic reforms.

U.S. Senate approved legislation, 74–22, to tighten embargo on American trade with Cuba and punish other countries that insist on continuing such trade; Canada, Russia, and the European Union condemned the measure.

The Organization of American States, at its annual meeting in Panama, approved a resolution criticizing U.S. extension of economic embargo of Cuba as a probable violation of international law.

Mexican president Ernesto Zedillo, visiting Canada, and Canadian prime minister Jean Chretien criticized U.S. effort to penalize foreign firms that trade with Cuba.

UN investigation concluded that Cuba's downing in February of two light civilian aircraft flown by Cuban-Americans occurred over international waters.

Leaders of fifteen European Union countries criticized U.S. legislation that would impose economic penalties on foreign companies that invest in Cuba, Iran, and Libya.

The Clinton Administration stroke for first time against foreign companies doing business in Cuba, informing top executives and biggest shareholders of Canada's Sherrit International Corp. that they and their families will be barred from the United States.

Fugitive U.S. financier Robert L. Vesco, who had been in Cuba for several years, was tried and sentenced to thirteen years in jail.

President Clinton granted Americans the right to sue foreign companies using American plants seized by Cuba more than thirty-five years ago but immediately suspended filing of suits for six months.

The Clinton Administration, unable to gain international support for strong action against Cuba over the downing in February of two civilian planes flown by Cuban-Americans, got United Nations Security Council backing for only a mild resolution of regret over the incident.

Cuba expelled American diplomat Robin Meyer for activities incompatible with diplomatic status.

Cuba rejected part of planeload of food aid for Hurricane Lili victims sent by Cuban-Americans because some of the packages carry "counter-revolutionary" slogans.

Fidel Castro attended annual Ibero-American Summit Conference in Santiago, Chile. Latin leaders end summit denouncing moves by U.S. to isolate Cuba, while pressing Fidel Castro to make democratic changes on the island.

John Paul II met with Fidel Castro for first time at the Vatican and accepted an invitation to visit Cuba in 1997.

The European Union urged Cuba to improve its policies on human rights and political freedoms, clearing the way for President Clinton to once again waive the most controversial part of new law intended to punish foreign companies that use confiscated American property in Cuba.

Cuba countered Helms-Burton Act, which toughened U.S. economic embargo on the country, by declaring invalid any claim made under the law and saying Americans seeking to make claims will be excluded from any possible settlement of the property issue by Cuba.

1997   President Clinton announced a suspension in the implementation of Title III of the Helms-Burton Act.

Canada's foreign minister, Lloyd Axworthy, on an official visit to Cuba, signed with his Cuban counterpart, Roberto Robaina, a joint declaration establishing fourteen areas of bilateral cooperation, including human rights, as part of Canada's policy of constructive engagement toward Cuba.

President Clinton made public his plan for a Cuba without Castro. Called "Support for a Democratic Transition in Cuba," it included a special appeal to the Cuban armed forces and an aid package of $4 to $8 billion.

The White House approved licenses for ten press organizations interested in establishing bureaus in Havana. The Cuban government approved only CNN.

In an official visit to Cuba, Peruvian President Alberto Fujimori signed an agreement of cooperation between the two countries. The Cuban government stated its willingness to mediate the hostage crisis and receive the MRTA group if Peru and Japan should ask it to do so.

The Italian group STET doubled its investments in Cuba when taking over Grupo Demo's telephone investment, while compensating AT&T to avoid Helms-Burton sanctions.

Human Rights Watch, Rapporteurs Sans Frontiers, and the Interamerican Press Association denounced persistent harassment against independent press in Cuba.

Foreign affairs ministers from the Non-Aligned Movement reiterated their demand to the United States to put an end to the embargo against Cuba.

ETA, a Spanish terrorist organization seeking a separate Basque homeland, established its Cuartel General (General Headquarters) in Havana.

Roberto Robaina's tour throughout Southeast Asia is reported as being very successful in terms of diplomatic recognition and cooperation agreements with Thailand, Singapore, Malaysia, Indonesia, and Brunei.

The president of the Spanish government, Jose M. Aznar, declared that Spain is against the Helms-Burton Act and advocated for a peaceful and democratic transition in Cuba.

Fidel Castro admitted publicly that the sugar harvest would not achieve its goal of 4.4 million tons. Instead it will be 4.2 million tons.

Percival Patterson, Jamaica's prime minister, paid an official visit to Cuba as part of an increased relationship between CARICOM countries and Cuba.

Bombs exploded in several hotels in Havana.

The United States made a public statement advising countries not to become involved in supporting the electro-nuclear project in Cuba (Juragua).

Decree 172 created the Banco Central de Cuba (Cuba's Central Bank).

The president of the Basque government paid an official visit to Cuba and met with Fidel Castro.

The Dominican Republic and Cuba restored consular relations.

Some dissident leaders challenged the official platform of the Fifth Congress of the Communist Party of Cuba and made public their own platform, "La Patria es de Todos."

The first public Mass since 1959 was held in Havana.

Four dissident leaders, the authors of "La Patria es de Todos," were arrested in Havana. They are Vladimiro Roca, Social Democrat Party; Felix Bonne Carcases, Cuban Civic Current; Raul Gomez Manzano, Independent Lawyers Agramonte's Current; and Marta Beatriz Roque, Independent Economists.

A new round of negotiations on immigration was held between the United States and Cuba.

Cuba celebrated the fourteenth World Youth & Students Festival with some 15,000 participants.

Cuba and Honduras agreed to establish interests sections as part of the normalization of bilateral relations.

The tourist industry was officially acknowledged as Cuba's number one industry.

Ministry of Interior announced the capture of a Salvadorian citizen responsible for the bombings and blamed the Cuban-American National Foundation.

The Fifth Party Congress took place in Havana. The Central Committee was reduced from 225 to 150 members; the Politburo from 26 to 24. Raúl Castro was ratified as successor to Fidel Castro.

Communists from Latin America met in Havana to plan a return to power "when capitalism fails."

Division General Alvaro Lopez Miera, fifty-three, was appointed new chief of the general staff, replacing General Ulises Rosales del Toro, who became minister of the sugar industry.

United Nations General Assembly voted against the U.S. embargo on Cuba by 143 votes against, 17 abstentions, and only 3 in favor, the largest majority ever achieved.

Fidel Castro received criticism and some support in Margarita's Ibero-American summit.

President Clinton declared that "an improvement of relations between his country and Cuba depends on the political changes that may be set in motion by the government of Fidel Castro."

Raúl Castro paid an official visit to China that lasted two weeks, stopping briefly in Italy on his return to Cuba.

German foreign affairs minister Helmut Schafter concluded a four-day official visit to Cuba with a meeting with Fidel Castro; both parties emphasized the need to further enhance bilateral relations.

Jorge Mas Canosa, chairman of the Cuban-American National Foundation, passed away.

The United States and Cuba held a new round of negotiations on immigration in Havana.

The Russian chief of the general staff, Anatoly Kvashnin, paid an official visit to Cuba with the purpose of signing agreements on bilateral cooperation, on the Lourdes station, and on Russian military supplies and spare parts, to help Cuba to maintain the combat readiness of its armed forces.

The official program for the pope's visit in January 1998 was announced in Havana, including a Holy Mass at José Martí Revolution Square. Castro allowed Christmas celebrations for the first time.

1998   Pope John Paul II visited Cuba.

President Clinton eased restrictions on travel to Cuba and on the export of medical supplies.

Raúl Castro assumed a greater role in the management and control of Cuban society.

Fidel Castro visited Jamaica, Barbados, Grenada, and South Africa.

The United Nations World Food Program made an emergency food-aid appeal to help drought-stricken eastern Cuba, but the drought was ended by Hurricane George.

The European Union dropped its legal challenge to the Helms-Burton Act.

The four members of the Internal Dissidence Working Group were threatened with five to six years' imprisonment despite appeals from the Vatican and elsewhere abroad.

The United Nations Human Rights Commission, in a vote of 19–16, rejected a U.S.-led effort to censure Cuba's human rights abuses.

Cuba admitted to the Asociación Latinoamericana de Integración (ALADI).

Alina Fernandez discussed her disenchantment with her father, Fidel Castro, both as a father and as Cuba's leader, which was the subject of her new book, *Castro's Daughter: An Exile Memoir of Cuba.*

1999 The death penalty was extended to armed robbery, attacks on the police, corruption of minors, and some drug offenses. Cuba also introduced the harshest penalties ever for engaging in political activities.

Vladimiro Roca, Felix Bone, Rene Gomez Manzano, and Marta Beatriz Roque were sentenced to three to five years in prison for publicly criticizing Cuba's system of government.

Sugar harvest of 3.6 million tons was just enough to stave off default on Cuba's international debts.

Cuba adopted the Euro as its official currency for trading with Europe.

Smith Kline Beacham signed an agreement with Cuba to distribute meningitis B vaccine on the world market.

Cuba came in second (after the United States) in the Pan American Games after its four gold-medal winners were disqualified for drug use following urine tests.

The Cuban government sold the right to make deep-water searches for galleon wrecks to Canadian Visa Gold Exploration.

Spain protested the U.S. threat of sanctions against the Sol Melia hotel chain for occupying American-owned land in Varadero.

Castro replaced his ministers of foreign relations, labor, and tourism.

Former U.S. Defense Department counter-terrorism expert John More told UPI that Cubans, militant Palestinians, Hezbollah, and even advisers from Venezuela are all active in Colombia.

The ninth Ibero-American Conference was held in Havana. Castro was criticized for human rights abuses and political repression.

An asylum dispute over Elían González, a six-year-old refugee picked up at sea near Florida after his mother perished in a Cuba-to-Miami voyage, caused major strains in U.S.-Cuban relations.

Niall Connelly, an Irish Republican Army (IRA) representative, was living in Cuba and representing the IRA for Latin America.

2000   The first major trial of a Cuban dissident in over a year ended with the sentencing of Dr. Oscar Elias Biscet to three years in prison—for hanging the nation's flag upside down.

The United States deported Cuban diplomat Jose Imperatori on espionage charges.

Jose Imperatori, the Cuban diplomat expelled from the United States, left Canada after overstaying his Canadian transit visa by almost three days. In a negotiated departure, Imperatori left the Cuban embassy in Ottawa and then boarded a Cubana Airliner jet sent to take him to Havana.

Scores of leaders from Africa, Asia, and Latin America gathered in Havana for one of the largest Third World meetings ever held, intended to set a new, united agenda for narrowing global wealth inequalities. More than sixty-five heads of state from the 133 member nations of the Group of 77 attended the five-day meeting led by Fidel Castro.

Castro told leaders of the world's poorer nations meeting in Havana that the capitalist system had caused suffering comparable to that of the Holocaust.

Angry over European criticism of its human rights record, Cuba canceled the planned visit to Havana by senior European Union officials. A delegation lead by the Portuguese cooperation minister, Luis Amado, had intended to have talks on issues including trade and human rights.

The government freed Rene Gomez Manzano, a dissident lawyer, from prison in the third early release of a prominent anti-government activist. The early release of Gomez, fifty-six, who was serving a four-year sentence for anti-government activities, followed the freeing over the previous two weeks of two of his close dissident colleagues, Felix Bonne, sixty, an academic, and Marta Beatriz Roque, fifty-five, an economist.

House Republican leaders agreed to end four decades of sanctions on sales of food to Cuba, but Cuban-American lawmakers managed to place severe restrictions on the bill. American farmers and agricultural businesses could sell directly to Cuba, but the federal government and American bankers could not provide any financing to the Castro regime.

Elían González returned to Cuba with his father and other family members aboard a chartered jet hours after the Supreme Court declined to hear an appeal brought by Miami relatives who wanted an asylum hearing for the boy.

The State Department accused Cuba of causing widespread suffering by refusing to let Cubans leave the island even if they held United States visas. Separately, officials said, the United States told Ricardo Alarcon, the president of the Cuban National Assembly, that he cannot attend a meeting of international lawmakers at the United Nations in New York.

Ending a two-month suspension, Cuba agreed to resume talks on legal migration of Cubans to the United States under accords signed in 1994 and '95. The agreements grant visas to 20,000 Cubans a year.

The *Chicago Tribune* and the *Dallas Morning News* learned that they would be allowed to open offices in Havana, joining the Associated Press and CNN as the only United States news organizations with bureaus in the country.

Fidel Castro, on a visit to the United Nations, denounced the American economic embargo against his country and presented a bleak vision of the world's future before thousands of cheering and flag-waving supporters gathered at Riverside Church in Manhattan.

Testifying in Washington before the International Trade Commission, Cuba's top diplomat in the United States, Fernando Ramirez de Estenoz, called for an end to all sanctions on Havana rather than the smaller step now being debated in Congress for limited sales of American food and medicine. The rare appearance by a Cuban official before a federal agency was protested by two Florida lawmakers. The ITC concluded that Castro's policies, not the embargo, are the main cause of Cuba's economic problems.

Reacting to the United States decision to give asylum to nine Cuban defectors, Castro and thousands of protesters converged on a Havana plaza in front of the American diplomatic offices. The nine fled in a small plane that crashed into the sea.

Pedro Riera Escalante, a longtime Cuban intelligence official who had broken with his government and sought refuge in Mexico, was arrested and deported to Cuba.

After years of deadlock, creditor nations in the so-called Paris Club were willing to try to reschedule the estimated $3.5 billion debt Cuba has with them. Cuba's total hard-currency foreign debt at the end of 1999 was just over $11 billion.

The Senate approved a bill easing nearly four decades of sanctions on the sale of food to Cuba, all but assuring the measure would become law. While the vote was viewed as a victory for farming groups, the legislation was not expected to lead to large sales of food products to Cuba any time soon.

Havana, retaliating against a bill in the United States Congress that makes use of Cuban money frozen in the United States, levied a 10 percent tax on the cost of telephone calls between Cuba and the United States.

Fidel Castro began his first official visit to Venezuela in four decades. He and President Hugo Chavez, an ally and friend, signed an agreement to let Cuba import oil from Venezuela at a discount and with long-term credits.

For the ninth year, the United Nations General Assembly called by a wide margin for the lifting of the United States embargo on Cuba. The vote was 167 to 3, with 4 abstentions. Only Israel and the Marshall Islands voted with the United States. El Salvador, Latvia, Morocco, and Nicaragua abstained.

Cuba and Venezuela sought the extradition of Luis Posada Carriles, a Cuban exile who Fidel Castro said planned to kill him during the Ibero-American summit meeting in Panama City.

Castro refused to join the other Ibero-American heads of state in condemning ETA terrorism at the 2000 meeting in Panama.

President Vladimir V. Putin of Russia, on a visit to the island, and Fidel Castro pledged to reinvent their countries' relationship, which foundered after the Soviet Union's demise. It would be based on a modest agenda of trade and commerce and a bit of ideological alignment.

Russia and Cuba agreed to abandon an incomplete nuclear-power plant at Juragua on the southern coast of Cuba.

During the trial of several Cuban spies in Miami, one of the accused, Alejandro Alonso, revealed on December 30 that he was instructed by Cuba's intelligence officers to locate areas in South Florida "where we can drop people as well as things, including arms and explosives."

2001   President Vaclav Havel of the Czech Republic called for the immediate release of two prominent Czechs being held in Cuba for meeting dissidents opposed to Fidel Castro. Cuba said former finance minister Ivan Pilip and a former student leader, Jan Bubenik, would be tried for plotting on behalf of American interests. Having been held for more than three weeks, the Czechs were released after they admitted breaking Cuban law, signing an admission drawn up before diplomats from several nations.

The U.S. Treasury Department authorized the release of $96.7 million in frozen Cuban funds to families of three Miami-based pilots shot down by Cuban fighter jets in 1996.

Fidel Castro met in Havana for the first time with veterans of the Bay of Pigs, at a three-day conference organized by American historians, scholars, and open-government advocates who uncovered secret archives of American, Cuban and other governments.

The Argentine government withdrew its ambassador to Cuba to protest comments by Fidel Castro that characterized President Fernando de la Rua's government as "bootlickers of the Yankees."

Fidel Castro made his first visit to Iran and was welcomed in grand style with a guard of honor at the former imperial palace. Discussions were expected to focus on bilateral cooperation and new ways to improve the effectiveness of the G-77 group of developing nations, which is currently headed by Iran.

Senators Jesse Helms and Joseph I. Lieberman offered a bill to send $100 million in aid to government opponents in Cuba over four years.

Five Cubans were convicted of conspiring to spy on the United States for Cuba; Gerardo Hernandez, the group's leader, was found guilty of contributing to the deaths of four members of Brothers to the Rescue, a Cuban exile group, whose plane was downed by Cuban jets in international airspace in 1996. Others convicted were Ramon Labanino, Antonio Guerrero, Fernando Gonzalez, and Rene Gonzalez; five other indicted members of the group pleaded guilty and four others are fugitives.

The U.S. House of Representatives voted, 240 to 186, for a measure that would effectively lift the ban on most travel to Cuba; the vote reflected growing sentiment in Congress that many sanctions on Castro's government have outlived their usefulness. Members of the House Republican leadership who oppose lifting the sanctions are expected to intervene and make certain that the measure dies this year, as they did with a similar measure last year.

Smugglers dropped 55 Cubans in the Florida Keys, bringing to 107 the number of such immigrants who arrived there over three days.

The U.S. government arrested and charged Ana Belen Montes, the Pentagon's top intelligence analyst for Cuba, with spying for the Cuban government; she had provided Havana with highly classified information, including American assessments of Cuban military readiness.

Russian president Vladimir V. Putin said Russia will abandon its largest electronic eavesdropping post in the West, at Lourdes, Cuba, and spend much of the savings on modern weapons for its armed forces.

Havana is negotiating a deal with American producers to buy food and agricultural products to replenish stocks destroyed by a recent hurricane; this would be the first such transaction in four decades, since the United States imposed trade sanctions against Cuba. The small value of the purchases suggested that Cuba might be using the catastrophe to cut into the American embargo rather than seek actual relief.

Four American companies became the first in four decades to sign trade deals with Cuba; Archer Daniels Midland, Cargill, Riceland Foods, and ConAgra will supply food to help the recovery from Hurricane Michelle.

The widow and four children of Howard F. Anderson, an American businessman executed in Cuba more than forty years ago on charges of conspiring against Castro's revolutionary government, filed a wrongful death suit against the Cuban government.

The leader of a Cuban spy ring was sentenced to life without parole for conspiracy to commit espionage and conspiracy to commit murder. Gerardo Hernández was convicted of trying to obtain U.S. military secrets by seeking to infiltrate military bases at Boca Chica Naval Base and U.S. Southern Command and for his involvement in the 1996 downing of two American civilian aircraft by Cuban MiGs over international waters.

The first shipment of American goods to be purchased by the Cuban government since the trade embargo was imposed arrived in the Havana harbor. The purchase was made possible by legislation passed in Congress that exempted food and medicine from the trade embargo.

SUGGESTED READING

Although numerous books, periodical articles, and newspapers in various languages were consulted in the preparation of this volume, only books in English have been included in the following list, which is intended mainly as a guide to further reading. Entries marked with asterisks are also available in paperback.

Aguila, Juan del. *Cuba: Dilemmas of a Revolution.* Boulder, Colorado: Westview Press, 1984.

A short but insightful analysis of the course of Cuban history and the impact of the Castro revolution.

Aguilar, Luis E. *Cuba 1933: Prologue to Revolution.* Ithaca, New York: Cornell University Press, 1972.

Based upon extensive and original research and on personal experiences, the author analyzes the revolution of 1933 and its possible linkages to the Castro revolution.

Ameringuer, Charles D. *The Cuban Democratic Experience.* Gainesville: University Press of Florida, 2000.

An exhaustive and scholarly appraisal of the two Auténtico administrations, 1944–1952.

Batista, Fulgencio. *The Growth and Decline of the Cuban Republic.* New York: Devin-Adair Co., 1964.

An apologetic narrative by the former dictator, highlighting his own role in Cuban history.

Benglesdorf, Carolle. *The Problems of Democracy in Cuba.* New York: Oxford University Press, 1994.*

An examination of the relationship between socialism and democracy, in classical Marxist theory and in the practice of the Cuban revolution.

Benjamin, Jules R. *The U.S. and Cuba: Hegemony and Dependent Development, 1880–1934.* Pittsburgh: University of Pittsburgh Press, 1977.

A scholarly study of U.S. policy during the first decades of the Cuban Republic.

Blight, James G., and David A. Welch. *On the Brink: Americans and Soviets*

Reexamine the Cuban Missile Crisis. New York: Hill and Wang, 1989.
A fresh and illuminating portrait of how those who bore ultimate responsibility grappled with the gravest threat of nuclear war in our time.

Blutstein, Howard I., et al. *Area Handbook for Cuba*. Washington, D.C.: United States Printing Office, 1971.
Prepared by the Foreign Area Study of American University and designed for use by the United States military, this handy volume contains a variety of basic facts on the social, economic, political, and military institutions of Cuba.

Bonachea, Rolando, and Nelson Valdés, eds. *Che: Selected Works of Ernesto Che Guevara*. Cambridge, Massachusetts: MIT Press, 1969. A carefully selected volume of Guevara's speeches and writings, introduced by a brief and vivid account of his career.

————. *Revolutionary Struggle: The Selected Works of Fidel Castro*. Cambridge, Massachusetts: MIT Press, 1971.
A compilation of the speeches and writings of Fidel Castro, with a fine introduction by the editors.

Bonsal, Philip W. *Cuba, Castro and the United States*. Pittsburgh: University of Pittsburgh Press, 1971.
An account by the last U.S. ambassador to Cuba of his experiences during the first two years of the revolution and of his relations with Castro and other Cuban officials. Ambassador Bonsal discusses in particular his attempts to find a basis for a rational relationship between Cuba and the United States, Castro's rejection of those attempts, and the United States' abandonment of a policy of non-intervention, which the ambassador had advocated.

Buell, Raymond L., et al. *Problems of the New Cuba*. New York: Foreign Policy Associates, Inc., 1935.
Written by a committee of the Foreign Policy Association, this book is one of the finest studies of Cuba's economic, social, and political situation in the 1930s.

Bunck, Julia Maria. *Fidel Castro and the Quest for a Revolutionary Culture in Cuba*. Pennsylvania: The Pennsylvania State University Press, 1994.*
An excellent study of the attempt of the Castro government to change traditional Cuban culture and of the costly social experimentation that took place in Cuba for twenty years.

Burks, David D. *Cuba under Castro*. New York: Foreign Policy Association, 1964.
A short but interesting *Headline Series* monograph discussing Castro's rise to power, his relations with the Communist world, and his conflict with the United States.

Carbonell, Nestor T. *And the Russians Stayed: The Sovietization of Cuba*. New

York: William Morrow & Co., 1989.

A first-hand account of the rise of Soviet-backed totalitarianism in Cuba.

Casuso, Teresa. *Cuba and Castro*. New York: Random House, 1961.

A first-hand portrait of Castro's revolutionary activities in Mexico, as well as of his personal relationship with those around him, by a former Castro supporter.

Chapman, Charles E. *A History of the Cuban Republic*. New York: The Macmillan Company, 1927.

A quite useful political survey of Cuban history with special emphasis on the first quarter of the twentieth century.

Chester, Edmund A. *A Sergeant Named Batista*. New York: Henry Holt, 1954.

This book, by Batista's public relations man, provides much interesting material, particularly about the 1933 revolution.

Corwin, Arthur. *Spain and the Abolition of Slavery in Cuba, 1817–1886*. Austin: The University of Texas Press, 1967.

A most important and well-documented study that skillfully interrelates the problem of Cuban slavery with international diplomacy, Spanish colonial policy, and Cuban domestic politics.

Crassweller, Robert D. *Cuba and the U.S.: The Tangled Relationship*. New York: Foreign Policy Association, 1971.

A short but well-thought-out analysis of the events and factors influencing the Cuban revolution and its anti-American posture, and particularly of Castro's impact on the nature and course of the revolution.

Dewart, Leslie. *Christianity and Revolution: The Lesson of Cuba*. New York: Herder and Herder, 1963.

A good study of some historical aspects of Cuba's Roman Catholic Church and of its confrontation with Castro.

Diaz Briquets, Sergio, and Jorge Perez-Lopez. *Conquering Nature: The Environmental Legacy of Socialism in Cuba*. Pittsburgh: University of Pittsburgh Press, 2000.

The only book-length analysis of the environmental situation in Cuba. An excellent study of the impact of forty years of Communist rule on the island.

Dominguez, Jorge I. *Cuba: Order and Revolution*. Cambridge, Massachusetts: Harvard University Press, 1978.

A thorough and scholarly analysis of politics in twentieth-century Cuba with an emphasis on the Castro revolution.

———. *To Make the World Safe for Revolution: Cuban Foreign Policy*. Cambridge, Massachusetts: Harvard University Press, 1989.

An authoritative examination of Castro's foreign policy and its impact on Cuba and the course of international affairs.

Draper, Theodore. *Castroism: Theory and Practice*. New York: Praeger, 1965.

———. *Castro's Revolution: Myths and Realities*. New York: Praeger, 1962.

Two well-researched and highly analytical studies essential to an understanding of Castroism.

Dubois, Jules. *Fidel Castro. Rebel, Liberator, or Dictator?* Indianapolis: Bobbs-Merrill, 1959.
A valuable book for the information it contains on Castro's insurrection against Batista.

Dumont, René. *Socialism and Development.* New York: Grove Press, 1970.
The author, a French Marxist agronomist and former adviser to Cuba who visited the island on various occasions, discusses in this book Castro's economic policies, criticizing the acceleration of collectivization, the highly centralized system of planning, the nationalization of small enterprises, the growing bureaucracy and inefficiency, the disdain for material incentives, and the militarization of society.

Erismen, Michael. *Cuba's Foreign Relations in a Post-Soviet World.* Gainesville: University Press of Florida, 2000.
A study of Cuba's adjustments since the fall of communism and confrontation with the U.S.

Estep, Raymond. *The Latin American Nations Today.* [Maxwell Air Force Base,] Alabama: Air University Documentary Research Study, 1964.
Contains a short but fine summary of Cuban development in the post–World War II period.

Fagen, Richard R., et al. *Cubans in Exile: Disaffection and the Revolution.* Stanford, California: Stanford University Press, 1968.
An interesting study of the Cuban exile population with special emphasis on their political orientation and social composition.

————. *The Transformation of Political Culture in Cuba.* Stanford, California: Stanford University Press, 1969.
A systematic and objective analysis of political socialization and cultural changes in Castro's Cuba.

Falk, Pamela. *Cuban Foreign Policy.* Lexington, Kentucky: D.C. Heath, 1986.
A superb analysis of Cuba's foreign policy in a complex international context.

Fauriol, George, and Eva Loser, eds. *Cuba: The International Dimension.* New Brunswick: Transaction Publishers, 1990.
A collection of essays by some of the best scholars on Cuba, analyzing various aspects of Cuba's foreign policy.

Fermoselle, Rafael. *The Evolution of the Cuban Military, 1972–1986.* Miami: Ediciones Universal, 1987.*
A chronicle of the most important events in Cuban military history with special emphasis on the changes that have taken place since the Castro revolution.

Fernandez, Damian. *Cuba's Foreign Policy in the Middle East.* Boulder, Colorado: Westview Press, 1988.

A comprehensive and well-researched study of Castro's involvement in the Middle East.

Fitzgibbon, Russel H. *Cuba and the United States, 1900–1935*. Menasha, Wisconsin: George Banta Publishing Company, 1935.
A useful and careful study of U.S.-Cuban relations in the first decades of the century.

Foner, Philip. *A History of Cuba in Its Relations with the U.S.* 2 vols. New York: International Publishers Co., Inc., 1963.
Extending only until 1895, these are useful volumes, although strongly biased against the United States.

Franqui, Carlos. *Diary of the Cuban Revolution*. New York: Viking Press, 1976.
Written by Castro's close collaborator and director of propaganda, the book offers an authoritative account of events from the beginnings of the Castro revolution in 1953 to Fidel's rise to power.

———. *Family Portrait with Fidel*. New York: Random House, 1984.
An impressive and important memoir by one of Castro's close associates and editor of the influential newspaper *Revolucion*.

Fuente, Alejandro de la. *Race, Inequality and Politics in Twentieth Century Cuba*. Chapel Hill: The University of North Carolina Press, 2001.
An examination of the impact of race on Cuban politics contending that racism and anti-racism coexisted within Cuba's nationalism.

Geyer, George Anne. *Guerrilla Prince: The Untold Story of Fidel Castro*. Boston: Little, Brown & Co., 1991.*
An excellent biography of Castro with new information about his childhood and youth.

Goldenberg, Boris. *The Cuban Revolution and Latin America*. New York: Praeger, 1965.
An important study by a sharp European observer who resided in Cuba for many years.

Gonzalez, Edward. *Cuba: Clearing Perilous Waters*. Santa Monica: The Rand Corporation, 1996.*
An assessment of the major leaders and institutions and the role of an emerging civil society, including proposals for U.S. strategy and scenarios for change.

———. *Cuba Under Castro: The Limits of Charisma*. Boston: Houghton Mifflin, 1974.
An excellent study of Castro's role in the political process and of revolutionary politics in general.

———. *Partners in Deadlock: The United States and Castro, 1959–1972*. Santa Monica, California: The Southern California Arms Control and Foreign Policy Seminar, 1972.
A short but perceptive study of U.S.-Cuban relations that also examines the origins of Cuban nationalism and provides specific policy alternatives for a Cuban-U.S. rapprochement.

Gray, Richard B. *José Martí: Cuban Patriot.* Gainesville: University of Florida Press, 1962.

A scholarly and interesting book, with special emphasis on Martí's charismatic appeal and his development as a national hero and political symbol in the twentieth century.

Grupo Cubano de Investigaciones Economicas. *A Study on Cuba.* Coral Gables, Florida: University of Miami Press, 1965.

Prepared by a group of Cuban economists in exile, this volume contains excellent material on Cuba's economic history, despite the rosy view of economic development presented by the authors.

Guerra y Sánchez, Ramiro. *Sugar and Society in the Caribbean.* New Haven, Connecticut: Yale University Press, 1964.

An excellent study of the development of the sugar industry and its related socioeconomic problems, with a perceptive foreword by Sidney W. Mintz.

Guerra y Sánchez, Ramiro, et al. *A History of the Cuban Nation.* 10 vols. Habana: Editorial Historia de la Nacion Cubana, S.A., 1958.

A comprehensive and detailed history of all phases of Cuban development written by a group of Cuba's most distinguished writers and intellectuals.

Gunn, Gillian. *Cuba in Transition.* New York: Twentieth Century Fund, 1993.*

A perspective on how U.S. policy toward Cuba can best serve U.S. interests.

Halperin, Ernst. *Castro and Latin American Communism.* Cambridge, Massachusetts: Center for International Studies, MIT, 1963.

———. *The Ideology of Castroism and Its Impact on the Communist Parties of Latin America.* Cambridge, Massachusetts: Center for International Studies, MIT, 1961.*

Two analyses, with much insight of Castroism and its relation to Latin America, by a longtime student of Communist affairs.

Halperin, Maurice. *The Rise and Decline of Fidel Castro.* Berkeley: University of California Press, 1972.

An analysis of Castro's foreign policy during 1959–1964 placed in the context of domestic policy and conditions.

Hart, Phillips R. *Cuban Sideshow.* Havana: Cuban Press, 1935.

Written by a former *New York Times* correspondent in Havana, this book provides an interesting eyewitness account of Cuba in the early 1930s.

Horowitz, Irving L., and Jaime Suchlicki, eds. *Cuban Communism.* New Brunswick, New Jersey: Transaction Books, 2000.

An excellent collection of essays on most aspects of the revolution, now in its tenth edition.

International Bank for Reconstruction and Development. *Report on Cuba.*

Washington, D.C.: International Bank for Reconstruction and Development, 1951.
An extensive and carefully done volume emphasizing the economic problems Cuba faced as it entered the 1950s.

Jackson, D. Bruce. *Castro, the Kremlin, and Communism in Latin America.* Baltimore: The Johns Hopkins Press, 1969.*
A carefully researched study of Castro's foreign policy toward Latin America and of the interaction and conflicts of Soviet and Cuban policies in the area.

James, Daniel. *Che Guevara: A Biography.* New York: Stein and Day, 1969.*
A detailed biography of Che with special emphasis on his exploits and his death in Bolivia.

Jenks, Leland. *Our Cuban Colony.* New York: American Fund for Public Service Studies in American Investment Abroad, American Imperialism Series, 1928.
An interesting study of Cuban-U.S. economic relations, highly critical of U.S. involvement in Cuba.

Johnson, Haynes. *The Bay of Pigs.* New York: W. W. Norton, 1964.
A valuable and highly readable account based on the stories of the Cuban leaders of the expeditionary force.

Jordan, David C. *Revolutionary Cuba and the End of the Cold War.* New York: University Press of America, 1993.
An analysis of Cuba's attempt to be a "free state" within an imperial international environment with emphasis on the post-Soviet era.

Jorge, Antonio. *A Reconstruction Strategy for Post-Castro Cuba.* Coral Gables, Florida: University of Miami, 1991.*
A fine attempt to offer observations and suggestions for strategies for the reconstruction of the island in a post-Castro period.

Karol, K. S. *Guerrillas in Power.* New York: Hill and Wang, 1970.
A controversial book by a European journalist and longtime student of world communism who visited Cuba several times between 1961 and 1968. With a strong pro-Chinese bias, Karol discusses the many problems facing the Cuban Revolution and blames many of them on Castro's dependence on the Soviet Union.

Kaufman, Purcell, Susan and David Rothkopf, eds. *Cuba: The Contours of Change.* Boulder, Colorado: Lynn Reiner, 2000.*
A collection of updated analysis of Castro's internal challenges and of U.S.-Cuban relations.

Klein, Herbert. *Slavery in the Americas.* Chicago: Quadrangle Books, 1967.
An excellent study of slavery in Virginia and Cuba, suggesting that U.S. slavery was harsher than other slave systems, analyzing the effects slavery had on Cuban and American societies.

Knight, Franklin W. *Slave Society in Cuba During the Nineteenth Century.*

Madison: University of Wisconsin Press, 1970.

Examines the conditions that maintained slavery in Cuba in the nineteenth century and analyzes the sociological effects of the institution on the island's politics, culture, and economy.

Kozolchyk, Boris. *The Political Biographies of Three Castro Officials*. Santa Monica: The Rand Corporation, 1966.*

Short but fascinating and incisive biographies of Fabio Grobart, a leading Cuban Communist organizer and theoretician; Raúl Roa, Castro's former minister of foreign relations; and René Anillo, a former student leader and later a Castro technocrat.

Langley, Lester D. *The Cuban Policy of the U.S.: A Brief History*. New York: John Wiley & Sons, 1968.

A concise but well-done history of American policy toward Cuba from Washington to Kennedy.

LaVesque, Jacques. *The U.S.S.R. and The Cuban Revolution: Soviet Ideological and Strategic Perspectives*. New York: Praeger, 1978.

A comprehensive survey of how the Cuban Revolution influenced Soviet perceptions of the world.

Levine, Barry B. *The New Cuban Presence in the Caribbean*. Boulder, Colorado: Westview Press, 1983.

A valuable collection of essays by several Caribbean specialists exploring the history and nature of Cuba's influence in the Commonwealth Caribbean, Mexico, and Central America.

Le Riverend Brusone, Julio. *Economic History of Cuba*. Havana Book Institute, 1967.

A Marxist interpretation of Cuba's economic development from the earliest Spanish colonial days by a well-known Cuban economist.

Liss, Sheldon B. *Fidel! Castro's Political and Social Thought*. Boulder, Colorado: Westview Press, 1994.

A fine effort to explain Castro's thoughts and ideology, organized by topics.

Lizaso, Felix. *Martí: Martyr of Cuban Independence*. Albuquerque: The University of New Mexico Press, 1953.

A fine biography of Cuba's great leader.

Llerena, Mario. *The Unsuspected Revolution: The Birth and Rise of Castroism*. Ithaca, New York: Cornell University Press, 1978.

A lucid and penetrating account of the Cuban revolution by an insider who was an early supporter of Fidel Castro.

Lockmiller, D. A. *Magoon in Cuba*. New York: Greenwood Press, 1969.

An interesting and useful study of the United States intervention in Cuba 1906–1909.

Lopez-Fresquet, Rufo. *My Fourteen Months with Castro*. New York: World Publishing Co., 1966.

A perceptive and revealing account of life in Cuba during the first year of the revolution by Castro's former minister of the treasury.

Lynch, Grayston L. *Decision for Disaster: Betrayed at the Bay of Pigs.* Washington, D.C.: Brassey's, 1998.
A CIA official challenges the historical record and blames the Kennedy administration for the Bay of Pigs disaster.

McCauley, Neill. *A Rebel in Cuba: An American's Memoir.* Chicago: Quadrangle, 1970.
A first-hand account, scholarly and incisive, of the author's guerrilla experiences under Castro.

MacGaffey, Wyatt, and Clifford R. Barnett. *Cuba: Its People, Its Society, Its Culture.* New Haven, Connecticut: Human Relations Area Files, Inc., 1962.
A useful one-volume introduction to Cuban history and culture.

Mallin, Jay, ed. *Che Guevara on Revolution.* Coral Gables, Florida: University of Miami Press, 1969.*
A compilation of the full texts of Guevara's most important writings and speeches. The editor's fine introduction provides biographical information on Che and analyzes his theoretical works and his various roles as a guerrilla leader and economist.

Mañach, Jorge. *Martí. Apostle of Freedom.* New York: Devin-Adair, 1950.
An excellent study of Martí and his role in organizing a war of independence, by one of Cuba's most distinguished intellectuals.

Mazarr, Michael. *Semper Fidel: America and Cuba, 1776–1988.* Baltimore: The Nautical and Aviation Publishing Company of America, 1988.
A comprehensive, well-written history of Cuban-U.S. relations with emphasis on the Castro period.

Mesa-Lago, Carmelo, ed. *Revolutionary Change in Cuba.* Pittsburgh: The University of Pittsburgh Press, 1971.
A comprehensive and authoritative collection of essays on most major aspects of socialist Cuba.

———. *The Economy of Socialist Cuba.* Albuquerque: The University of New Mexico Press, 1981.*
An analysis of the successes and failures of the economy during the revolution. Rich in economic data.

———. *Market, Socialist and Mixed Economies.* Baltimore: The John Hopkins University Press, 2000.
A comparative analysis of the economies of Chile, Cuba, and Costa Rica convincingly showing the superiority of market economies.

Millet, Allan Reed. *The Politics of Intervention: The Military Occupation of Cuba, 1906–1909.* Columbus: Ohio State University Press, 1968.
A fine study of the second U.S. intervention in Cuba, pointing out that U.S. policy, although well-intentioned, was impractical.

Montaner, Carlos Alberto. *Fidel Castro and the Cuban Revolution*. New Brunswick, New Jersey: Transaction Press, 1989.

A penetrating analysis of Castro's personality and policies, an important effort to understand the character of Fidel and his regime.

———. *Journey to the Heart of Cuba*. New York: Algore Publishing. 2001.

An analysis of the causes and impact of the Castro revolution with a chapter on post-Castro Cuba.

Nelson, Lowry. *Cuba: The Measure of a Revolution*. Minneapolis: University of Minnesota Press, 1972.

A valuable assessment of the social, political, and economic impact of the Cuban revolution, which concludes by pointing out that the Castro regime has been a tragedy for Cuba and its people.

———. *Rural Cuba*. Minneapolis: University of Minnesota Press, 1950.

Based on field research in Cuba in the mid-1940s, this book is the best study of the pre-Castro Cuban countryside.

Ortíz, Fernando. *Cuban Counterpoint: Tobacco and Sugar*. New York: Knopf, 1947.

A classic book by one of Cuba's most distinguished writers and anthropologists, it interprets the development of Cuban culture and society and the mingling of ethnic strains.

Osgood, Cornelius. *The Ciboney Culture of Cayo Redondo, Cuba*. New Haven, Connecticut: Yale University Press, 1942.

One of the few studies, and a fine one, of Cuba's early inhabitants.

Paterson, Thomas G. *Contesting Castro*. New York: Oxford University Press, 1994.*

An analysis of the relationship between Cuba and the U.S. seeking to explain the origins of the U.S. collision with revolutionary Cuba.

Payne, Richard T. *Opportunities and Dangers of Soviet-Cuban Expansion: Toward a Pragmatic U.S. Policy*. Albany: State University of New York Press, 1988.

Examines the conduct of U.S. foreign policy against the backdrop of Cuban/Soviet involvement in Angola, Afghanistan, Nicaragua, and the Caribbean and prescribes alternative policies to deal with the Soviets.

Perez, Louis A. *Army Politics in Cuba, 1898–1958*. Pittsburgh: University of Pittsburgh Press, 1976.

A scholarly and detailed account of the role of the military in Cuban politics.

———. *Cuba Between Reform and Revolution*. New York: Oxford University Press, 1995.

A comprehensive study that provides an excellent foundation for the understanding of contemporary Cuban politics.

———. *On Becoming Cuban: Identity, Nationality and Culture*. Chapel Hill: University of North Carolina Press, 2000.

A cultural history of the relations between the United States and Cuba and the impact on Cuba's identity.

Perez-Stable, Marifeli. *The Cuban Revolution.* New York: Oxford University Press, 1993.*
A critical analysis of the Cuban revolution and of U.S. policy by a Cuban-American scholar.

Plank, John N., ed. *Cuba and the United States: Long Range Perspectives.* Washington, D.C.: The Brookings Institution, 1967.
A collection of articles on various aspects of the revolution, and from differing perspectives.

Pratt, Julius. *Expansionists of 1898.* New York: P. Smith, 1964.
A challenging study originally published in 1936, analyzing the motives behind the Spanish-American War and the opposition of American business to the war.

Ratliff, William E. *Castroism and Communism in Latin America: 1959–1976.* Washington, D.C.: American Enterprise Institute, 1976.*
Examines the theories and practices of Marxist-Leninist organizations in Latin America and the rivalries between Castroite, pro-Soviet, and pro-Chinese groups in the area. The ideas and writings of Fidel Castro, Che Guevara, and Regis Debray are examined.

Roca, Sergio. *Cuban Economic Policy and Ideology.* Beverly Hills: Sage, 1976.
A penetrating analysis of economic problems and development since the revolution.

Ruiz, Ramon Eduardo. *Cuba: The Making of a Revolution.* Amherst, Massachusetts: The University of Massachusetts Press, 1968.
An interesting and controversial study of nationalism and anti-Americanism and its impact on the Cuban Revolution and its leaders.

Seers, Dudley, ed. *Cuba: The Economic and Social Revolution.* Chapel Hill: The University of North Carolina Press, 1964.
A group of English and Chilean economists contrast pre-Castro Cuba with the changing situation since 1959 in the fields of agriculture, industry, and education.

Short, Margaret I. *Law and Religion in Cuba.* New Brunswick, New Jersey: Transaction Publishers, 1998.
An excellent study of the clash between religion and Marxism in contemporary Cuba.*

Smith, Robert E, ed. *Background to Revolution: The Development of Modern Cuba.* New York: Alfred A. Knopf, 1966.*
A well-selected and highly relevant collection of excerpts from books and articles written by United States and Cuban historians, with a fine introduction by the editor.

Smith, Robert F. *The United States and Cuba: Business and Diplomacy.* New York: Bookman Associates, 1961.

A well-documented study of the effects of business interests on U.S.-Cuban relations from 1917 to 1960.

Suarez, Andres. *Cuba: Castroism and Communism, 1959–1966.* Cambridge, Massachusetts: MIT Press, 1967.*
A well-researched and carefully written book on Castro's relations with the Soviet Union and with the Cuban Communists, indispensable for an understanding of Castroism.

Suchlicki, Jaime. *Historical Dictionary of Cuba.* Metuchen, New Jersey: The Scarecrow Press, Inc., 2001.
A reference book presenting essential historical facts and events as well as biographies of prominent leaders in Cuban history, culture, and economic development from pre-Columbian times to the present. Includes a chronology from Columbus to Castro and an extensive bibliography.

———. *University Students and Revolution in Cuba.* Coral Gables, Florida: University of Miami Press, 1969.
A study of the role of university students in Cuban politics from the 1920s to the Castro revolution.

———. ed. *Cuba, Castro and Revolution.* Coral Gables, Florida: University of Miami Press, 1972.
An important collection of essays on various internal and external aspects of the revolution by ten specialists.

———. ed. *Problems of Succession Cuba.* Coral Gables, Florida: University of Miami Press, 1985.*
A collection of essays by prominent Cuba scholars analyzing the various aspects of a succession crisis in Cuba.

———. *The Cuban Military Under Castro.* Coral Gables, Florida: University of Miami Press, 1989.*
A collection of essays by specialists analyzing the mission, organization, and strength of the Cuban military, as well as civil-military relations and Cuban-Soviet military relations.

———, and Antonio Jorge, eds. *Investing in Cuba: Problems and Prospects.* New Brunswick, New Jersey: Transaction Publishers, 1994.*
A collection of essays discussing the challenges and problems faced by foreign investors interested in penetrating the Cuban market.

Szulc, Tad. *Fidel: A Critical Portrait.* New York: William Morrow & Co., 1989.
A perceptive and well-written biography of Castro.

Taber, Robert. *M-26: Biography of a Revolution.* New York: Lyle Stuart, 1961.
An extremely sympathetic book by a CBS reporter who interviewed Castro in the mountains and later became one of the leaders of the Fair Play for Cuba Committee. Contains valuable information on the anti-Batista struggle.

Thomas, Hugh. *Cuba: The Pursuit of Freedom.* New York: Harper and Row, 1971.

A monumental and scholarly volume by an English historian, exploring the whole sweep of Cuban history, from the English capture of Havana until the Castro revolution.

Triay, Victor Andres. *Bay of Pigs. An Oral History of Brigade 2506.* Gainesville: University of Florida Press, 2001.

The story of the invasion, told in the words of the participants.

Wilkerson, Loree. *Fidel Castro's Political Programs: From Reformism to Marxism-Leninism.* Gainesville: University of Florida Press, 1965.*

A small but incisive book tracing the origins of Castro's ideology and analyzing the factors that led to his conversion to Marxism-Leninism.

Wood, Bryce. *The Making of the Good Neighbor Policy.* New York: W. W. Norton, 1961.*

The best-documented study of U.S. policy in the 1920s and 1930s, with two chapters devoted especially to Cuban-U.S. relations.

Wright, Irene A. *The Early History of Cuba, 1492–1586.* New York: The Macmillan Co., 1916.

An old but still valuable and interesting volume on Cuba's early history.

Wyden, Peter. *Bay of Pigs: The Untold Story.* New York: Simon & Schuster, 1979.

A complete, detailed account based on documentary evidence as well as interviews with eyewitnesses.

Zeitlin, Maurice. *Revolutionary Politics and the Cuban Working Class.* Princeton, New Jersey: Princeton University Press, 1967.*

Based on interviews with Cuban workers in 1962, the author attempts to analyze the social determinants of the workers' political attitudes and the workers' perception of the Cuban Revolution and their role in the revolutionary process.

INDEX

Note: **ph** in page references refers to photographic insert.

ABOUT THE AUTHOR

JAIME SUCHLICKI, one of the world's foremost scholars on Latin America, is Emilio Bacardi Moreau professor of history and director of the Institute for Cuban and Cuban-American Studies at the University of Miami's School of International Studies. He was the editor of the *Journal of Inter-American and World Affairs* (1982–1996) and a consultant to the U.S. government and the private sector. His previous books include *Mexico: From Montezuma to the Fall of the PRI, University Students and Revolution in Cuba,* and *Historical Dictionary of Cuba*. Dr. Suchlicki lives in Coral Gables, Florida.